DIALOGUE WITH BAKHTIN ON SECOND AND FOREIGN LANGUAGE LEARNING

NEW PERSPECTIVES

DIALOGUE WITH BAKHTIN ON SECOND AND FOREIGN LANGUAGE LEARNING

NEW PERSPECTIVES

Edited by

Joan Kelly Hall
Pennsylvania State University

Gergana Vitanova
University of Central Florida

Ludmila Marchenkova
The Ohio State University

LAWRENCE ERLBAUM ASSOCIATES, PUBLISHERS
2005   Mahwah, New Jersey   London

Lawrence Erlbaum Associates, Inc., Publishers
10 Industrial Avenue
Mahwah, New Jersey 07430

Cover design by Kathryn Houghtaling Lacey

Library of Congress Cataloging-in-Publication Data

Hall, Joan Kelly.
Dialogue with Bakhtin on second and foreign language
learning : new perspectives / edited by Joan Kelly Hall,
Gergana Vitanova, Ludmila Marchenkova.
p. cm.
Includes bibliographical references and index.
ISBN 0-8058-5021-X (alk. paper)
1. Language and languages—Study and teaching. 2.
Bakhtin, M. M. (Mikhail Mikhaælovich), 1895–1975—
Views on foreign language study and teaching I. Vitanova,
Gergana.   II. Marchenova, Ludmila.   III. Title.

P51.H288 2004
418'.0071—dc22   2004046968
                                             CIP

Printed in the United States of America
10 9 8 7 6 5 4 3 2 1

Contents

Preface

The idea for this volume emerged from our mutual interests in Mikhail Bakhtin and language learning, discovered via discussions begun at the 2002 meeting of the American Association for Applied Linguistics. We found out then that, having read much of his work, we were each quite attracted to Bakhtin's philosophy of language and interested in exploring its implications for the learning of languages. This volume is a result of our collective desire to share these interests with others in the field. To our knowledge, this volume is the first to explore links between Bakhtin's ideas and second and foreign language learning.

With the exception of chapter 7, all the chapters are original, written specifically for this volume. Together, they address a range of contexts, including elementary and university-level English-as-a-second-language and foreign language classrooms and adult language-learning situations outside the formal classroom. Because the chapters are situated within a coherent conceptual framework, we expect them to be of interest to a broad audience of scholars with interests in second and foreign language learning. Moreover, given their significant pedagogical implications, we anticipate that teacher educators and language teachers will also find the volume useful.

ACKNOWLEDGMENTS

We acknowledge with much gratitude the chapter authors' goodwill in responding to our many requests and meeting all deadlines. Their combined efforts in enhancing our understandings of Bakhtin's philosophy and its implications for language learning make a significant contribution to the field of second and foreign language learning. We would also like to thank

Naomi Silverman for her constant encouragement and patient assistance and Lori Hawver, Erica Kica and the other folks at Lawrence Erlbaum Associates for their care and attention in bringing the volume to fruition. Thanks must also go to the two reviewers of the manuscript, Diana Boxer, University of Florida and Terry A. Osborn, University of Connecticut, who provided much helpful feedback. Finally, we extend our appreciation to family, friends, colleagues, and students, who inspire us to constantly seek out new opportunities for mutual understandings. We are excited to present this volume to readers and look forward to continuing the dialogue.

Contributors

Riikka Alanen is a senior researcher working at the Centre for Applied Language Studies. She runs a project called "Situated Metalinguistic Awareness and Foreign Language Learning." Her expertise includes Vygotskyan approaches to language learning, and she currently focuses on the notion of transfer in foreign language learning.

Karen Braxley received her PhD in TESOL from the University of Georgia. For the last 6 years she has taught English as a second language in the university's intensive English program and has also worked as a writing tutor in the university's Learning Center, where she works with graduate and undergraduate students from many different countries. Her research interests include ESL composition, qualitative research methodology, and sociocultural theory based on the work of Bakhtin and Vygotsky. Her dissertation focuses on the ways that international graduate students meet the challenge of writing academic English.

Ruth Devlin is an artist and writer who teaches primary English Language Learners (ELLs) at Paradise Professional Development School in Las Vegas, NV, and is an adjunct faculty member at the University of Nevada, Las Vegas. She has been teaching and working with ELL students for the past 14 years. She received her MS in Curriculum and Instruction in 1996 and continues to maintain her TESOL endorsement. Her research has focused on the connections among art, writing, and meaning-making of young language learners as they work in English dominant environments. She has published a book entitled *Desert Seasons: A Year in the Mojave* (2004, Stephens Press).

Hannele Dufva works as a senior research at the Centre for Applied Language Studies, University of Jyväskylä, Finland. She specializes in issues dealing with language and cognition, and her framework is dialogical, based on Bakhtinian thought.

Joan Kelly Hall is Professor of Applied Linguistics and Education at Pennsylvania State University. Her work is based on a sociocultural perspective of language and learning and centers on two overarching goals. The first is to understand the conditions by which language learners' involvement in the various constellations of their classroom practices is shaped, and how such involvement affects both what is learned and how it is learned. The second is to use this understanding to help create effectual classroom communities of language learners. Her most recent publications include *Teaching and Researching Language and Culture* (2003, Pearson) and *Methods for Teaching Foreign Languages: Creating a Community of Learners in the Classroom* (2002, Prentice Hall).

John Haught is a visiting professor at the University of Nevada, Las Vegas, where he is completing his PhD. He returned to teach in the United States after 10 years in Central America. His research interests include cultural historical activity theory, Latino issues, and the role of drama and other artistic activities in the identity formation of second language learners.

Chris Iddings is Assistant Professor of Language and Literacy at the University of Nevada, Las Vegas. Her scholarly interests include second language and literacy learning and sociocultural theory. Her latest research focuses on the social and cognitive processes of second language learning as learners learn language and literacy in integrated mainstream classrooms and as they become legitimate participants of their learning environments. Of particular interest to her are collaborative interactions between native speakers of English and non-native speakers.

Alex Kostogriz is on the Faculty of Education at Monash University in Australia. He has been involved in EFL and ESL education in eastern Europe and Australia and has published in areas of sociocultural psychology and language learning. His research interests include cultural–historical activity theory, cultural semiotics, New Literacy Studies, and postcolonial studies.

Angel M. Y. Lin obtained her PhD from the Ontario Institute for Studies in Education, University of Toronto, Canada. Her research and teaching have been centered on the connections between local face-to-face interactions and the larger institutional, sociocultural, historical, socioeconomic, and political contexts in which they are situated. With a background in ethnomethodology, conversation analysis, and social theory, her theoretical orientations are phenomenological, sociocultural, and critical. She has published research articles in *Curriculum Inquiry*; *TESOL Quarterly*; *Linguistics and Education*; *International Journal of the Sociology of Language*; *Journal of Pragmatics*; *Journal of Language, Identity, and Education*; *Canadian Modern Language Review*; *Language, Culture and Curriculum*. She serves on the editorial advisory boards of *Linguistics and Education*, *Critical Discourse Studies*, and *Critical Inquiry in Language Studies*. She started the publication of *TESL-HK* (http://www.tesl-hk.org) in 1997 and is currently as associate professor in the Department of English and Communication, City University of Hong Kong.

Jasmine C. M. Luk is a lecturer in English as the Hong Kong Institute of Education. She obtained her doctoral degree from Lancaster University, UK. She has been researching classroom interactions between native-English-speaking teachers and Hong Kong students. She is an experienced English teacher and teacher educator for both primary and secondary levels. Her research interests included cross-cultural dialogic interaction practices, culture, and second and foreign language learning.

Ludmila Marchenkova is completing her doctorate at the Ohio State University, where she also teaches ESL composition courses. The main emphasis of her dissertation is on Mikhail Bakhtin's theory of dialogue and its application to second language learning. She worked as a teacher educator and taught EFL and ESP courses for both undergraduate and graduate students in Moscow, Russia. She is particularly interested in sociolinguistics, cultural–historical theory, second language acquisition, intercultural communication, and philosophy of language.

Jeffery Lee Orr works with students from around the world. They enliven his spirit and enrich his ESOL composition instruction at Southern Polytechnic State University, where he directs the ATTIC—Advising, Tutoring, Testing/Disability Services, International Student Center. His interests in language include social cultural theory; discourse analysis, and matrices of popular culture, social identities, and composition theory. He is a PhD student at the University of Georgia in Language Education, concentrating in TESOL.

Elizabeth Platt is Associate Professor in Multilingual/Multicultural Education at Florida State University, where she teaches such graduate courses as applied linguistics, FL/SL curriculum, and psycholinguistics. On her own and with her colleague, Frank B. Brooks, she has conducted research on early second language learning, particularly from a sociocultural perspective. Another line of research entails collaboration with other Florida ESOL professionals to document various state and federal policies and mandates as they affect the fate of English-language learners in Florida's schools. She has found convergence of her two research interests by studying the linguistic minority child in various classroom contexts in light of the teacher's beliefs and practices. More recently, she has begun teaching and conducting research on migrant workers from Mexico, hoping to understand processes by which these students solve problems in their second language.

Gergana Vitanova is Assistant Professor at the University of Central Florida, where she teachers TESOL and applied linguistics courses. She has also taught ESL courses at the University of Cincinnati, Harvard University, and Ohio State University. Her research interests encompass critical approaches to second language learning involving gender, agency, and discursive practice.

Lindsay Amthor Yotsukura is an Associate Professor and Coordinator of the Japanese Language Program at the University of Maryland, College Park. She also serves as Graduate Director for the new MA degree program in Japanese Second Language Acquisition and Application. Her research interests include discourse and conversation analysis, pragmatics, pedagogical linguistics, and teaching with technology. Recent publications include *Negotiating Moves: Problem Presentation and Resolution in Japanese Business Discourse* (Elsevier Science, 2003); "Reporting Problems and Offering Assistance in Japanese Business Telephone Conversations," in *Telephone Calls: Unity and Diversity of Conversational Structure across Languages and Cultures* (K. K. Luke and T. Pavlidou, Eds., John Benjamins, 2002); "Bakhtin's Speech Genres in a Japanese Context: Business Transactional Telephone Calls," in *Bakhtinian Theory in Japanese Studies* (J. Johnson, Ed., Edwin Mellen Press, 2001).

Chapter 1

Introduction:
Dialogue With Bakhtin on Second and Foreign Language Learning

Joan Kelly Hall
Pennsylvania State University

Gergana Vitanova
University of Central Florida

Ludmila Marchenkova
The Ohio State University

Scholarship in second and foreign language learning has traditionally looked to the fields of linguistics and psycholinguistics for its epistemological foundations. One assumption in particular that has exerted much influence over the years on research concerned with language learning is a formalist view of language. Drawn from mainstream linguistics, this view considers language to be a set of abstract, self-contained systems with a fixed set of structural components and a fixed set of rules for their combination. Moreover, the systems are considered objects of study in their own right in that they can be extracted from their contexts of use and studied independently of the varied ways in which individuals make use of them.

Drawing on this formal view of language, investigations of language learning have ranged from identifying structural differences among language systems for the purposes of predicting those patterns that could cause difficulty in learning to describing the components of learners' *interlanguage system*, the transitional system posited to be developed by language learners as they move from beginning to more advanced stages of knowledge of the target language system. Also of interest has been the various forms of pedagogical interventions to determine the most effective way to facilitate learners' assimilation of new systemic knowledge into known knowledge structures. Given the view of language as stable, autonomous systems, it has been assumed that the best that teaching could do is to help learners make more effective use of an otherwise-immutable process.

Concerns with the limitations of this view for understanding fully language learners' experiences have recently increased, with scholars calling for explorations into other disciplinary territories in search of new ways to conceptualize the field (Firth & Wagner, 1997; Hall, 1993, 1995). These explorations have been productive, yielding insights into the nature of language and learning that challenge the traditional, formalist perspective typical of earlier research.

One of the more significant sources of current understandings of language can be found in the work of Mikhail Bakhtin, a Russian literary theorist. Bakhtin developed his ideas in response to early Russian formalists. In contrast to an understanding of language as sets of closed, abstract systems of normative forms, Bakhtin viewed it as comprising dynamic constellations of sociocultural resources that are fundamentally tied to their social and historical contexts. These collections, which are continuously renewed in social activity, are considered central forms of life in that not only are they used to refer to or represent our cultural worlds, but they also are the central means by which we bring our worlds into existence, maintain them, and shape them for our own purposes. Voloshinov (1973, p. 95) stated that "*Language acquires life and historically evolves precisely here, in concrete verbal communication, and not in the abstract linguistic system of language forms, nor in the individual psyche of speakers.*"[1]

One concept that is crucial to Bakhtin's conceptualization of language is the *utterance*, our concrete response to the conditions of the moment. For Bakhtin, the utterance is always a two-sided act. In the moment of its use, at one and the same time, it responds to what precedes it and anticipates what is to come. When we speak, then, we do two things: (a) we create the contexts of use to which our utterances typically belong and, at the same time, (b) we create a space for our own voice.

Bakhtin used the term *speech genres* to capture what is typical about utterances. According to Bakhtin, genres provide the history of an utterance. They bring to the moment a set of values and definitions of the context, or a way of thinking about the moment (Morson & Emerson, 1989). Bakhtin (1986, p. 87) noted:

---

[1]Current views of Russian Bakhtinists hold that the texts written by Voloshinov and Medvedev were actually dictated by Bakhtin to these individuals. Because of space and topic constraints, we cannot include a historical accounting of the debate here but instead refer readers to Emerson (1997).

A speech genre is not a form of language but a typical form of utterance; as such the genre also includes a certain typical kind of expression that inheres in it. In the genre the word acquires a particular typical expression. Genres correspond to typical situations of speech communication, typical themes, and to particular contacts between the meanings of words and actual concrete reality under certain typical circumstances.

When we speak, then, we do so in genres—that is, we choose words according to their generic specifications. At the moment of their use, we infuse them with our own voices.

Bakhtin used the term *dialogic* to capture the meaning-making process by which the historical and the present come together in an utterance. All utterances are inherently dialogic; they have, at the same time, a history and a present, which exist in a continually negotiated state of "intense and essential axiological interaction" (Bakhtin, 1990, p.10). It is in the dynamic tension between the past and the present that gives shape to one's individual voice. Such a view of language removes any a priori distinction between form and function and between individual and social uses of language. Just as no linguistic resource can be understood apart from its contexts of use, no single utterance can be considered a purely individual act. Thus, rather than being considered peripheral to our understanding of language, dialogue is considered its essence.

Bakhtin's conceptualization of language has several significant implications for current understandings of second and foreign language learning. First, it helps us to see language as a living tool—one that is simultaneously structured and emergent, by which we bring our cultural worlds into existence, maintain them, and shape them for our own purposes. In using language to participate in our activities, we reflect our understanding of them and their larger cultural contexts. At the same time, we create spaces for ourselves as individual actors within them.

Second, it locates learning in social interaction rather than in the head of the individual learner. In learning a language, we appropriate signs that are laden with meaning, "drenched in community experience" (Dyson, 2000, p. 129), and so, at the same time that we learn to use specific linguistic resources, we appropriate their histories and the activities to which they are associated. Learning language, then, does not mean accumulating decontextualized forms or structures but rather entering into ways of communicating that are defined by specific economic, political, and historical forces (Holquist, 1990).

From this perspective, the act of learning other languages takes on special meaning. For Bakhtin, it is only through knowing others that we can come to know ourselves. The more opportunities we have for interacting with others, the wider and more varied our experiences with different genres are. The more encounters with different genres we experience, the more enriched is our ability to understand and participate in social life. For, according to Bakhtin, in orienting toward us, others' utterances project a potentially new space for us that we can evaluate, draw on, and make our own. Where there are few possibilities for others to orient to us, "there are no tools for living in that place" (Emerson, 1997, p. 223). Thus, it is only by entering into dialogue with "a diversified array of others" (Emerson, 1997, p. 223) who are different from us that we can flourish.

OVERVIEW OF THIS BOOK

This edited volume presents 10 chapters that draw on Bakhtin's insights about language to explore theoretical and practical concerns with second and foreign language learning and teaching. The chapters begin with the premise that learning other languages is about seeking out different experiences for the purposes of developing new ways of understanding ourselves and others and becoming involved in our worlds. The text is arranged into two parts. Part I contains 7 chapters that report on investigations into specific contexts of language learning and teaching.

Braxley's chapter (chap. 1) uses Bakhtin's concepts of dialogism and speech genres in investigating how international graduate students in a North American program master the task of academic writing in English as a second language. Arguing that dialogue is a critical component of the process through which non-native speakers negotiate the complexity of academic genres, Braxley presents data from a qualitative study with five female students from east and southeast Asia. The data, collected through open-ended interviews, revealed several important patterns. Most important, Braxley discovered that although mastering the genre of academic English was challenging both cognitively and emotionally for her participants, it was facilitated by dialogues with peers, instructors, and with texts. The findings also reveal that students were able to appropriate the genres of their own academic fields; however, the mastery of one genre did not extend to the mastery of other genres. Braxley concludes her chapter with a discussion of what she considers to be some significant pedagogical implications arising from these findings.

In chapter 2, Iddings, Haught, and Devlin examine mutual relations among sign, meaning, and language learning that involve two second language students in an English-dominant third-grade classroom. They apply Bakhtin and Vygotsky's views on meaning-making, supplemented by Bakhtin's concept of dialogism, in order to understand how these novice learners of English reorganize and develop semiotic tools to create meaning through interaction with each other. Their findings indicate that the students' engagement in multimodal representations facilitated their access to the social life in the classroom, which in turn opened the door to the learning of English. Iddings et al. conclude that the most important factor in creating meaning was the developing relationship between the two interactants, in which they used various signs, such as drawings, block patterns, and ornate designs.

Orr considers in chapter 3 Bakhtin's concept of utterances to be particularly fertile for the field of English as a second language composition. In his study of a freshman composition classroom, he demonstrates how objects of popular culture function as utterances that carry ideological and cultural meanings. The ESL students in this classroom had to select, analyze, and respond to bumper stickers as artifacts of popular culture. In the essays they wrote, followed by letters to friends and the owner of car with the bumper stickers, students actively engaged in dialogic relationships with others' utterances. They evaluated these utterances on the basis of their own ideologies and the ideologies of their first-language communities. Orr's findings reveal that these ESL composition students exhibited a keen awareness of the interactive nature of utterances, and they understood how these are politically and socially situated. This realization—that language is not a neutral medium, according to the author—can significantly enhance access to the second language and increase L2 proficiency.

In chapter 4, Lin and Luk take as their point of departure Bakhtin's analyses of the liberating power of laughter. They use Bakhtin's ideas to address the issue of teaching English in post- and neocolonialist contexts. They then present a discourse analysis of classroom interactions video recorded in two Hong Kong secondary schools. The analysis demonstrates that English lessons may be uncreative parroting sessions for students. In contrast, Lin and Luk discuss how students use their native language styles in more creative learning situations. They conclude the chapter by arguing that Bakhtin's ideas can help English teachers to be more aware of the ideological nature of their own teaching practices and to use dialogic communication with their students. A special role in such communication, they emphasize, belongs to students' uses of local linguistic styles, social languages, and creativity.

Chapter 5, by Dufva and Alanen, combines Bakhtin's notion of dialogicality with neo-Vygotskyan approaches to language learning in their ongoing study of a small group of Finnish schoolchildren. Drawing on dialogical and Vygotskian perspectives, Dufva and Alanen critique purely cognitivist views on children's metalinguistic awareness and suggest that the latter is simultaneously a social and individual/cognitive phenomenon. *Polyphony* is another Bakhtinian concept that Dufva and Alanen extend to their analysis of metalinguistic awareness. By arguing that young children develop their knowledge of native and foreign languages in a variety of settings and interactions, they explain that children's awareness emerges as a multivoiced, rather than a unified, construct. Dufva and Alanen's analyses demonstrate that the child's metalinguistic awareness is, in a significant way, a *heteroglossic* phenomenon, as Bakhtin would term it. In other words, it reflects traces not only of different dialects, registers, and styles but also of values and beliefs that are picked up in everyday life contexts. By embedding metalinguistic awareness in Bakhtinian terms, the chapter prompts language researchers to rethink this complex construct and contends that metalinguistic awareness develops through socialization practices into the discourses of one's settings.

In Platt's chapter 7, the concept of dialogism elaborated by Bakhtin serves as a theoretical framework for analyzing the performance of a problem-solving (information gap) task in a new language. The focus of her study is on two novice learners of Swahili who establish intersubjectivity, construct meaning, and come to recognize their language-learning selves in negotiating this challenging task. Using multiple sources of data, Platt demonstrates the differences between the participants in terms of their perspectives on language, procedural preferences, and goals for accomplishment. She also describes the gradual processes of a successful completion of the task by both participants, revealing how, as a result of their dialogic activity, one of the learners, Majidah, comes to recognize herself as a good language learner.

In chapter 8, Vitanova explores how adult immigrants author themselves and how they act as agents in contexts and discourses alien to them. Vitanova's understanding of agency is grounded in the Bakhtinian framework of subjectivity, in which agency is shaped by creative answerability and marked by emotional–volitional tones. To illustrate, Vitanova draws on narrative discourse examples from three eastern European immigrants. She examines how the participants reauthor and re-create their selves through dialogic relations with others, in responding creatively to the others' voices and practices. She concludes the chapter by calling for microsocial linguistics articulated by Bakhtin that views personhood as a continuous creative process.

The three chapters that comprise Part II, "*Implications for Theory and Practice,*" present broader discussions on second and foreign language learning using Bakhtin's ideas as a springboard for thinking. In chapter 9, Marchenkova outlines a much-needed parallel between Bakhtin and Vygotsky. In it, she argues that, despite their different theoretical backgrounds—philosophical and literary theory for Bakhtin and developmental psychology for Vygotsky—the two scholars' frameworks enrich and complement each other. In delineating the similarities and differences between the two Russian scholars, she focuses on three interrelated areas: (a) the notion of language, and how it is conceptualized in the two frameworks; (b) the role of culture in the development of intercultural understanding; and (c) the formation of self and the role of the other in this process. Of particular interest to L2 researchers and teachers, however, is not merely the theoretical parallels between Vygotsky's and Bakhtin's approaches to language and the self; rather, it is Marchenkova's suggestion of how linking these two compatible—and, at the same time, distinct—frameworks can provide a fruitful ground for L2 pedagogy.

Kostogriz's chapter, 10, also espouses Bakhtin's notions of dialogue, culture, and the other. Its focus, however, is on L2 literacy learning in multicultural classrooms. Kostogriz argues that Bakhtin's theory, with its strong emphasis on the social nature of language and consciousness, equips language researchers with a critical and ideological tool with which to approach ESL education. For instance, according to Kostogriz, dialogue, in a Bakhtinian sense, can be used as a unit of analysis of intra- and intercommunication. On the basis of these and other theoretical considerations, he advocates that we need to formulate a thirdspace pedagogy of ESL literacy that involves multiple perspectives of knowledge and recognizes issues of power, resistance, and transformation.

In the final chapter of this volume, chapter 11, Yotsukura explores a particular genre, Japanese business telephone conversations, and shows how it may be used for the development of language learners' pragmatic competence in Japanese. Drawing on Bakhtin's understanding of speech genres, she discusses some important features of Japanese business telephone conversations in terms of their thematic, structural, and stylistic similarities, with special attention paid to opening segments. Yotsukura presents a number of excerpts from these segments are presented to show how participants negotiate interactional tasks on the telephone. Using these excerpts as a springboard, Yotsukura proposes that second and foreign language students may benefit in learning preferred interactional strategies in Japanese from authentic conversations. Students will derive further benefits, she argues, from the use of the Bakhtinian notion of addressivity "as a heuristic to explore how participants design appropriate utterances for their audiences."

As Bakhtin (1986) noted, all words, all utterances, all texts, are unfinalizable in that they want to be heard and responded to. And so it is with this volume. We invite readers to enter into dialogue with the chapters here. Such experiences entail, as Bakhtin noted, not just reaching an understanding of the authors' words from their points of view but also taking the authors' words and supplementing them with the readers' own voices as they move to engage in other discourses, at other times, for other purposes.

REFERENCES

Bakhtin, M. M. (1986). *"Speech genres" and other essays* (M. Holquist & C. Emerson, Eds., V. McGee, Trans.). Austin: University of Texas Press.

Bakhtin, M. M. (1990). *Art and answerability* (M. Holquist & V. Liapunov, Eds.). Austin: University of Texas Press.

Dyson, A. (2000). Linking writing and community development through the children' forum. In C. Lee & P. Smagorinsky (Eds.), *Vygotskian perspectives on literacy research* (pp. 127–149). Cambridge, England: Cambridge University Press.

Emerson, C. (1997). *The first hundred years of Bakhtin.* Princeton, NJ: Princeton University Press.

Firth, A., & Wagner, J. (1997). On discourse, communication, and (some) fundamental concepts in SLA research. *Modern Language Journal, 81,* 277–300.

Hall, J. K. (1993). The role of oral practices in the accomplishment of our everyday lives: The sociocultural dimension of interaction with implications for the learning of another language. *Applied Linguistics 14,* 145–166.

Hall, J. K. (1995). (Re)creating our world with words: A sociohistorical perspective of face-to-face interaction. *Applied Linguistics, 16,* 206–232.

Holquist, M. (1990). *Dialogism: Bakhtin and his world.* New York: Routledge.

Morson, G. S., & Emerson, C. (Eds.). (1989). *Rethinking Bakhtin: Extensions and challenges.* Evanston, IL: Northwestern University Press.

Voloshinov, V. N. (1973). *Marxism and the philosophy of language* (L. Matejka & I. R. Titunik, Trans.). New York: Seminar.

PART I

INVESTIGATIONS INTO CONTEXTS OF LANGUAGE LEARNING AND TEACHING

Mastering Academic English: International Graduate Students' Use of Dialogue and Speech Genres to Meet the Writing Demands of Graduate School

Karen Braxley
University of Georgia

In the last few decades, American colleges and universities have seen an influx of international graduate students. These students believe that a graduate degree from an American university will open doors for them, either in the United States or at home, and are willing to spend considerable time, effort, and money to attain their academic goals. American educational institutions welcome such students both for their academic prowess and, it must be admitted, for the welcome income they bring, especially in times of budget constraints. The end result is that "American educational institutions are to the modern world what Alexandria in Egypt was to the ancient world" (Ubadigbo, 1997, p. 2).

When international students arrive in American universities, they face the challenge of simultaneously adapting to a new country, language, culture, and educational system. For graduate students, the challenge is particularly great as they are often expected to produce scholarly writing within a short period of their arrival. This can be especially daunting when such students may have had little experience of writing in English (Dong, 1998; Rose & McClafferty, 2001) and may have expectations that are different from those of their professors (Belcher, 1994; Fishman & McCarthy, 2001; Fox, 1994). Despite the difficulties they face, many international graduate students are able to rise to the challenge of writing academic English. How they are able to do so is the focus of the study I report in this chapter, which used Bakhtin's concepts of *dialogism* and *speech genres* as a theoretical framework for understanding how international graduate students master the genre of academic writing.

My motivation for conducting this study was my realization that many of the more successful graduate students with whom I have worked as a writing tutor in a university learning center seemed to share a certain characteristic: They tended to seek out opportunities for interaction in order to improve their written work. To determine how these students learned through their interaction and to investigate the other factors that led to their success in academic writing, I designed a research study in which I used Bakthin's theories of *dialogism* and *speech genres*—two concepts that seemed particularly apposite for investigating how such students learned to master the genre of academic English—as a theoretical lens to bring these students' learning experiences into sharper focus.

In the first part of this chapter, I review the concepts of dialogism and speech genres and discuss how they are relevant to the problem of learning to write the genres of academic English. In the second part of this chapter, I introduce the study, discuss its findings and implications, and make suggestions for further research.

DIALOGISM

Dialogism is the term Bakhtin (1981, 1986) used to describe the interaction between a speaker's words, or utterances, and the relationship they enter into with the utterances of other speakers. The concept of dialogism was of fundamental importance to Bakhtin and has implications for the way we understand all spoken and written communication.

Inherent in Bakhtin's notion of dialogism is the idea of a speaker and a listener. In Bakhtin's (1986) view, the speaker is always responding to others' words:

> Any speaker is himself a respondent to a greater or lesser degree ... he presupposes not only the existence of the language system, but also the existence of preceding utterances, his own and others'—with which his given utterance enters into one kind of relation or another .... Any utterance is a link in a very complexly organized chain of other utterances. (p. 69)

The trope of the utterance as a link in a chain of utterances was extensively used by Bakhtin. As I understand it, this chain has both temporal and spatial dimensions. In Western thought, the link of utterances stretches back in time to the words (and rhetorical models) of ancient Greeks, Romans, and Hebrews and forward in time to utterances that have yet to be spoken. The chain also stretches out to other fields, other genres, and other languages so that we can see, in Bakhtin's own work, for example, how the fields of linguistics, literary criticism, and philosophy enter into dialogue with each other and interanimate one another. Bakhtin's insights show us that dialogue ranges far and wide, through time and space.

Implicit in the idea of dialogue is the desire to elicit a response; we may even have a particular respondent in mind. Bakhtin (1986) called this concept *addressivity*, because the utterance is always directed at someone; it is not designed to dissipate in a vacuum. In everyday conversation, the addressee will (probably) be the person to whom we are speaking, but in writing, even though we may be removed in distance or time from our respondent, we still have a respondent in mind, from whom we wish to elicit a response. In Bakhtin's (1986) conception of dialogism, the listener, too, is always an active respondent: "When the listener perceives and understands the meaning of speech, he simultaneously takes an active, responsive attitude toward it. He either agrees or disagrees with it, augments it, applies it, prepares for its execution and so on" (p. 68). The listener may be the next link in the chain, or a future link. Even if an utterance does not evoke an immediate response on the part of a listener, the listener will respond eventually, either in words or in action.

In the genres of academic writing, especially in academic writing for publication in journals, dialogue is an essential part of the process a writer goes through to write an article. Often it is the author's reading of previous research that provides the impetus for conducting new research. Moreover, in writing an article, the author will almost certainly review the literature and, by doing so, will allow others to speak through his or her work and will add his or her voice to theirs, thereby adding another link to the chain.

Even the format of the typical research article has a kind of internal dialogism built into it. As Bakhtin (1986) himself pointed out, "In secondary speech genres, especially rhetorical ones .... Quite frequently within the boundaries of his own utterance the speaker (or writer) raises questions, answers them himself, raises objections to his own ideas, responds to his own objections and so on" (p. 72). Although the above-mentioned practices do not represent true dialogism—they are a rhetorical device rather than true dialogue—they do show how fundamental dialogue is to the practice of argumentation: To make an effective argument, it is important to anticipate and respond to the reader's response.

In a peer reviewed journal, dialogism is built right into the writing and publication process: The journal editor sends the article to various reviewers, who will write their comments on it, and the author is then required to respond to these comments if he or she wishes to have the article published. If the author is invited to revise and resubmit the article, this process may then start over again and, if the process stretches on long enough, the author will also need to rewrite the article to include the voices of other researchers who have been published since the process began.

Often, a journal will continue the dialogue after publication of an article by publishing others' responses to the original article. For example, in preparing to write this chapter, I researched how others had used Bakhtin's theories in their work and came across an article titled *"Individualism, Academic Writing, and ESL Writers,"* by Ramanathan and Atkinson (1999), published in the *Journal of Second Language Writing*. I also found Peter Elbow's (1999) response to this article, published in the same journal 6 months later and, published another 6 months later, Atkinson's (2000) response to Elbow's article. No doubt the dialogue will continue, and merely by referencing these articles I am adding another small link to the chain.

Amidst so much dialogue it is difficult to answer the question James Wertsch (1998) asked when analyzing Bakhtin's theories: Who is doing the talking? Wertsch (1998) pointed out that, from a Bakhtinian perspective, there will always be more than one voice. This presents both an opportunity and a challenge to a writer of English as a second language (ESL): by engaging in dialogic reading and writing she may come to understand (and hence to write) her subject better, but with so many voices echoing in her head she may find it difficult to make herself heard; she may even no longer be able to distinguish her own voice from those of others. This situation was described poignantly by Jieming, a Chinese graduate student in Helen Fox's writing class, in a note she handed in with her research paper:

> Note: ... It is hard for me to say from which resources I have drawn any ideas to put into this paper. However, one thing is clear; that all the knowledge and the ways I used to think and write are what I have learned from my teachers and others, although I have used my own mind to absorb and integrate them. I am very grateful to those who gave me knowledge and let me know how to recognize the world. And I am very sorry that I did not put any references at the end of this paper. (Fox, 1994, p. 64)

SPEECH GENRES

At first glance, the term *speech genre* seems singularly inapposite to use as a framework for analyzing the genre of academic *writing*. However, for Bakhtin, a speech genre is by no means limited to speaking alone; although

Bakhtin used words such as *speech*, *speaker*, *listener*, and *speech communication* throughout his work, he made it clear that his concepts apply equally to writing, writer, reader, and written communication (1986, p. 69).

Bakhtin saw language as a site of struggle wherein the collision of centripetal and centrifugal forces results in a condition of heteroglossia, in which context and the dialogic relationship between a speaker and other participants in speech communication are all important. On the one hand, centripetal forces play a normative role, ensuring that speakers of a language will be able to understand one another. On the other hand, centrifugal forces keep a language alive and allow for the creation of new genres.[1] Speech genres, then, are an outcome of the clash between centripetal and centrifugal forces, which causes language to fracture into new genres.

Although Bakhtin (1986) described speech genres as "relatively stable," he also noted their extreme heterogeneity. In discussing the links between style and genre, he pointed out that genre and style must be studied in their sociohistorical context: "Each sphere has and applies its own genres that correspond to its own specific conditions" (1986, p. 64). Moreover, "the specific conditions of speech communication specific for each sphere give rise to particular genres" (Bakhtin, 1986, p. 64). It would be mistaken, then, to see genres as engraved in stone, and it would be equally mistaken to see academic writing as composed of one monolithic, unified genre. From a Bakhtinian perspective, there might be considerable variation in the written genres even of closely related fields. To understand why this is so, it is important to take into account their sociohistorical context.

Atkinson and Ramanathan's (1995) ethnography of two writing programs within the same university illustrates this point. The motivation for conducting the study was Atkinson's realization that the students he taught in the English Language Program (ELP) were perceived by the instructors in the University Composition Program (UCP) as having poor writing abilities. Moreover, certain characteristics that were emphasized in the first program (ELP) seemed to be criticized in the second (UCP).

After conducting a 10–month-long ethnographic study of the two programs, Atkinson and Ramanathan (1995) found some key differences between them. Several of these differences can be attributed to the differing writing genres favored by the two departments. For example, the instructors in the UCP felt that form should serve the writer's purpose (not vice versa) and favored subtle writing characterized by the use of imagery, metaphor, and personification. The ELP, in contrast, favored a clear, straight-

---

[1]Some examples of centripetal forces are dictionaries or freshman composition classes that teach traditional models of rhetoric; some examples of centrifugal forces are new technologies such as the Internet and popular art forms such as hip-hop.

forward, "workmanlike" prose and generally taught a deductive essay format. The most striking difference between the two programs, however, was that the ELP embraced the five-paragraph essay, a form that was despised by the UCP.

Atkinson and Ramanathan (1995), echoing Santos' (1992) earlier comments, suggested that the differences between the two programs stemmed from their different origins: All the faculty in the ELP had backgrounds in applied linguistics, whereas those in the UCP had backgrounds in composition and rhetoric. Both programs presumably intended to prepare their students for the writing they would have to do in college, but the two programs clearly favored different genres of academic writing. As a result, Atkinson and Ramanathan found that students moving from one context to the other may "experience a significant disjuncture" (p. 563). As Bakhtin (1986) suggested, an investigation of the sociohistorical background of the two departments is useful in explaining the difference.

My own experience in moving between departments leads me to suspect that such disjunctures are not uncommon. As a graduate student moving from the field of literature to the field of education, I had great trouble adapting to the genre and style of a typical research article in the social sciences; such articles initially seemed to me to be as dry and unpalatable as week-old French bread. Only later did I learn that their generic form reflected social scientists' desire to ally themselves with the hard sciences and to appreciate how the form facilitated clear presentation of research and aided comparison between articles.

Newly arrived graduate students may also experience a similar disjuncture—but to a much greater degree, especially if the written genres valued by their own cultures differ considerably from American academic genres. There have been many excellent discussions of the ways in which international students' cultures and expectations may clash with those of their American professors and of the ways in which this clash affects their writing (see, e.g., Fishman & McCarthy, 2001; Fox, 1994; Ivanic & Camps, 2001; Ramanathan & Atkinson, 1999). In the study reported in this chapter, I hope to show how international graduate students are able to win the struggle to appropriate the new genres to which they are exposed.

Because of their divergent historical development and differing aims, academic writing genres differ from one another considerably with respect to the amount of individuality they allow to writers within the genre. Bakhtin (1986) pointed out that

> Not all genres are equally conducive to reflecting the individuality of the speaker in the language of the utterance, that is, to an individual style. The most conducive genres are those of artistic literature: here the individual style enters directly into the very task of the utterance .... In the vast majority

of speech genres, the individual style does not enter into the intent of the utterance, does not serve as its only goal, but is, as it were, an epiphenomenon of the utterance, one of its by products. (p. 63)

In researching this chapter, I found considerable differences among the ways that scholars use Bakhtin's concepts in their work, especially with regard to their focus on individuality in writing. Many researchers in the field of first-language composition focus on Bakhtin's notion of voice, which has been strongly linked to the notion of individuality and individual style (Baynam, 1999; Bialystosky, 1998; Farmer, 1995; Ritchie, 1998). This is in keeping with the genre of writing favored in most college composition classes, the instructors of which see individual voice as an important part of the genre.

By contrast, several ESL researchers reject the notion of voice, asserting that it is a Western construct unshared by members of non-Western cultures (Johns, 1999; Ramanathan & Atkinson, 1999; Ramanathan & Kaplan, 1996). ESL researchers tend rather to focus instead on other Bakhtinian concepts, especially dialogue. This book is no exception. That researchers in English composition and researchers in ESL tend to draw on different concepts from Bakhtin indicates that they may value different characteristics in writing; thus, it is not surprising that the academic writing taught in ESL classes and in freshman composition classes may be different genres (Atkinson & Ramanathan, 1995).

One further point is of importance to the study reported in this chapter. Bakhtin pointed out that, because of the extreme heterogeneity of genres, no one can master every speech genre. In the following example, he illustrated how mastery is usually limited to a few genres:

Frequently a person who has an excellent command of speech in some areas of cultural communication, who is able to read a scholarly paper or engage in a scholarly discussion, who speaks very well on social questions, is silent or very awkward in social conversation. Here it is not a matter of an impoverished vocabulary or of style, taken abstractly: this is entirely a matter of the inability to command a repertoire of genres of social conversation. (Bakhtin, 1986, p. 80)

Only when we master genres can we use them freely and express our own individuality within them (Bakhtin, 1986, p. 80), yet mastery of genres is a struggle that may take years, and even then it is by no means assured, especially for non-native speakers.

Another point essential to mastery of the genre of academic writing is the ability to write authoritatively within the genre. Bakhtin (1981) discussed authority mostly in terms of *authoritative discourse*, which, for him, had particular qualities: It does not open itself to dialogue as do other forms of discourse (termed by Bakhtin as *internally persuasive discourse*); instead, it insists that one must either accept or reject it. One of the examples Bakhtin gave of authoritative discourse is "acknowledged scientific truth" (1981, p. 343). I suggest that the voice of scientific truth does have relevance to the genre of academic writing, especially for writing in the social sciences, which often carries with it the trappings of science in its use of terminology. For example, in social science writing (especially in studies that use a quantitative methodology), we often speak of theories, we pose research questions, and we prove or disprove hypotheses.

By using such expressions, we evoke the language of science to lend authority to our writing, and some research suggests we learn to do so at an early age. Wertsch (1991, 1998) has offered two examples of how children are able to gain control of the conversation by evoking the language of science. In one example, Wertsch (1991) analyzed a segment of classroom discourse (a fourth-grade science class) and found that one student's use of the scientific words—*lava* and *atmosphere*—had a profound effect on his classmates, who thought his response was "smart" although, in fact, the student's answer had very little to do with the question he was trying to answer. In another example, Wertsch (1998) analyzed a segment of dialogue in which a child was able to deflect her father's irritatingly authoritative questioning about how many sides a pyramid has by invoking the voice of an even higher authority, that of science. She did this by stating, "I'm used to Euler's formula" (p. 68).[2] Her invocation of these seemingly magical words gave her the authority to control the conversation, or at least to change its direction.

Our use of "scientific" language in our writing has a similar effect by allowing us, rightly or wrongly, to ally ourselves with the authoritative discourse of science. All writers wish to receive the accolade of being said to write with authority, but few of us are able to do so, especially those of us who are novice writers or who are writing English as a second language. In this study, I wished to determine what factors led international graduate students to become successful writers, and I expected that success in academic writing would be aided by at least being able to give the appearance of writing with authority.

In this review I have discussed some concepts that I believe are relevant to the problem of writing academic English in a second language: the dialogic nature of academic writing; the fact that genres reflect their sociohistoric development and thus vary, even between closely related fields; and the notion that, in order to write with authority, students might call on particular forms of discourse, for example, the authoritative discourse of science. In the next section, I will briefly review the challenges stu-

---

[2]This is a method for calculating the number of faces of polyhedra.

dents face in writing English as a second language and introduce a study I conducted to investigate how students are able to meet these challenges.

THE PROBLEMS OF WRITING ACADEMIC ENGLISH
IN A SECOND LANGUAGE

Writing English as a second language is a difficult, almost overwhelming, task for many international students. The difficulties such students face in writing in American colleges and universities have been well documented in second language writing research (Ferris & Hedgcock, 1998; Fox, 1994; Silva, 2001; Zamel & Spack, 1998). However, most studies of second language writing have focused on the writing of undergraduates in college composition classrooms (Atkinson & Ramanathan, 1995; Harklau, 2000; Warschauer, 1998) and in the content areas (Fishman & McCarthy, 2001; Leki, 2001; Leki & Carson, 1994, 1997). Comparatively few studies have focused on the challenges faced by international students writing at the graduate level (Prior, 1998, 2001, is an exception), and some of those that do tend to focus on the writing of theses and dissertations (Dong, 1996, 1998). However, international graduate students in many programs, especially those in the humanities and social sciences, are expected to do copious amounts of writing long before they reach the stage of writing a thesis or dissertation. For these students, the first years of graduate school are the most challenging, because there is often a huge gap between the level and amount of writing they have done so far and that which is now expected from them. In Bakhtin's (1981, 1986) terms, these students must appropriate and eventually master the genre of academic writing required by their field of study.

THE STUDY

To determine how international graduate students are able to bridge this gap—to raise the level of their writing to that required in graduate school— I conducted a qualitative interview study of five female graduate students whom I considered to be successful writers.[3] The participants in this study were five east and southeast Asian female graduate students, aged between 25 and 32. I selected Asian participants because, in the university where the research was conducted, most graduate students come from Asian countries. I chose female participants because I believed they would be more

---

[3]I defined these students as successful because they reported that, although writing English had initially been a struggle for them, they now received positive evaluation from their professors on their writing, as was evidenced by their high grade-point averages. Moreover, all the participants held research or teaching assistantships, and most had already published in their fields.

willing than men to discuss situations with a female researcher they might have found humiliating. One more point is important: my relationship with the participants. Prior to (and after) the study, I worked with three of the students (Anne, Becky, and Keiko—all pseudonyms) as a writing tutor in the university's learning center. This relationship is likely to have influenced the nature of their responses.

I collected data by means of open-ended interviews in which I asked the participants to tell me about their educational backgrounds, the kinds of writing they had to do in graduate school, and how they were able to meet the writing requirements of their programs. I analyzed the data using techniques based on grounded theory (Charmaz, 2000, 2002; Glaser & Strauss, 1967; Strauss & Corbin, 1998), and through constant comparison and recursive analysis I identified themes that I used to develop questions for a second round of interviews and a group discussion with all the participants. I collected follow-up data through e-mails and telephone conversations, often initiated by the participants themselves.

On the basis of my analysis, I identified the following themes in the data:

- Writing the genre of academic English is extremely challenging, but students were able to meet the challenge by creating opportunities for dialogue with (a) peers, (b) a writing tutor or an instructor, and (c) texts.
- Most of the graduate students believed that having an individual style or voice was not a key component in writing in their fields.
- The students believed that authority in writing came mostly from thorough knowledge of their fields, but they felt that having limited proficiency in English undermined their ability to write with authority.
- Although students were able to successfully appropriate the genres of their fields, mastery of this one genre did not lead to mastery of other genres.

THE DIFFICULTY OF WRITING ACADEMIC ENGLISH AT THE GRADUATE LEVEL

Do you remember your first assignment in graduate school?

I was almost crying. (Keiko)

Even the word W-R-I-T-E just, you know, made me nervous. (Becky)

I got, you know, feedback from professors. It's kind of scratched out on every pages. You know red scratched out on every pages. I was really upset. [sighs and blushes deeply]. So I realized my English writing really have serious problems. (Anne)

I remember in the first semester when I had to write the first, very first, writing assignment. It's difficult [sighs and shakes her head]. Like to get one page is so hard. (Sangthien)

As the preceding excerpts show, the participants found writing academic English extremely challenging, both cognitively and emotionally. One reason they found their first experience of writing in graduate school so difficult was that they generally had little or no experience of writing academic English before coming to graduate school. Most of the writing they had done in college English classes in their own countries had been informal and expressive:

[In Korea] we wrote like diaries, journals, essays about what your ideal husband look like ... it's totally different [from here]. (Becky)

We only wrote like a paragraph, so writing a thesis—long paper—[for her U.S. master's degree] was so hard. [In Japan] we practiced a lot of writing about feelings—we wrote journals every day. (Mizuki)

For most of these students, exposure to the genre of academic writing did not occur until they entered graduate school in America. It is no wonder, then, that their first writing assignment came as such a shock, as they described:

I thought I was doing right. Then all of a sudden I got this paper back and it's horrible. That was kind of my awakening moment. (Becky)

Before getting feedback from professors, I knew I have mistakes in my writing—but the real reality was different from my imagination. I was very upset. (Anne)

Moreover, the students recognized that the academic writing genres in which they were now expected to write were different from the academic genres they had been familiar with in their own countries. Mizuki described how she used to get confused between writing in English and Japanese academic style: "I got mixed up with Japanese composition, which is like totally opposite—you can never be clear about things—they're totally different styles." All of the students were able to describe differences between American academic writing and the academic writing style in their own countries, as Becky illustrated:

[In America] you put the topic sentence at the beginning of the paragraph. [In Korea] we don't do that much. We put the important sentence at the end of the paragraph. It is considered more humble, a humble way to express yourself, and you should be humble as a scholar … so I did that [in America] because it's what I'm used to. But nobody noticed what I'm saying!

Considering how little exposure to academic writing in English most of these students had before attending graduate school in the United States, it is surprising that the students were able to adjust as well as they did. One practice that the students found instrumental in helping them meet the writing requirements of their programs was seeking out opportunities for dialogue with friends, instructors or writing tutors, and with the text.

Dialogue With Friends

The students used dialogue with friends and classmates to help them in various ways, and the nature of the help they needed seemed to determine which friends they went to for help: When they needed help with understanding the subject matter, the participants often went to other international students for help, as Keiko described:

> I usually studied with another international student who was very serious and helped me. Also there's a wonderful Japanese graduate student in statistics, and he can always help me with everything.

However, when they needed help with writing in English, they usually went to American friends. In the following passage, Becky explains how she was able to learn from her American friends:

> I learn to use different words, like *argue* or *claim*—not the same word all the time … and I learn things like parallel structure.

However, although they did ask their friends and classmates for help, the students reported that were often hesitant to do so, either because they felt embarrassed at showing others their "poor" writing or because they didn't want to waste their friends' time. One student, Anne, reported that although she occasionally asked friends for help, she felt that she didn't learn from their help:

> Even though I asked a student in my department to read my paper, I think writing skill is different …. I think I need to talk to expert in English writing for international students … experts in English can help me through the conversation with me—help me reorganize my paper. If I ask a friend in my department, she can't explain *why*. It's not really understandable to me.

Anne felt the need to speak to someone who could not only correct her errors but could also explain them, and for this she sought help from a writing tutor.[4]

Dialogue With Tutors and Instructors

Anne was not alone in thinking the help she could get from a writing tutor was qualitatively different from the help she received from friends. Both Keiko and Becky felt that discussing the paper with a tutor helped them to get a new perspective on their writing:

> Before I show some work to you, I may think it's okay, and then, when I explain it to you, I notice it's not really good. I need to rewrite some parts ....
> Sometimes I notice after I write something, if it's not clear to you, it's not clear to anybody. That's when there's a better way to explain it. (Keiko)

> We just go through and you ask me questions like "What do you mean by this sentence?" you know, "Why do you use this word here?" And that makes me think about my whole structure, so after I come back and I tear it down and I rewrite it. It really helps me to structure clearly. (Becky)

These passages suggest that dialogue with a tutor meant more than just proofreading; by discussing their paper with another person the students were not only reorganizing their papers or acquiring new words but also developing their thoughts.[5]

Sangthien, the only student who already had experience of doing academic writing in English before coming to America, reported taking part in another kind of dialogue, an internal dialogue with an English instructor who had taught her several years earlier. Whenever she wrote, she heard in her head the voice of the man she called "my scary English teacher":

> Whenever I'm writing, I hear his voice: "Show don't tell! This sounds unnatural! You are sounding Thai!" It's horrible, but it's a good warning; it's like stuck on the back of my head.

Although Sangthien disliked hearing the injunctions of her English teacher ringing in her head whenever she wrote, she felt that hearing his voice did make her a better writer. When she wrote, she was always responding to his comments, whether she wanted to or not.

---

[4]In the cases of Anne, Becky, and Keiko, I was the tutor with whom they worked. As a result, they may have overstated the importance of the help they received from a tutor in order to make me feel appreciated.

[5]This is an example of the development that occurs when working in Vygotsky's zone of proximal development. See Vygotsky (1978) for a full discussion.

When the participants asked their content area instructors for help, they received a variety of responses. The participants all reported that although they could get help on the content of their papers (e.g., their understanding of the theories and concepts they were studying), they did not often feel they could get help on how to write their papers. The most common response from instructors was a suggestion that the students get editing help from friends, classmates, or writing tutors. A few instructors, however, were willing to help by going through papers with the students, especially if the assignment was an important one: Becky reported that her advisor invited her to his home, where he spent several hours going through her master's thesis with her. Other professors made allowances for their non-native speaking students by focusing on content rather than on surface errors. This last response, although well intentioned, sometimes led the students to have a false impression of their writing ability, as Becky described:

> The worst thing about my first semester is my professor gave me lots of writing assignment and he never correct any. He tried to understand what I'm saying and he gave me a good grade .... Then another professor, he's really picky, you know—correct everything. So I got my paper back and I was just shocked!

Although the students reported that their professors seldom gave them explicit help in appropriating the academic writing genre, they all reported getting help elsewhere: from the academic texts they read.

Dialogue With the Text

When I asked Sangthien how she had learned to write in the genre of her field, her response was immediate: "I learned it from reading!" All the participants reported learning through dialogue with the text and, in describing to me how they approached their writing assignments, all of them mentioned going back to the text throughout the writing process. It was Sanghthien who articulated most clearly the dialogic nature of her reading, and this point is particularly striking if one compares her comments with those of Bakhtin (1986):

> If I have no idea how I'm going to do it [a writing assignment], I'll have to ask the classmates. Yeah, I'll talk with my classmates, [say], "How would you do it?" And then if it's still not clear, I'll ask the professor. And then I go to the library to find the articles of something else on that topic. *I need to see what other people think about that. And then I kinda make notes about other peoples' opinions on the topic and I use that in my writing ... and kinda like, I think along the same lines, like do I agree with this? Or this is not good* (italics added).

When the listener perceives and understands the meaning of speech, he simultaneously takes an active, responsive attitude toward it. He either agrees or disagrees with it, augments it, applies it, prepares for its execution and so on. (Bakhtin, 1986, p. 68)

In the preceding passage, we can see that Sangthien goes through various kinds of dialogue in responding to a challenging writing assignment: She talks with friends, with the instructor, and with the texts themselves. Clearly, her reading is a very dialogic process, as she interrogates the authors she reads and then interrogates herself about her response to the readings. I believe that the dialogic process Sangthien goes through in writing plays a major role in helping her to be the accomplished writer that she is.

INDIVIDUALITY IN ACADEMIC GENRES

When I asked the participants if individuality and originality were important in the genres in which they wrote, they responded differently according to their fields. The four students in the social sciences responded quite definitively, "no": Although it was important to have original ideas, it was not important to show originality in expressing those ideas. In other words, they did not consider individual writing style to be important in the genres in which they wrote.

However, Becky, the graduate student in history, believed that original ideas and individual writing style were both important, and she said that the degree to which individual writing style was valued depended on where the history department was located:

Sometimes history departments are located in social sciences and sometimes in the arts. My history department is located in the college of arts, so I have to try to write in an artistic way. I have to try to be individual, but some professors say you can learn that by finding someone whose style you like and imitating it. Then you can find your own style. I am trying to find my own style, but it's hard! I didn't find it yet!

Becky's words echo Atkinson and Ramanathan's (1995) findings about the different genres found in English classes depending on whether they are located in English or applied linguistics departments. They also support Bakhtin's (1986) notion that in order to understand a genre it must be studied in its historical context.

While the four students in the social sciences did not feel the need to express individuality in their writing, they did feel some tension between expressing others' ideas and expressing their own ideas, and nowhere was this more apparent than in writing the literature review, which all five students thought was the most difficult part of writing a research paper. In the following passage, Mizuki expresses the frustration she felt about having to reproduce others' ideas. She said that in writing the literature review, she often felt as though she were "stealing" others' ideas rather than dialoguing with others:

> The literature review is soooo hard for me. Put all the quotes together but not quote, just put in my own words. I feel like I'm creating something I'm not supposed to. *I feel like I'm stealing.* You know, people say, you have to use your own words, but I have to use *someone else's academic writing* pattern anyway, so it's not really my own words—I'm just copying people anyway.

In this passage, Mizuki seems to feel constrained, not just by having to reproduce others' words but by having to write in a writing pattern, or genre, that is not her own. Mizuki frequently expressed her desire to be original and creative, and we can infer from her words above that she felt constrained by this particular characteristic of the genre.

A Bakhtinian perspective on Mizuki's frustration is that she is caught up in the struggle to appropriate those others' words without losing her own. "Language," Bakhtin wrote, "is not a neutral medium; it is populated—overpopulated—with the intentions of others. Expropriating it, forcing it to submit to one's own intentions and accents, is a difficult and complicated process" (1981, p. 294). The fact that all the students in this study mentioned (unsolicited) that they found the literature review the most difficult section to write shows that they were all caught up in this struggle. As non-native speakers, they found the struggle to simultaneously wrest these words from others and reaccentuate them with their own intentions very challenging, especially as they had to balance the genre's demand for acknowledging the research of others with presentation of their own original ideas. This is a difficult challenge even for experienced writers writing in their first language.

WRITING AUTHORITATIVELY WITHIN THE GENRE

On the question of what lends authority to one's writing, the participants were united in their opinion: Authority comes from comprehensive knowledge of the field and from having original ideas:

> If you can show you read all the important sources, even secondary ones, and you really know your field, you can have authority. (Becky)

Contrary to my expectations, the participants did not feel that using the jargon or terminology of their fields lent authority to their writing, possibly because they took using such language for granted as it is so much a part of the genre. As Anne put it, "I have to use those important words and expressions anyway." They did agree, however, that an essential way of lending authority to their work was to cite the important scholars in their field. This is in line with previous findings about the use of citations in academic writing (Baynam, 1999; Dong, 1996; Swales, 1990).

One factor that all participants agreed prevented them from writing authoritatively was their level of English proficiency. Sangthien and Becky,[6] who both mentioned that they often thought about their readers as they wrote, worried about how their readers would judge them. Becky felt that her English proficiency was the major factor that both undermined her authority and prevented her from developing a more distinctive style:

> When I write, I feel timid. I want to use some creative expression, but I think maybe [the readers] will not understand me, so I write simple and clear. It makes me timid.

Even though these students felt confident about their knowledge of their fields and the originality of their ideas, they felt hampered by the fear that their readers would misunderstand them. It was this fear that made several of the participants state that seeking assistance from a writing tutor was invaluable. Keiko said that working with a writing tutor "improves the quality of my written work so people can focus on content—not about English problems."

MASTERY OF GENRES IS LIMITED

On the basis of the high grades these students received on their papers, the assistantships they held, and the articles some of them had already published, all of them had succeeded in mastering the genres of their fields. However, they all mentioned that spending so much time immersed in these genres affected their use of other speech genres: Keiko reported being very critical of the vocabulary and argumentation in everything she read, even in fiction; moreover, influenced by the quantitative methodology that predominates in her field, she repeatedly tried to rephrase the interview questions I asked her so that she could give me a quantitative response. Becky reported a tendency to use American rhetorical style ("Give a thesis statement, then support!") even in conversation with friends. However, four of the students reported spending a lot of time with Ameri-

---

[6]Although Sangthien and Becky worried about how readers might judge their work, their awareness of audience may well have contributed to their being the most skilled writers among the group.

can friends and thus had plenty of opportunities to acquire different speech genres, especially those of casual conversation. For one student, though, the case was otherwise: Anne reported that the only genre in which she felt proficient was the genre of academic writing. Like the scholarly man referenced by Bakhtin (1986, p. 80), Anne felt at a loss when she had to speak or write "in layman's terms":

> This is a really drastic thing to me: Sometimes we have to write out the study results in layman's terms, because we need to report to workers in the site, so we need to write really easy to read. It is really difficult for me to write layman's expressions. My professor asked me, "Please write easily—this is really academic." So nowadays I realize my writing skills or patterns are really extreme—too academic—so that's not good for me.

Anne's solution to this problem was to try to find time to read non-academic books (she mentioned *Who Moved My Cheese?* [Spencer, 1998] and the *Harry Potter* books), and she hoped that by reading such books she would be able to master more everyday speech genres. Perhaps this problem was more severe for Anne because, unlike the others, she reported that she spent most of her time reading the literature of her field, and she said that when she socialized with others, it was mostly with Korean-speaking friends. Whereas the other students had mastered a variety of speech genres, Anne felt that she had mastered only the genre of academic writing.

IMPLICATIONS

Mastering speech genres is, as Bakhtin (1981) maintained, a struggle. For non-native speakers of English it is still more challenging. In describing speech genres, Bakhtin (1986) compared the way we acquire them to the way we learn our native language:

> We are given these speech genres in almost the same way that we are given our native language, which we must master long before we begin to study grammar. We know our native language—its lexical composition and grammatical structure—not from dictionaries and grammars but from the concrete utterances we hear and that we ourselves reproduce in live speech communication with others around us. (p. 78)

However, non-native speakers of English rarely have the opportunity to acquire English speech genres in the same way that they acquire the speech genres of their native language. All too often, they have learned much of their English from dictionaries and grammar books. A major implication of this study, then, is that such speakers should have the opportunity to acquire the genre of academic English through dialogue, and not only through dialogue with the texts they read. The students in this study sought out opportunities for dialogue with friends, with writing tutors, and with their professors; however, not all students are willing or able to do so.

To encourage students to find opportunities to dialogue with others, we need to build opportunities for dialogic interaction into their writing classes and, ideally, into their content courses. Although collaboration is now gaining a toehold in writing classes, many writing instructors, perhaps motivated by fear of plagiarism and by Western notions of individualism (Pennycook, 1996; Scollon, 1994; Ramanathan & Atkinson, 1999), still believe that their students should "do their own work" rather than dialogue with others. One way to make composition classes more dialogic would be for their instructors to arrange for students to work with tutors in a writing laboratory or learning center. By working with tutors, students will create zones of proximal development (Vygotsky, 1978) in which they can develop their thoughts and organize their ideas. Through dialogue with a tutor they can also gain a better sense of audience, as their reader (i.e., the tutor) will be able to give them immediate feedback on their work.

In the case of international graduate students, access to tutoring services is still more important, as working with a tutor may be the only opportunity they have to focus on improving their writing skills, and academic writing *per se* is seldom explicitly taught in their departments. Tutoring also has an affective dimension, which should not be overlooked (Krabbe & Krabbe, 1993; Lepper, Woolverton, Mumme, & Gurtner, 1995). Mastering academic English is challenging both emotionally and cognitively. In my work as a tutor, I have often met international graduate students who are overwhelmed by the challenges they face. Knowing that they have somewhere to turn for help is an immediate relief, and when the emotional burden is lightened, they are more able to meet the cognitive challenge.

Teaching writing at the graduate level is also of critical importance. Rose and McClafferty (2001) called for the teaching of writing in graduate education; I would go further and suggest teaching a writing class specifically for international graduate students. Considering how little exposure the students in the present study had had to academic writing in English before coming to the United States, they could all have benefited from such a class. The class I envision would have both whole-class and one-on-one activities and, rather than writing assignments specifically for the class, students would be able to work on assignments from their content areas, thus benefiting from scaffolded learning about the characteristics of their academic genres and from opportunities for individual tutoring. Such a class would also be an ideal setting to encourage students to read and write in a more dialogic way.

In this study, two of the most skilled writers I interviewed had taken classes (in their content areas) that had encouraged a dialogic approach to reading and writing. Sangthien had taken a class in which she had been required to critique others' work and to find support for her critiques in the literature. Although she found it a tough class, she said it had taught her to read more analytically and to respond to others' work more critically. Becky took a class in which she was always encouraged to write with a reader in mind (a real reader, not just the instructor) and to imagine how the reader would respond to her writing. Teaching students these kinds of dialogic strategies has the benefits of challenging students to think more deeply and to write more persuasively.

In terms of understanding the dialogic processes these students went through to master the written genres of their fields, Bakhtin's (1981, 1986) theories of dialogism and speech genres provided a useful analytical lens for the present study. However, there is much more in Bakhtin's work that is relevant to the study of second language learning. Bakhtin has much to teach us about the vital importance of context, an area that has sometimes been overlooked in the area of second language acquisition. Future research could also incorporate concepts such as addressivity, voice, and double voicing—concepts that have generally been addressed only in first-language writing research. Bakhtin has much to offer the field of second language teaching and research; his contribution to the study of language is unique and, to use his own favorite metaphor, his utterances forged links in a chain that is likely to stretch far beyond him. I encourage readers to add their own links to the chain.

REFERENCES

Atkinson, D. (2000). On Peter Elbow's response to "Individualism, Academic Writing, and ESL writers" by Vai Ramanathan and Dwight Atkinson. *Journal of Second Language Writing, 9*(1), 71–76.

Atkinson, D., & Ramanathan, V. (1995). Cultures of writing: An ethnographic comparison of L1 and L2 university writing/language programs. *TESOL Quarterly, 29*, 539–568.

Bakhtin, M. (1981). *The dialogic imagination.* Austin: University of Texas Press.

Bakhtin, M. (1986). *Speech genres and other late essays.* Austin: University of Texas Press.

Baynam, M. (1999). Double-voicing and the scholarly "I": On incorporating the words of others in scholarly discourse. *Text, 19*, 485–504.

Belcher, D. (1994). The apprenticeship approach to advanced academic literacy: Graduate students and their mentors. *English for Specific Purposes, 13*, 23–34.

Bialystosky, D. (1998). Liberal education, writing, and the dialogic self. In F. Farmer (Ed.), *Landmark essays on Bakhtin, rhetoric, and writing* (pp. 187–197). Mahwah, NJ: Lawrence Erlbaum Associates.

Charmaz, K. (2000). Grounded theory: Objectivist and constructivist methods. In N. K. Denzin & Y. S. Lincoln (Eds.), *Handbook of qualitative research* (2nd ed., pp. 509–535). Thousand Oaks, CA: Sage.

Charmaz, K. (2002). Qualitative interviewing and grounded theory analysis. In J. Gubrium & J. A. Holstein (Eds.), *Handbook of interview research* (pp. 675–694). Thousand Oaks, CA: Sage.

Dong, Y. R. (1996). Learning how to use citations for knowledge transformation: Non-native doctoral students' dissertation writing in science. *Research in the Teaching of English, 30,* 428–455.

Dong, Y. R. (1998). Non-native graduate students' thesis/dissertation writing in science: Self-reports by students and their advisors from two U.S. institutions. *English for Specific Purposes, 17,* 369–390.

Elbow, P. (1999). Individualism and the teaching of writing: A response to Vai Ramanathan and Dwight Atkinson. *Journal of Second Language Writing, 8,* 327–338.

Farmer, F. (1995). Voice reprised: Three etudes for a dialogic understanding. *Rhetoric Review, 13,* 304–320.

Ferris, D., & Hedgcock, J. (1998). *Teaching ESL composition: Purpose, process, and practice.* Mahwah, NJ: Lawrence Erlbaum Associates.

Fishman, S., & McCarthy, L. (2001). An ESL writer and her discipline-based professor. *Written Communication, 18,* 180–228.

Fox, H. (1994). *Listening to the world: Cultural issues in academic writing.* Urbana, IL: National Council of Teachers of English.

Glaser, B. G., & Strauss, A. (1967). *The discovery of grounded theory: Strategies for qualitative research.* New York: Aldine de Gruyter.

Harklau, L. (2000). From the "good kids" to the "worst": Representations of English language learners across educational settings. *TESOL Quarterly, 34,* 35–67.

Ivanic, R., & Camps, D. (2001). I am how I sound: Voice as self-representation in L2 writing. *Journal of Second Language Writing, 10,* 3–33.

Johns, A. (1999). Opening our doors: Applying socioliterate approaches to language minority classrooms. In L. Harklau, K. Losey & M. Siegal (Eds.), *Generation 1.5 meets college composition: Issues in teaching writing to U.S. educated learners of ESL* (pp. 159–171). Mahwah, NJ: Lawrence Erlbaum Associates.

Krabbe, J. L., & Krabbe, M. A. (1995, February). *Tutor training enhanced by knowledge of tutee expectations.* Paper presented at the 19th annual conference of the National Association for Developmental Education, Chicago, IL.

Leki, I. (2001). "A narrow thinking system": Nonnative-English-speaking students in group projects across the curriculum. *TESOL Quarterly, 35,* 39–67.

Leki, I., & Carson, J. (1994). Students' perceptions of EAP writing instruction and writing needs across the disciplines. *TESOL Quarterly, 26,* 81–101.

Leki, I., & Carson, J. (1997). "Completely different worlds": EAP and the writing experiences of ESL students in university courses. *TESOL Quarterly, 31,* 39–69.

Lepper, M. R., Woolverton, M., Mumme, D. L., & Gurtner, J. L. (1993). Motivational techniques of expert human tutors: Lessons for the design of computer-based tutors. In S. P. Lajoie & S. J. Derry (Eds.), *Computers as cognitive tools* (pp. 75–105). Hillsdale, NJ: Lawrence Erlbaum Associates.

Pennycook, A. (1996). Borrowing others' words: Text, ownership, memory and plagiarism. *TESOL Quarterly, 30*(2), 210–230.

Prior, P. (1998). *Writing/Disciplinarity: A sociohistoric account of literate activity in the academy.* Mahwah, NJ: Lawrence Erlbaum Associates.

Prior, P. (2001). Voices in text, mind, and society: Sociohistoric accounts of discourse acquisition and use. *Journal of Second Language Writing, 10,* 55–81.

Ramanathan, V., & Atkinson, D. (1999). Individualism, academic writing, and ESL writers. *Journal of Second Language Writing, 8,* 45–75.

Ramanathan, V., & Kaplan, R. B. (1996). Audience and voice in current L1 composition texts: Some implications for ESL student writers. *Journal of Second Language Writing, 5,* 21–34.

Ritchie, J. (1998). Beginning writers, diverse voices and individual identity. In F. Farmer (Ed.), *Landmark essays on Bakhtin, rhetoric, and writing.* Mahwah, NJ: Lawrence Erlbaum Associates.

Rose, M., & McClafferty, K. A. (2001). A call for the teaching of writing in graduate education. *Educational Researcher, 30,* 27–33.

Santos, T. (1992). Ideology in composition: L1 and ESL. *Journal of Second Language Writing, 1*(1–15).

Scollon, R. (1994). Authorship and responsibility in discourse. *World Englishes, 13*(1), 33–46.

Silva, T. (2001). Toward an understanding of the distinct nature of L2 writing: The ESL research and its implications. In T. Silva & P. K. Matsuda (Eds.), *Landmark essays on second language writing.* Mahwah, NJ: Lawrence Erlbaum Associates.

Spencer, J. (1998). *Who moved my cheese? An amazing way to deal with change in your work and in your life.* New York: Putnam's.

Strauss, A., & Corbin, J. (1998). *Basics of qualitative research: Techniques and procedures for developing grounded theory* (2nd ed.). Thousand Oaks, CA: Sage.

Swales, J. M. (1990). *Genre analysis.* Cambridge, England: Cambridge University Press.

Vygotsky, L. S. (1978). *Mind in society: The development of higher psychological processes.* Cambridge, MA: Harvard University Press.

Ubadigbo, F. (1997, February). *Recruitment dynamic of foreign students into United States post-secondary institutions: The implications for education and international development.* Paper presented at the 20th annual conference of Community Colleges for International Development, Orlando, FL.

Warschauer, M. (1998). Online learning in a sociocultural context. *Anthropology and Education Quarterly, 29,* 68–88.

Wertsch, J. V. (1991). *Voices of the mind: A sociocultural approach to mediated action.* Cambridge, MA: Harvard University Press.

Wertsch, J. V. (1998). *Mind as action.* New York: Oxford University Press.

Zamel, V., & Spack, R. (1998). *Negotiating academic literacies: Teaching and learning across languages and cultures.* Mahwah, NJ: Lawrence Erlbaum Associates.

Chapter 3

Multimodal Rerepresentations of Self and Meaning for Second Language Learners in English-Dominant Classrooms

Ana Christina DaSilva Iddings
Vanderbilt University

John Haught
University of Nevada, Las Vegas

Ruth Devlin
Paradise Professional Development School and University of Nevada, Las Vegas

Central to Bakhtin's (1981) thinking about knowledge was the preoccupation with capturing human behavior through the observation of the use of language (in a broad sense),[1] particularly in dialogue. His explanations of dialogue were both profound and complex, encompassing myriad theoretical constructs and guiding a variety of disciplines, such as anthropology, literary studies, linguistics, and so on. Schematically, for Bakhtin dialogue is composed of an utterance; a reply; and, most important, a relation between the two. This emphasis on the relational aspects of language underscores the sharedness of human experience, the simultaneity of *self* and *other*, and the relativity of meaning (concepts which we will further explore later in this chapter). Moreover, and simply put, Bakhtin's interpretation of dialogue included above all the dialogue be-

---

[1]Bakhtin (1981, p. 430) defined language as "any communication system employing signs that are ordered in a particular manner."

tween mind and world. That is, it is through the dialogue between mind and world that, according to Bakhtin, the artificial dualisms between the inner and outer spheres of being are dismantled. Within these theoretical parameters the human activity of meaning-making is inextricably connected to social interactions, which occur in a particular social, cultural, and political context and at a particular point in history. For Bakhtin, all of those aspects of a given interaction must be given full consideration. In many of those respects, his ideas were deeply implicated in the theoretical assumptions of some of his contemporaries, such as Lev Vygotsky, as well as others who theorized from a sociocultural perspective. Therefore, in this chapter we use aspects of both dialogical and sociocultural theoretical constructs to illuminate our understandings of the data we present here and ultimately to provide us with insights into the processes of second language learning.

For Bakhtin, as well as for other sociocultural theorists, second language learning is considered to involve the reorganization and redevelopment of semiotic tools from the native language to the second language, through participation in social practices. According to this view, language emerges from engagement in social and cultural activity and later becomes internalized (i.e., reconstructed internally, as psychological processes, e.g., ways of thinking, modes of learning). These activities are mediated by signs (i.e., semiotic tools)—for example, linguistic and nonverbal elements (e.g., gestures, facial expressions). As these semiotic tools and resources become reorganized and redeveloped, individuals become transformed (Kramsch, 2000; Lantolf, 2000).

Although the recent research in this area shows a growing preoccupation with the transformation processes one undergoes in learning a second language (Belz, 2002; DaSilva Iddings & McCafferty, 2003; Kinginger, 2002; Kramsch, 2000; Lantolf, 2000; Lantolf & Pavlenko, 2001; McCafferty, 2002), little has been documented with regard to how this process actually takes place for children with little or no English proficiency included in English-dominant school environments. Therefore, for this study we were interested in observing (a) how second language students with very preliminary levels of English proficiency began to reorganize and to develop semiotic tools for meaning-making when they entered a multilingual classroom in which English was the primary medium of instruction and (b) how these processes related to the development of intersubjectivity and to second language learning. Our observations focused primarily on two second language students in a third-grade classroom. One of these students was from Laos, and spoke both Thai and Laotian; the other student was from Cuba and was a native speaker of Spanish. Both of these students were new to the United States at the time of data collection, and neither one spoke English; however, they often engaged in lengthy interactions, giggling, playing, and working together for extensive periods of time as they relied on multimodal ways of representation to communicate with each other and with others in the class. It became noticeable that, through engagement in these activities, a process of transformation was taking place over time as the students negotiated tensions that arose from multiple and competing perspectives. In sum, the mutual relations among sign, meaning, and language learning involving these two students were the focus of this investigation. To better understand these complex relations, we begin by exploring Bakhtin's (1981) concept of *dialogism*[2] in relation to language.

DIALOGISM: THE SHAREDNESS OF HUMAN EXPERIENCE

Bakhtin rejected the then-predominant view of language derived from *abstract objectivism*, "[a philosophy that] treats language as a pure system of laws governing all phonetic, grammatical, and lexical forms that confront individual speakers as inviolable norms over which they have no control" (Holquist, 1990, p. 42). Bakhtin was also opposed to *individualistic subjectivism*—the idea that all aspects of language can be explained in terms of each individual speaker's voluntarist intentions. Although each of those views are characterized by the relations of self and others, abstract objectivism sees meaning as *other* dominant and completely originated outside the individual, whereas in the philosophy of individualistic subjectivism it is the individual, the *I*, who controls the meaning—here, language originates completely inside the individual. Bakhtin was skeptical of both of those understandings about language and instead he wished to accentuate the *intersubjective*[3] aspects of language by proposing that an *utterance*,[4] rather than language alone, is the fundamental unit of investigation for those interested in studying language. Bakhtin's perspectives regarding the intersubjective aspects of an utterance were discussed by V. N. Voloshinov (1929/1986)[5] in *Marxism and the Philosophy of Language*:

> In the verbal medium, in each utterance, however trivial it may be, [a] living dialectical synthesis is constantly taking place between the psyche and ideology, between the inner and the outer. In each act, subjective experience perishes in the objective fact of the enunciated word-utterance, and the enunciated word is subjectified in the act of responsive understanding in order to generate, sooner or later, a counterstatement. (pp. 40–41)

---

[2]*Dialogism* is a term never used by Bakhtin himself (Holquist, 1990).

[3]*Intersubjectivity* refers to the inextricable relations between self and other and thus to the inescapable sharedness of human experience.

[4]For Bakhtin, an *utterance* refers to "text" having a particular meaning that is "social, historical, concrete, and dialogized" (Bakhtin, 1981, p. 433).

[5]V. N. Voloshinov is believed to be one of the pseudonyms under which Bakhtin published his work.

This intersubjective aspect of language brings us perforce to the topic of *self–other* relations, which must be viewed not as binary (either–or) but as a relation of *simultaneity*, a continuum of degrees in which otherness is manifested in a self through the medium of language—or, more precisely, through utterances. Bakhtin's notion of simultaneity implies that self and other must not be viewed as absolute concepts because they are always relative to each other through "simultaneous unity of differences in the event of an utterance" (Holquist, 1990, p. 36). That is, although the self and other are always different from one another as occupants of different times and spaces, the self cannot exist without the other; the other is what gives meaning to the self. Bakhtin (1981) explained: "I cannot do without the other, I cannot become myself without the other; I must find myself in the other, finding the other in me" (p. 185). For the philosopher, then, the constructs of self and other clearly must be viewed as shared existence: Existence is always cobeing.

SIGN-MAKING ACTIVITY: THE RELATIVITY OF MEANING

At the core of Bakhtin's (1981, p. 426) concept of dialogism is *heteroglossia*, or the notion that everything means and is understood as part of a greater whole in which there is constant interaction among meanings, all of which have the potential to influence the others. This construct underscores the extent to which inhabitants of a given discourse community, in any given time, condition and are conditioned by the social, cultural, historical, and institutional contextual elements as well as by each other, as they participate in social activity. Because these conditions are highly unstable, an utterance will always differ from another, even if one person repeats the same words as the other person. From this perspective, Bakhtin is opposed to viewing language as a static communications system with fixed correspondence between words and objects; instead, he ascribes to language a much more dynamic role. Meaning-making and sign-making activity is an integral part of this process.

For Bakhtin, meaning comes about both intra- and interpersonally through the medium of signs. He contended that something exists only insofar as it has meaning (even if it at any particular point it has only a potential meaning) and that understanding comes about as a response to a sign with signs (Holquist, 1990).

Although Bakhtin's views reflect a clear emphasis on the dialogicality of sign mediation and on the multiplicity of meaning, for this study (and in relation to second language learning) we also drew from Vygotsky's views, which emphasize meaning-making as a revolutionary process of transformation (tool and result) and thus is *a precondition for language-making*. That is, for Vygotsky, the process of meaning-making is completed—not derived—by language (Newman & Holzman, 1997). This is an important point for our study, because the two participating second language students were newly arrived to the United States and therefore had no proficiency in English. For these students, the process of meaning-making seemed to be embodied in their drawings, block structures, art projects, and so on, as they engaged in dialogical activities involving the making of new signs by combining and recombining already-known signs (DaSilva Iddings & McCafferty, 2003; Kramsch, 2000, Kress, 1997; McCafferty, 2002).

THE STUDY

Participants and Setting

The observation site for this study was Ruth Devlin's third-grade classroom, in a professional development school in a large Southwestern city. The school is of recent construction, built on the campus of the local research university, and is located within one of the city's urban areas. Although the school is affiliated with a university, the student population is drawn from the surrounding neighborhoods and is not considered a laboratory school with a special population.

Ruth's classroom comprises of English language learners with varying degrees of English language proficiency. The primarily immigrant population tends to be highly transitory, with frequent changes in the classroom roster. All of the 22 students were Spanish-speaking Latinos (2 from Cuba; 1 from El Salvador; 12 from Mexico; 1 from Tahoe, Nevada; and 5 from various cities in California), except for 1 child, who was a Laotian national and spoke both Thai and Laotian at home with her family.

Ruth's classroom has a highly interactive environment. Desks are arranged in two rows of double desks that face each other, thus inviting dialogue and collaboration among students. Learning centers were placed around the room where students often worked in pairs, independently from the teacher. These centers included a computer station, equipped with a variety of educational software; an art center; a listening center, where students listened to prerecorded books; a beanbag chair, where students would often go in pairs to read and reread some of the books they had read in class; and an open carpeted area, where the children often sat as a group to build with blocks, to engage in dramatic play, or work in pairs to catch up on class assignments.

The highly interactive nature of the classroom environment was propitious to our investigations as we were interested in capturing instances of naturally occurring dialogue among the second language learners. Also, when working in the learning centers, students were afforded high levels of agency. They were often given choices regarding at what center they wished to work, with whom they wanted to work, and as to how they would go about resolving the tasks that Ruth had set up for them. Student agency was an important element to this investigation as we were interested in observing students as they participated in authentic classroom activities.[6] In addition, Ruth was very diligent in creating a cohesive community in her classroom, which was conducive to the forming of friendly relationships among the students. This fact was helpful in the observations of our topics of interest.

Overall, the climate of the school and of the classroom in which we made our observations could be generally described as both nurturing and vastly active. For the most part, the children appeared to enjoy being at school, tackling their activities with enthusiasm and engagement. On one occasion a girl burst into tears when sent home by the school nurse, because she wanted to remain in school. This seemed to be a reflection of the comfort level and sense of community that Ruth had engendered within her classroom.

The two girls we specifically observed were both recent immigrants. Fatima (pseudonyms are used for all participants) was an 8-year-old Cuban girl who was already able to read and write in her native Spanish language. Pia was a 9-year-old Laotian who had grown up on the Mekong River and lived for some time in Thailand. Of the students in the room, Pia was the only one with virtually no prior formal educational experience. A family interview determined that approximately 6 months of schooling had occurred during her first 9 years of life. The level of those months of schooling was somewhat indeterminate, and Pia arrived in the United States with very little in the way of literacy skills. Both girls were cooperative with all adults with whom they came in contact, and they eagerly shared their drawings and other creations with us.

Mode of Inquiry: A Dialogical Perspective

Unlike proponents of traditional modes of conducting ethnographies, which look for general regularities in complex human activities, often detaching these activities from their sociocultural and historical context, Bakhtin recognized the dynamic and conflictual nature of culture; the historical and ideological character of dialogue; and the inseparability of mind and activity from the historical, cultural, political, and social contexts in which activity occurs. In conducting research from a dialogical perspective, the dialectical interrelationships between thought and the material world, individual and society, are foregrounded.

---

[6]Activity is regarded here as cultural–historical frames, for example, what is supposed to happen in classrooms under a particular system of education in combination with the particulars of what actually happens.

Bakhtin (1981) argued that the key conceptual tool for analysis of human activity is the utterance. However, we should emphasize that language from this perspective is viewed as inextricably tied to the social medium in which meaning is conveyed. This focus on meaning forces one to understand language as a social process, rather than as isolated instances of linguistic sounds. In describing language as social activity, Bakhtin further suggested that individuals internalize language into inner speech and that, because thought is carried out by inner speech, *consciousness*[7] arises from this ongoing process of social communication.

It is not surprising that, considering his theoretical emphasis on the dynamic nature of sign, context, and meaning, Bakhtin viewed the world as activity and regarded existence as an ever-changing event. This dynamic conceptualization of the individual's relation to the world provides an important theoretical advance in that it presumes that individuals have agency in affecting the communication process and hence in continuing the ongoing reshaping of the sociocultural context which they inhabit. Thus, in acknowledging the agentive potential of the individual, dialogical modes of inquiry reinforce the transformational nature of human activity. Research conducted according to this paradigm disregards the idea that education must be socially reproductive and instead places great value in transformative processes. In observing the creative and innovative means of interactions used by the participants in this study, we hoped to discover how their activities served to shape and reshape their understandings about the new sociocultural environment in which they were immersed.

Data Collection

Data collection for this study was part of a larger research project that lasted for approximately 7 months, in which Chris Iddings and Ruth had collaborated for the purpose of learning more about ways to best structure an effective learning environment for second language students. In the course of that project, Ruth described the unusual friendship that had sprung up between the Laotian girl (Pia) and one of the Cuban students (Fatima) and the innovative ways they engaged with each other. It was agreed that observing the girls' engagement during regular classroom activities would prove to be a valuable case study. John Haught was then invited to participate in this particular study, which lasted for approximately an additional 5 months.

John visited the classroom on a regular basis, usually two or three times a week for an hour or more during the time scheduled for learning centers. Chris came to the classroom one additional time a week to interview the chil-

---

[7]According to a dialogical perspective, consciousness is said to be, in relative (not absolute) terms, the differential relation between a center and that which is not a center.

dren and to speak to Ruth, who kept a teacher journal with notes concerning her observations of Pia and Fatima. Data gathering consisted of videotaping student activity; taking field notes; conducting interviews with the students and Ruth; and collecting artifacts, such as student journals. These forms of data collection allowed for close examination of complex relationships among the students, activity, and context, both in moment-to-moment interaction and over time. The process of analysis was continuous and ongoing throughout all the phases of data collection as well as after completion of the fieldwork. Approximately 10 hours of video footage was searched for exceptional moments of interaction, involving both verbal and nonverbal interactions; however, for the sake of conciseness we analyzed only the episodes that were related to the key epistemological concepts that shaped this inquiry. To reiterate, we were particularly interested in how Pia and Fatima reorganized and developed semiotic tools to create meaning through their interactions with each other.

RESULTS AND DISCUSSION

With the preceding considerations in mind, we now consider the multimodal ways of representation that Pia and Fatima used to communicate with each other and to make sense of their new contexts. We will examine the students' activities while they jointly participated in creating journal drawings, creating block structures, and ornate designs.

Journal Drawings

From the very beginning of the school year, Pia and Fatima seemed to enjoy each other's company. Perhaps bounded by a sense of solidarity in being newcomers to the school and to the United States, they often chose to sit across from one another and to stay near each other during lunch and playground activities. Unable to effectively communicate linguistically, the two students relied on nonverbal forms of communication: They smiled, nodded, and frequently touched each other. For example, on one occasion early in the school year, Ruth reported that she had observed Pia and Fatima placing their hands in each other's mouths to get a tactile sense of each other's teeth.

In observing their interactions during regular classroom activities, it was particularly interesting to us that, over time, Pia and Fatima actively appropriated many features of whatever the other was doing (in a "copycat" kind of way). For example, during the first few months of school, Fatima would recurrently draw landscapes that resembled her homeland. Present in her pictures were often green trees with rounded tops and red apples, as well as colorful butterflies and houses that resembled her actual home in Cuba. Those features were equally present in free drawing journal activities and in drawings that were assigned as part of a class project. On one occasion during the month of November, Ruth read a folk tale to the class and asked the students to draw a picture in response to the story. Fatima began by drawing a house where the main character of the story lived. In drawing this house, Fatima took several minutes to meticulously draw intricate roof patterns (see Fig. 3.1). When Chris, during an informal interview on that same day,

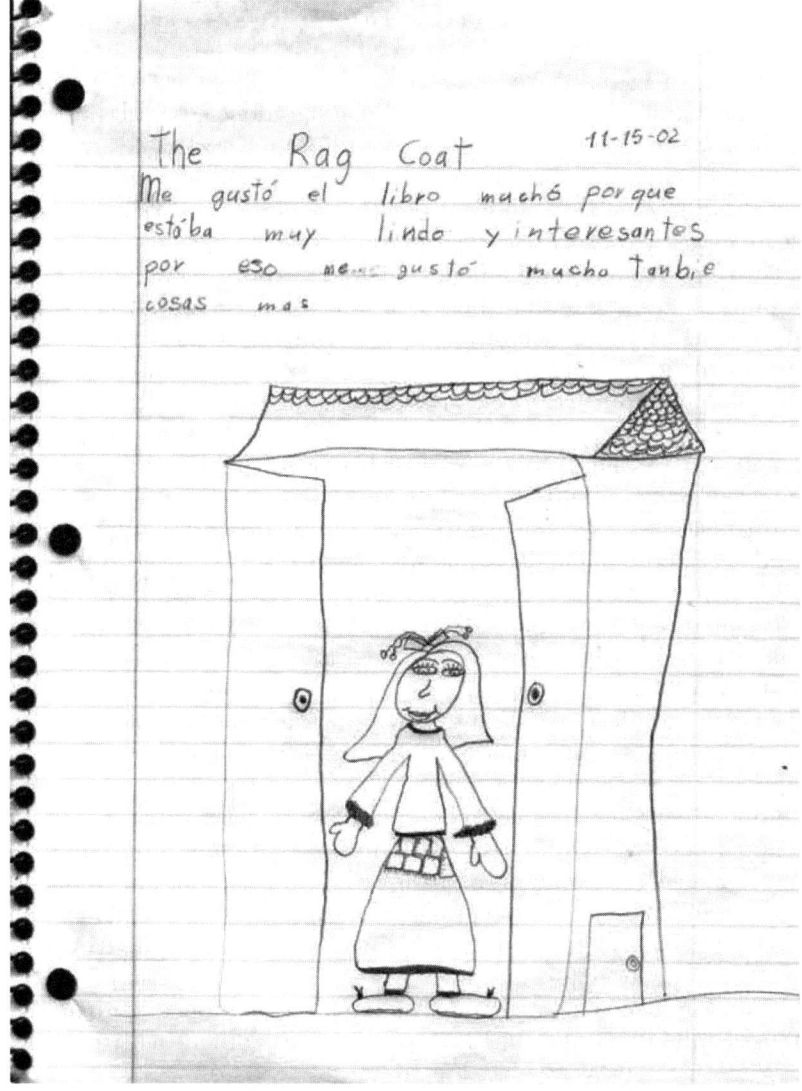

FIG. 3.1. Fatima's representation of a house resembles her home in Cuba.

asked Fatima to explain her drawing, she smiled and answered: "Esa es la casita de la niña [en el cuento]. Mira! Se parece con mi casa en Cuba! Mi casa tenia su tetio bien asi" ["This is the home of the girl (in the story). Look! It looks like my home in Cuba. My house had the roof just like this"].

Pia, on the other hand, in the beginning of school, often drew landscapes that resembled her homeland, with pointy trees, large flowers, and water-falls. However, over time, as the students began to develop high degrees of intersubjectivity, those landscapes became intricately combined. For exam-ple, on a journal entry dated in early October, Pia drew her typical pointy tree, a waterfall, and a large flower (see Fig. 3.2). Fatima, while conserving her customary rounded tree, butterflies, and clay roof patterns, began imi-tating Pia's drawings of a waterfall, to which she added colorful fish (see Fig. 3.3). Pia, in turn, had already begun drawing butterflies in the same fashion as the ones present in Fatima's drawings. Also, plants with dotted flowers, and apple trees with rounded tops, characteristic of Fatima's pictures, began appearing in Pia's artwork (see Fig. 3.4).

The way the two girls drew people in their pictures also was interesting to us. In the beginning of the school year, Pia drew people with slanted eyes, who wore hats that were pointy on top and wide on the sides. Fatima, on the other hand, initially drew her people with no or very little hair and no eyes (see Fig. 3.2). However, by October, Fatima was then drawing her people who were wearing pointy hats that were wide on the sides and who had slanted eyes[8] (see Fig. 3.5). Pia, in turn, had begun drawing her people with more rounded eyes and no hair (see Fig. 3.4).

Also of interest were the features of American urban and suburban land-scapes (e.g. shopping malls; WalMart; chain restaurants, such as Pizza Hut, Panda Express, McDonald's, etc.) that gradually began to appear in similar basic dimensions and content in both of Pia's and Fatima's drawings as they came to experience the new environment (see Fig. 3.6).

As Pia and Fatima continually appropriated features and imitated each other in their different ways of representing their social and cultural envi-ronments, they changed, innovated, and experimented with different sign compositions that reified the dialogical processes in which they engaged. In addition, their journal drawing became a kind of a record of the develop-ment of intersubjectivities between them. However, it is important to note that these new combinations of form and meaning cannot be understood ahistorically. Many of the integral elements of each child's original home-land historicities remained present in their drawings throughout the course of our investigation. This finding is in agreement with Bakhtin's (1981) ideas that individuals both condition and are conditioned by their social, cultural, and historical elements as well as by each other. In furthering this

---

[8]Also note Fatima's pointy tree.

FIG. 3.2. Pia's homeland landscape drawing.

idea, this finding is also in agreement with Vygotsky's claims that the task of psychology is the discovery of the historical child—that is, the task of psychology is the understanding of the linear history of a particular child, which is inextricably related to the activities in which he or she engages in (Newman & Holzman, 1997).

FIG. 3.3. Fatima's landscape drawing with appropriated features from Pia's drawings.

Dramatic Play

In addition to the journal drawings, the growing intersubjectivity between Pia and Fatima was aptly demonstrated in their interactions while playing in a free-time learning center. Again, these are largely of a nonverbal nature. We have chosen to present two episodes: the first appeared to be the initial time the girls had engaged in dramatic play of any sort, whereas the second demonstrates how the girls were enhancing their ability to make meaning together as they better understood and negotiated the intentions of their play.

Episode 1. The girls went to a learning station and began to play with uncolored wooden blocks of various shapes. Initially, Pia began to stack her blocks into familiar tower shapes. Fatima, on the other hand, began to form small, widely spaced forms consisting of just a few blocks. Pia

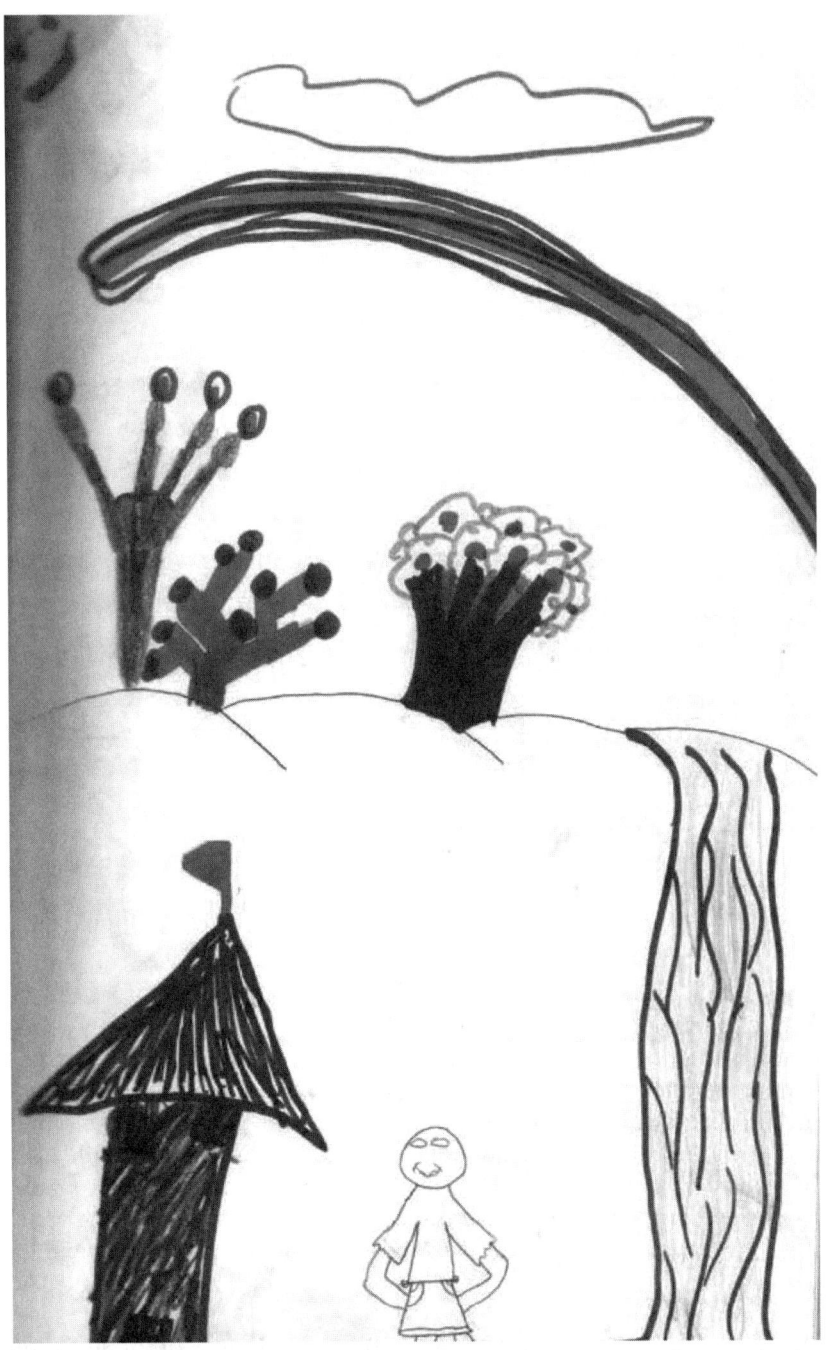

FIG. 3.4. Pia's landscape drawing with appropriated features from Fatima's drawings.

FIG. 3.5.   Fatima's drawing of people with features appropriated from Pia's drawings.

watched quietly until Fatima assembled several forms. Apparently recognizing what her companion was doing, Pia scooted closer on her knees and began assembling similar forms. At this point, Fatima then began to construct an archway, and it became apparent that the girls were assembling "furniture." Fatima began to lay out a floor plan as Pia began to build elaborate pillored entrances and walkways. Although no words were exchanged, Pia was able to discern the nature of the play activity in which Fatima was engaged and began to build entranceways that resembled Asian architectural structures and "furnish" the building with constructions similar to Fatima's (see Fig. 3.7).

By this point in the school year (March), the last month of the study, the girls shared some limited English vocabulary and were able to communi-

FIG. 3.6. Pia's drawings of the new environment.

cate in simple sentences supplemented by gestures. At one point, Pia objected to one of Fatima's constructions.

Pia [pointing]:	What's that?
Fatima:	TV.
Pia [frowning]:	Doesn't look TV.

Fatima considered for a moment, adjusted the construction, and they looked at each other and wordlessly nodded in agreement. The floor plan was completed and the girls chose smaller forms, which Fatima dubbed "Mom, Dad, Baby." The two girls began placing the figures within the

FIG. 3.7. Building entrance ways.

house and "walking" a figure along the walkways and through the archways. There was no conversation except an occasional directive, as when Pia told Fatima "No. Baby over there" (pointing). Another phrase they shared and invoked quite often was "Look at this," nearly always accompanied by indicating gestures. Often their agreements constituted nothing more than glances and smiles as they manipulated the figures within the floor plan. Although vocabulary and conversation were limited, the girls demonstrated their shared intentionality through gesture, eye contact, engagement, and physical proximity. As the activity progressed, the girls moved from two separate activities physically separated by approximately 2 feet of space to one unified activity with the girls side by side, touching each other to draw attention and building and manipulating forms within a shared play area. It wasn't until the girls were able to engage in similar meaning-making activity that they were able to communicate shared intentions. This underscores the inseparable dialectical unity between shared meaning-making and communicative activity. First, jointly arriving at a sense of the activity, facilitated communicative interactions. Meaning-making through available means, as found in this example, serves as a precondition for meaning-making through linguistic means.

Episode 2. In the second episode, Pia and Fatima returned to the block learning station. Without a word, they knelt side by side (see Fig. 3.8) and began to form the furniture shapes. Unlike in Episode 1, in which each girl had begun a separate activity before arriving at a mutual form of play, this time the girls understood the meaning of the forms and structures and jointly created a "home" for their block characters. Because their ability to make meaning together had been established through previous encounters, the activity progressed much more quickly, and soon the girls were manipulating the figures within the space. What was striking in this episode was how the girls would withdraw from their role playing to discuss or negotiate their play and then return to their side by side manipulations. Although the dialogue was largely unintelligible, the nonverbal elements of communication and the level of the students' interactions were growing increasingly lively and complex. In accord with Bakhtin's notion of dialogism, in both Episodes 1 and 2 the children's communication appeared to be purposeful and motivated, serving a central role in the mediation of all their activities and influencing each other's social interactions and understandings as well as affecting their own cognitive activity.

FIG. 3.8. Jointly creating a "home."

Ornate Designs

Another significant moment occurred when Pia and Fatima were involved in an art activity. The girls were seated side by side in the art station and began to assemble what appeared to be ornate envelopes or folders. Choosing two colors of construction paper, Fatima appeared to lead the way as she folded and trimmed the paper with edging scissors. Pia, rather than simply imitating Fatima's actions, appeared to choose similar design elements and the same colors, but she combined them in a different and almost complementary way. She would add original touches by choosing different edging scissors (i.e., blades with differently patterned) or different placement for the hearts and flowers.

During this independent work time, the two girls occasionally chose to make gifts for another classmate. In one instance, it was one of their handmade envelopes. After completing the envelope, they both walked over to Susanna (who spoke Spanish and English). Fatima gestured to Susanna what the envelope was to be used for. Pia held open the envelope as Fatima demonstrated putting an imaginary object inside. When the demonstration was completed, both girls took hold of an edge of the envelope and presented it to Susanna, smiled, and walked back to the art table. Fatima's choice not to speak in Spanish to her Spanish classmate seemed to be in solidarity with Pia, who was unable to participate in a conversation held in Spanish.

Fatima's ability to converse with the other Spanish-speaking students and her first-language literacy skills afforded her a definite advantage in negotiating the classroom activities. However, her loyalty to friend Pia appeared unwavering. During whole-class instruction, Ruth had observed that Fatima as well as other students who sat around Pia whispered answers to her so that she could raise her hand and participate in the discussions. The children were engaging in inclusionary activities that are sometimes at odds with conventional notions of schooling but are perhaps a necessary part of the emotional support Pia needed to be successful.

CONCLUSION

Our observations revealed that the engagement in multimodal representations facilitated Pia's and Fatima's access to participate with one another as part of the larger goal of gaining access to the social life of their English-dominant classroom. However, it was the dialogical use of semiotic tools that seemed to prove essential to the children's reorganization of self and meaning in the new context. Specifically, it was the relationship between the two interactants and their signs, as revealed in their utterances (drawings, block patterns, and ornate designs), that gave their activity meaning. Holquist (1990, p. 63), stated:

In so far as an utterance is not merely what is said, it does not passively reflect a situation that lies outside language. Rather, the utterance is a deed, it is active, productive: it resolves a situation, brings it to an evaluative conclusion (for the moment at least), or extends action into the future. In other words, consciousness is the medium and utterance the specific means by which two otherwise disparate elements—the quickness of experience and the materiality of language—are harnessed into a volatile unity. Discourse does not reflect a situation, it is a situation.

It is also important to point out that the interactions captured for this study illustrate the intentional, purposeful ways that the second language students expanded their communicative resources for making meaning—which, following Vygostky (1978), is a precondition for the use of language. Thus, more broadly speaking, in expanding their meaning-making capability through their dialogical use of semiotic tools Pia and Fatima were creating circumstances that were conducive to learning language. Moreover, it is important to note that the attention devoted to the observation and understanding of the dialogicality of these signs as a focus of the study departs from the yet prevalent view of second language learners immersed in English-dominant classrooms as deficient communicators and in fact suggests quite the opposite: that second language learners are multicompetent sign makers and users (see Belz, 2002).

In relation to the highly intersubjective relationship between Pia and Fatima in this study, we invoke Mahn and John-Steiner (2002), who explored how supportive interrelations between peers and mentors are crucial in enabling learners to have the confidence to engage in creative risk-taking. Furthermore, they argued that confidence is an essential aspect of lifelong learning. In our study, the emotional support that Pia and Fatima demonstrated toward each other induced a greater sense of confidence in how they negotiated classroom activities in general. Thus, in accord with Mahn and John-Steiner, our study also attests that the emotional support of friends and mentors can be critical to one's ability to transform within different sociocultural environments.

Future research may reveal more clues regarding how different class members alter their own activities in response to the presence of new class members who are linguistic newcomers to the context. However, we would like to further note that in this particular classroom the solidarity that Fatima demonstrated toward Pia was extended to other members of the class, who by the study's conclusion had also clearly adopted an attitude of caring for the one student, Pia, who did not share either of their spoken languages. This fact led us to realize that the dialogical nature of Pia's and Fatima's relationship was in effect *heteroglossic* in that it reached beyond the localized communicative actions between them—it affected and ultimately transformed the classroom community as a whole.

52   IDDINGS, HAUGHT, DEVLIN

In regard to more specific pedagogical implications of this study, we emphasize that the context that Ruth created in her classroom—the balance between structured and open-ended tasks she used with her students—and the way that she valued students' voice (in whatever modality) in her classroom propitiated opportunities for the interactions on which we focused. Pia and Fatima were allowed ample freedom to talk during learning center activities, a privilege often denied students in more traditional settings, as the noise level in the classroom environment is often misunderstood as off-task behavior. It is also relevant to point out that although the second language students were seemingly off task in performing some of the assigned tasks, one must consider that these children were actively and strategically seeking out ways to engage in dialogue with each other in an effort to author themselves through the new context. In this respect, Bakhtin's (1981) notion of *simultaneity*, or the differential relation between self and other, is implicated in the way the students mirrored, imitated, and changed elements of each other's utterances. Thus, we emphasize that multimodal means of representation should be considered for second language students, and especially for those who are newcomers to a culture, as an important part of the social fabric. Similar to linguistic forms of communication, multimodal signs are always present with a history and always belong to others. As such, these are meaningful tools for students in their processes of learning.

REFERENCES

Bakhtin, M. (1981). *The dialogic imagination: Four essays.* Austin: University of Texas Press.
Belz, J. A. (2002). Second language play as a representation of the multicompetent self in foreign language study. *Journal of Language, Identity, and Education, 1,* 13–39.
DaSilva Iddings, A. C., & McCafferty, S. (2003, February). *Language play and language learning.* Paper presented at the Georgetown Round Table for Language and Linguistics, Washington, DC.
Holquist, M. (1990). *Dialogism: Bakhtin and his world.* London: Routledge.
Kinginger, C. (2002). Defining the zone of proximal development in US foreign language education. *Applied Linguistics, 23,* 240–261.
Kramsch, C. (2000). Social discursive constructions of self in L2 learning. In J. P. Lantolf (Ed.), *Sociocultural theory and second language learning* (pp. 133–154). Oxford, England: Oxford University Press.
Kress, G. (1997). *Before writing: Re-thinking the paths to literacy.* London: Routledge.
Lantolf, J. P. (2000). *Sociocultural theory and second language learning.* New York: Oxford University Press.
Lantolf, J. P., & Pavlenko, A. (2001). (S)econd (L)anguage (A)ctivity theory: Understanding second language learners as people. In M. P. Breen (Ed.), *Learner contri-*

butions to language learning: New directions in research (pp. 141–158). Essex, England: Pearson Education.

Mahn, H., & John-Steiner, V. (2002). The gift of confidence: A Vygotskian view of emotions. In C. G. Wells & G. Claxton (Eds.), *Learning for life in the 21st century* (pp. 46–58). Oxford, England: Blackwell.

McCafferty, S. (2002). Gesture and creating zones of proximal development for second language learning. *Modern Language Journal, 86,* 192–203.

Newman, F., & Holtzman, L. (1993). *Lev Vygotsky: Revolutionary scientist.* New York: Routledge.

Voloshinov, V. N. (1986). *Marxism and the philosophy of language* (L. Matejka & I. R. Titunik, Trans.). Cambridge, MA: Harvard University Press. (Original work published 1929)

Vygostky, L. (1978). *Mind and society: The development of higher mental processes.* Cambridge, MA: Harvard University Press.

Chapter 4

Dialogic Investigations: Cultural Artifacts in ESOL Composition Classes

Jeffery Lee Orr
University of Georgia

Students who study English as a second or additional language travel from some location to the United States. Accordingly, they navigate, explore, and discover geographic and ideological terrain. Although their journeys have often been inspired by folklore ventriloquated through the ages within the voices of their lineage, and perhaps more currently through glossy covers of travel guides and in-flight magazines or technologically savvy university Web sites, it is their arrival in the United States that set upon them the tasks of localized ideological mediation. Such mediation is influenced by:

> heteroglot from top to bottom: it represents the co-existence of socio-ideological contradictions between the present and the past, between different epochs of the past, between different socio-ideological groups in the present, between tendencies, schools, circles and so forth, all given a bodily form. (Bakhtin, 1981, p. 291)

It is not surprising, then, that students in composition classes for English speakers of other languages (ESOL) bring their own ideology when they arrive in the United States. Through these journeys, concomitant schemas emerge that transcend finite spatial–temporal markers and traverse ideological continua. Those schemas position ESOL students as potentially and uniquely available to dialogic investigations. They already hold in dialogic association cultural influences: family, friends, religions, economies, politics, and philosophies (Savignon & Sysoyev, 2002).

These influences not only affect students' mediation of the sociocultural ideology they encounter in the United States but also inform their mediation of both cultures and both languages. The influences, the ideology, and the mediation provide promise for ESOL composition: promise for students to contribute to and learn from socially constructed language-learning environments and promise for instructors to draw on Bakhtinian theory and defer to student ideology. Instead of constructing composition syllabi as instruments primarily devoted to reducing ESOL learners' language deficiencies, and instead of requiring another one-topic-fits-all expository essay, instructors can guide students in exploring the myriad epistemologies and ideologes that ESOL students already hold. To foreground macro-level competence, however, is not to ignore micro-level challenges; that is, creating language learning opportunities that build on student knowledge does not negate attention to students' sentence-level linguistic competence. One goal of the study I report in this chapter was, therefore, to illustrate one ESOL activity that integrates Bakhtinian notions of utterance and addressitivity to reinforce the reciprocal sociocultural nature of language.

Bakhtin's (1986) theory of utterances seems particularly appropriate for ESOL composition instruction at the university level, because inherent in the theory is the social situatedness of communication. When considering communication as a social entity, ESOL students and instructors may experience the utterance as "a link in the chain of speech communication of a particular sphere" (Bakhtin, 1986, p. 91). Students may learn to make connections between their experiences in first-language speech spheres, especially if they have several years of first-language experience, and their developing second language experience in speech spheres. They may learn that speaking in various contexts or locales—for example, recreational settings with peers, educational settings with peers or instructors, religious ceremonies with family, and interviews with immigration officials—situate them as both contributors and respondents to speech, as speakers and listeners. "The speaker," noted Bakhtin (1986), "with his world view, his evaluations and emotions, on the one hand, and the object of his speech and the language system (language means), on the other—these alone determine the utterance, its style, and its composition" (pp. 90–91). The listener, affirmed Lähteenmäki (1998), "should be able to relate the position that the speaker's utterance represents to other positions expressed in a given discourse community" (p. 79).

Within one tenet of his theory, Bakhtin made succinct a philosophy for ESOL composition: What one says, and how one writes, link directly to one's epistemological, ideological fiber, fiber that all the while is socially situated. Bakhtin would find allies with composition theorists even though such theorists hail disparate ideologies: social constructionism (Bruffee, 1984, 1986) on the one hand, and expressivism (Elbow, 1973, 1986) and process (Emig, 1971; Flower & Hayes, 1980, 1981; Hairston, 1982; Zamel, 1983) on the other hand in composition and ESOL alike. What they would agree upon with relative certainty are expectations for composition students at the end of first-year composition studies. According to the Writing Program Administration (WPA), students should accomplish the following in regard to rhetoric (Yancey, 2001):

• Focus on a purpose.
• Respond to the needs of different audiences.
• Respond appropriately to different kinds of rhetorical situations.
• Use conventions of format and structure appropriate to the rhetorical situation.
• Adopt appropriate voice, tone, and level of formality.
• Understand how genres shape reading and writing.
• Write in several genres.

In regard to critical thinking, the WPA recommends that students:

• Use writing and reading for inquiry, learning, thinking, and communicating.
• Understand a writing assignment as a series of tasks, including finding, evaluating, analyzing, and synthesizing appropriate primary and secondary sources.
• Integrate their own ideas with those of others.
• Understand the relationships among language, knowledge, and power (Yancey, 2001).

Compositionists generally appreciate the skills named by the WPA, skills that challenge students to evoke a voice suitable to a given writing assignment, therefore acknowledging the existence of many voices. Likewise, Bakhtin (1981) claimed that "the prose writer as a novelist does not strip away the intentions of others from the heteroglot language of his works, he does not violate those socio-ideological cultural horizons ... he welcomes them" (p. 299).

Bakhtin's theory and students' increasing ideological development intersect in activities that require students to consider various language spheres and strategies of mediation of those spheres. Of note is the sociopolitical ideology embodied in various media. One prevalent medium Americans choose to illustrate ideology and frequently advocate social change is the bumper sticker. Bumper stickers, then, serve as significant sources for analyses of utterances, for bumper stickers in their ubiquitous representations enact "various spheres of human activity and communication" (Bakhtin, 1986, p. 62). People who speak through or write bumper stickers, and those who respond or listen, can attest to Bakhtin's (1986) assertion that "language enters life through concrete utterances (which manifest language) and life enters language through concrete utterances as well" (p. 63). Jacoby and Ochs (1995) reinforced the relevance of utterances to dialogic processes: "Utterances are also viewed as multivocal or heteroglossic in nature, informed by the ideas and representational styles of others" (pp. 173–174). A greater understanding of utterances warrants further consideration to response, the anticipated reaction to utterances. Utterances such as bumper stickers exist to resonate not singularly in a vast chasm but in dialogic relation to additional voices, additional cultures, representations, speakers, hearers—interlocutors, interpreters, privileged members of various communities. Such interlocutions render students as

> agents of culture rather than merely bearers of a culture that has been handed down to them and encoded in grammatical form. The constitutive perspective on indexicality incorporates the post-structural view that the relation between person and society is dynamic and mediated by language … while person and society are distinguishable, they are integral. Person and society enter into a dialectical relation in that they act on each other, and transform each other. In such paradigms, while society helps define a person, a person also helps to (re)define society (Ochs, 1993, p. 416).

The dialectic surrounding person and society affects one's ongoing awareness of multiple subjectivities (Weedon, 1987). Various influences affect those subjectivities—for example, social contexts affect language learners, and language learners affect social contexts. That reciprocal quality of the dialectic between person and society resembles closely Bakhtin's notion of dialogism: the associations between speaker and utterance, utterance and addressee, speaker and addressee, and utterance and response. The dialogic quality of bumper stickers discursively, contextually, and intertextually draws upon "languages of heteroglossia…specific points of view on the world, forms for conceptualizing in words, specific world views, each characterized by its own objects, meanings and values" (Bakhtin, 1981, pp. 291–292). Therefore, ESOL students in the composition classroom I taught in the fall of 2002—who extol and represent bodies of ideologies, sometimes static, sometimes fluid, often resonant of the discourse of their environments and of their cultures—are themselves cultural artifacts. As cultural artifacts—that is, beings informed not only by their cultural heritage and its inherent social languages (Bakhtin, 1981, p. 275; Hermans, 1999; Wertsch, 1991) but also by an increasing awareness of U.S. culture—these students investigated bumper stickers, exemplars of U.S. social language, by contemplating and interpreting them as vehicles of visual rhetoric, utterances originating from and contributing to culturally influenced subjectivities. Significant among these subjectivities is that of student in the United States.

ESOL students, like first-language students, in first-year writing courses in typical U.S. universities negotiate academic literacy (Spack, 1988; Zamel, 1988; Zamel and Spack 1998), whether thought of as discipline specific (Bridgeman & Carlson, 1983; Spack, 1988) or as competencies (Gajdusek & vanDommelen, 1993) or as behaviors (Blanton, 1994), in composition classes and throughout the academy. They encounter additional ways of knowing (epistemological stances) and additional ways of thinking about new knowledge (ideological stances; Ochs, 1993). These ESOL composition students begin to negotiate academic literacy as defined by competencies and behaviors of interpretation, evaluation, synthesis, and extra polation, mediated, in this instance, through the sociocultural text of bumper stickers. Bumper stickers—those sometimes-amorphous, polysemous, miniature mobile billboards, which traverse theoretical trajectories—offer these students opportunities to decipher what language can do, that is, how language presents and represents not only messages, messengers, and targets but also communities, societies, and philosophies in harmony and in discord, monologically, dialogically, and in ever-evolving rhetorical manifestations. Analyzing bumper stickers as culturally saturated text, these students investigate the polyvocaic qualities of utterances by exploring addressivity, audience, and intent to discover.

> The utterance is related not only to preceding, but also to subsequent links in the chain of speech communion … from the very beginning the utterance is constructed while taking into account possible responsive reactions, for whose sake in essence it is actually created. As we know, the role of the *others* … for whom my thought becomes actual thought for the first time (and thus for my own self as well) it is not that of passive listeners, but of active participants in speech communication. (Bakhtin, 1986, p. 94)

In the spirit of the dialogic, this study foregrounded strategies of response, informed by Bakhtian notions of utterance and addressivity, that the students in my ESOL composition class evoked to contextualize bumper stickers and participate in the cultural dialogues rendered through them.

The following research questions guided this study:

1. Do students' responses to bumper stickers demonstrate the dialogic nature of language? If so, how?
2. How do students' stances toward bumper stickers vary according to interactional context?
3. How do students' evaluations of bumper stickers contribute to their own developing ideologies?

RESEARCH CONTEXT

The site of the study was a freshman composition course designed for non-native speakers of English who study in a small, socially constructed learning environment characterized by intensive peer interaction and instructor–student interaction at an engineering technology university in a city in the southeastern United States. Students may select this course, may be referred to the course by other composition faculty, or register for a composition class with native English speakers. The course offers 3 credit hours and is the first of a two-course sequence in composition.

This study, an investigation of the ways five ESOL composition students responded to bumper stickers, took place during the fall semester of 2002. Of the five students enrolled in the course, two were from Brazil (one man and one woman, the only woman in the class), one was from northern Africa, one was from India, and one was from Pakistan. Each student self-selected the course during the semester of the study; I served as the instructor and researcher and designed the course in my role as ESOL instructor at the university. I chose this site because of convenient access to this population. The study emerged from my work with students as cultural artifacts mediating cultural artifacts. Through our class discussions, the students and I acknowledged being situated in and informed by culture.

Data sources comprise Portfolio No. 3, the third and final portfolio of the term that students had to complete: Each student chose three bumper stickers from the car of a professor who is also employed at the university. They wrote an essay on the selection and interpretations of bumper stickers in response to the following prompts:

1. Name the bumper stickers you chose.
2. Explain the reasons you chose the bumper stickers.
3. What do they say to you? What do these choices say about you?
4. What are the reasons you did not choose the other stickers?

Students read each others' essays, made suggestions for improvement, revised their own essays accordingly, and submitted them to me. Next, each student wrote a letter about bumper stickers to someone in his or her country. Students also wrote a letter to the professor who owns the car with the bumper stickers. They turned in the letters to me. I first analyzed the essays using content analysis to determine what stickers the students had selected and to determine whether there was any evidence indicating that ESOL students perceive such utterances as socially situated. The initial content analysis gave way to discourse analysis; that is, I coded the data first according to *what* students communicated and second according to *how* they communicated. Students explained their reasons for selecting particular bumper stickers by using indexicality. Therefore, I coded data according to students' indexed epistemological, ideological, behavioral, and affective stances. I analyzed students' letters using indexicality and discovered that students indexed according to rhetorical context and addressee, that is, the intended audience. Three of the five students created bumper stickers, and although I did not analyze them, I do report them here to indicate student ideology presented though the forum of bumper stickers.

RESULTS

The study revealed the following:

1. The students' responses to bumper stickers demonstrated the dialogic nature of language. They responded by indexing their epistemologies, ideologies, behavioral stances, and afffective stances.
2. The students indexed familiarity, dialogic history, and intent in letters addressed to someone in their home country. They indexed identification, intent, and evaluation when they wrote to the professor who owns the car.
3. The students used reciprocal discursive adaptation. They strategically customized their responses to particular contexts and demonstrated language innovation.

The students in this study responded to utterances of others, the speakers of the bumper stickers, oftentimes by calling on intertextual references to subjectivities and therefore ideologies of their first-language culture. They also communicated their initial responses to utterances primarily through indexicality (Cappelen & Lepore, 2002; Glenberg & Robertson, 1999; Ochs, 1996) by pointing some linguistic form toward some immediate context (Ochs, 1996). *Indexicality*, according to Cappelen and Lepore (2002), is the use of "linguistic expressions whose meaning remains stable while their reference shifts from utterance to utterance" (p. 271). Glenberg and Robertson (1999) asserted that "indexing, that is, referring words and phrases to objects (or analogical representations of objects) is required for comprehension" (p. 1). The students' responses mediate cultural context and demonstrate an increasing competence in dialogic participation.

The first research question was "Do students' responses to bumper stickers demonstrate the dialogic nature of language? If so, how?" Evidence of students' preliminary response occurs immediately: Students walked outside their composition classroom to a campus parking lot and observed a car with at least 12 bumper stickers. They looked at the car, looked at themselves, looked at me, and asked "Is this your car?" With this one initial question, the students began the work of debunking the *fictions* (Bakhtin, 1986, p. 66) of a one-dimensional flow from speaker to listener and thereby intuited a far more dynamic communicative system such that

> when the listener perceives and understands the meaning (the language meaning) of speech, he simultaneously takes an active, responsive attitude toward it. He either agrees or disagrees with it (completely or partially), augments it, applies it, prepares it for execution and so on. (Bakhtin, 1986, p. 68)

If "this" car belongs to me, then they have identified me as the speaker of particular utterances, endorser of particular ideologies, and, in this instance, they have attributed significance to consequences of ideological agreement or disagreement with me as the evaluator of their forthcoming assignment. Before they began the written work of response, however, they considered not only the utterances—objects of communicated thought—and their reactions to them but also objects derived from a source—in this case, me, their instructor—wrought with sociopolitical, cultural ideology. I informed them the car does not belong to me. Instead, it belongs to a professor in another department at the university.

After learning that the car was not mine, the students exercised reciprocal discursive adaptation. They took the two ascertained answers, the "who" and the "where," and began to ponder the "what," "when," and "why" in a basic journalistic approach, no longer encumbered by their initial assumptions about car ownership but now using what was later evidenced in their writing: the awareness that "any understanding of live speech, a live utterance, is inherently responsive, although the degree of this activity varies extremely. Any understanding is imbued with response and necessarily elicits it in one form or the other: the listener becomes the speaker" (Bakhtin, 1986, p. 68). Before they spoke, however, they considered the speaker(s) of the stickers as culturally, politically, and historically situated sources, inspired by ideology and agenda. They made inferences and assumptions and constructed their responses accordingly (see ADDRESSIVITY section). This, then, is reciprocal discursive adaptation: the implementation of a listener's customized communicative strategies contextualized by the listener's sociopolitical stances in response to a particular speaker's utterance. The listener, when generating a response, attempts to contextualize the speaker's ideology and intent, and the listener ultimately takes on the role of speaker and anticipates a response. In other words, when these students asked "Is this your car?" they were inquiring not merely the question of car ownership but were indexing their attribution of the car owner as speaker and the stickers as utterances, the messages spoken to them awaiting their responses. Their responses evolve through their implementations of reciprocal discursive adaptation. Tables 4.1 and 4.2 present details about the

TABLE 4.1
Bumper Stickers

Selected stickers	Students
1. HANG UP AND DRIVE	1, 2, 3, 5
2. FEMINISM IS THE RADICAL NOTION THAT WOMEN ARE PEOPLE	1, 4
3. SMILE WHAT COULD IT HURT	1, 3
4. EQUAL RIGHTS ARE NOT SPECIAL RIGHTS	4
5. WAR IS COSTLY, Peace is Priceless	5, 2, 3
6. It will be a great day when our schools get all the money they need and the air force has to hold a bake sale to buy a bomber	2
7. EVERYONE DOES BETTER WHEN EVERYONE DOES BETTER	5
8. Well-behaved women rarely make history	4

TABLE 4.2
Students

Student	Home country	Selected stickers
Endept	India	1-2-3
Paulo	Brazil	5-6-1
John	Africa	1-5-3
Serah	Brazil	4-2-8
Muhamed	Pakistan	1-5-7

bumper stickers, which bumper stickers the students selected, the students, and their home countries.

Among the various bumper-stickered utterances displayed on the car, the students collectively selected eight (see Tables 4.1 and 4.2). Their selections initiate response, whereas the reasons accompanying their selections perpetuate dialogism. Equally salient to the answer to the "who" question (i.e., "Who is speaking?") within and through the stickers is the answer to the "what" question. What is the utterance?" What is its significance? With what behavior does one associate it? What are "the overtures of the style...dialogic overtures" (Bakhtin, 1986, p. 92)? What are the "echoes and reverberations of other utterances to which it is related by the community of the sphere of the speech community" (Bakhtin, 1986, p. 91)? Such questions signal

Halasek's (1999) reading of Bakhtin: "The utterance, then, is defined in Bakhtinian terms by the interrelationships between and among speaker and subject, speaker and audience, and the audience and subject" (p. 63).

The reasons the students offered in support of why they selected certain stickers index the students' epistemological/ideological, behavioral, and affective stances (see Table 4.3). They repeatedly proclaim: "I know," "I understand," "I do not understand," "I believe," "I think," "I want," "I like," "I dislike." These proclamations indicate that the students' initial reciprocal involvement with utterances aligns with what Halasek (1999) wrote: "The audience's role is not, therefore, defined solely, or even primarily, by its position relative to the author, ... but also by its perspective on the subject of the discourse" (p. 63). Thus, the students contemplated the utterances and the speakers' relation to the utterances and formed their own reactions, which all "may be juxtaposed to one another, mutually supplement one another, contradict one another and be interrelated dialogically" (Bakhtin, 1981, p. 292).

First, the students responded according to epistemology and behavioral modification: Voloshinov (1973) contended that "Language, in the process of its practical implementation, is inseparable from its ideological or behav-

TABLE 4.3
Epistemic and Affective Stances

Student	Stances
Endept	I am cautious—I want others to think like me—I want them to do something—I am not a feminist—I see the funny side—I am jovial—not always—I do my best to smile.
Paulo	I care about important issues in the world, and I do my part to make the world a better place.
John	I have chosen three bumper stickers because I know more about them, also they reflect ... the world we live in today.
	My choices reflect my feeling ... they affect me ... people driving dangerously because they are talking on the cell phone ... America going to war with Iraq ... has political intentions and can hurt economy.
Serah	I chose ... because I completely disagree with because I am extremely against feminism and I am not afraid to defend my point of view.
Muhamed	All ... are based on things I believe in ... I was hit by a car ... the driver was on the phone ... current events in Iraq ...is not worth going to war and having people killed ... people can only help themselves and should not be looking for handouts.

ioral impletion" (p. 70). Students indexed what they know and behavior they desire. Endept, Paulo, John, and Muhamed selected HANG UP AND DRIVE—the sticker chosen more often than any other. It comments on people who "use their cell phone while driving, and concentrate more on the conversation. This can prove dangerous and I think one should not use a cell phone while driving ... it conveys something I want to tell people," stated Endept. Paulo affirmed, "It has been proved that drive and talk on mobile phone is dangerous." John claimed that "It is a distraction when we talk and drive at the same time. It leads to accidents most of the time," and Muhamed agreed: "People who drive on the phone are not really paying attention to the road." Although *it* and *this* demonstrate anaphora with their antecedents of HANG UP AND DRIVE, the sticker itself, and the dangerous act of driving and talking on the phone, respectively, "can prove dangerous" and "has been proved" index factual attributions even though students offer no support for these assertions. Endept most emphatically articulated his wish for behavioral modification when he exclaimed, "I want to tell people. I want others to think like me. I want them to do something." His desire to interact, to persuade, to motivate—all reasons he selected certain bumper stickers—also typify the reason one states an utterance: the anticipated response.

In addition to indexing epistemology and behavior, students index ideological stances. Stickers on war "send serious and important messages" and index ideological certainty. John, Paulo, and Muhamed all chose "WAR IS COSTLY, Peace is Priceless." John said he believed that "Going to war involves heavy arsenal, huge number of personnel deployment. War is synonym of destruction, pain, famine, disease ... [and] should be avoided." Muhamed declared, "War is costly not only financially, but it also cost people their lives .... Peace is priceless because it does not cost people their lives, and the cost of a human life is priceless," and Paulo admitted that "I chose 'WAR IS COSTLY, Peace is Priceless' and *it will be a great day when our schools get all the money they need and the air force has to hold a bake sale to buy a bomber* because they send serious and important messages." In addition to ideological certainty, Paulo indexed behavioral modification: "We should seek peace, not war, and put the money ... into important things like school ... instead of killing."

The third use of indexicals in response to the stickers is affect. Endept and Serah responded to FEMINISM IS THE RADICAL NOTION THAT WOMEN ARE PEOPLE. It "appealed to me, as it is humorous. It mocks strict feminists and gives ... a funny outlook when it is actually more serious," Endept avowed. Conversely, for Serah "EQUAL RIGHTS <u>ARE</u> <u>NOT</u> SPECIAL RIGHTS, FEMINISM IS THE RADICAL NOTION THAT WOMEN ARE PEOPLE, and 'Well-behaved women rarely make history'—Those bumpers all together defend the same argument ... feminism ... about the sociopolitical ideas of the car owner—a radical feminist."

"I liked SMILE WHAT COULD IT HURT as it tells me that a smile costs nothing to give but it means a lot to people receiving. It shows how significant a small thing can be," said Endept. John added, "Smiling makes people happier and comfortable ... get us out of daily stress .... People around you appreciate it."

When students explained the reasons they did not select certain stickers (see Table 4.4), they again indexed epistemology/ideology, behavior, and affect. Although "did not appeal to me," "did not make sense—were not funny," and "do not [send] important messages" contain *not*, suggesting some negative evaluation, the negative evaluation constitutes a response nevertheless. Moreover, "did not have an impact on me" constitutes misunderstanding, or at least an incomplete evaluation, because each of the reactions represents a response based on some impact, some consideration of the utterance.

ADDRESSIVITY

The second research question of the study considers ways students' stances toward bumper stickers varied according to interactional context. When students in this composition class write a letter to someone in their home country, they engage as authors of a particular text, the letter, to an addressee whom they view almost as "an immediate participant–interlouctor in an everyday dialogue" (Bakhtin, 1986, p. 95) even though they do not experience face-to-face interaction. The absence of immediate spatial proximity does

TABLE 4.4
Weighing Values (Reasons Why Stickers Were Not Selected)

Student	Reasons
Endept	They did not appeal to me nor did they make sense—were not funny and they did not have an impact on me.
Paulo	I do not think the other stickers sent important messages.
John	I am not familiar ... they could not catch my attention because they do not affect me ... lack of understanding behind the real messages, what the exactly the author intends to say.
Serah	I could choose other stickers also, but I chose those because they are very polemic.
Muhamed	A few did not make sense to me ... a few would be difficult to write about. I do not know why someone would put that (Apple) sticker ... maybe he/she works for Apple or ... is trying to cover a scratch. Some were too long.

not, however, negate the familiar. That awareness of familiarity affects the textual discourse markers students use to communicate their own experiences of having previously enacted the role of addressee, one of the masses whom the bumper stickers hail. What students write, what they say, and how they speak to their addressees reflect their understanding. "Understanding" for Bakhtin (1981, p. 282) "comes to fruition only in the response. Understanding and response are dialectically merged and mutually condition each other, one is impossible without the other." Understanding for these students, however, emerges synergistically as they contemplate the call—the speakers' utterances as voices with intention; their own responses, based on social, cultural, and political stances as juxtaposed to stances of others; and the responses these utterances may stimulate from their addressees, people whose ideologies have varyingly constituted schemas.

Dialogism emerges as a student responds to having been addressed, hearing a speaker—an author of a bumper sticker—whose "orientation toward the listener is an orientation toward a specific conceptual horizon, toward the specific world of the listener" (Bakhtin, 1981, p. 282). In response to the speaker, a student ventriloquates the speaker to his or her addressee just as the car owner ventriloquates the sticker writers when she displays the stickers on her car. These reflexive reciprocal instantiations constitute heteroglossia.

Students began the letters to someone in their country with greetings that indicate close emotional proximity despite the geographic distance from their addressees: "Dear," "Hey! How is it going?" "Hi how are you?" and "Hello." When students wrote a letter to the car owner, however, they hail an addressee whom they view not as a casual everyday interlocutor: "Dear Sir/Madam," "Hello," "To: The owner of the blue escort," "To: The President of the Feminist Group," and "Dear Professor that owns the Ford Escort with the bumper stickers on it." In the letters home, students generally used discourse markers to index familiarity, dialogic history, and intent, whereas in letters to the car owner students generally indexed identification, intent, and evaluation. To both addressees, students called on intertextuality and heteroglossia as they expanded dialogism.

FAMILIARITY AND DIALOGIC HISTORY

First and foremost, when writing to someone in their countries, the students indexed familiarity and dialogic history: "I am guessing your fine since you have not written to me in the past two months. I heard you changed your major from electrical engineering to architecture. Well I always told you that engineering was not your field." "I do miss you people a lot," Endept admitted. In an intertextual reference, Paulo wrote that he had seen "a car with many stickers, just like the back of your dad's truck" and cited dialogic history shared by his cousin, his uncle, and himself; they have all witnessed and responded on some level to the stickers on the truck. That response informs Paulo's responses to the professor's car. He revealed, "When I read the bumper sticker that says, WAR IS COSTLY, Peace is Priceless, I thought about you, because it reminded me [of] that famous MasterCard commercial that gives a list of things that you can buy with MasterCard, and in the end says what is priceless." He made an intertextual thematic connection to the invaluable. Intertextuality, "this forward and backward glance, the linking of one utterance to another…looks forward to the receiving audience, but also looks backward toward inceptive one(s)" (Halasek, 1999, p. 65). Paulo continued, " I know you like that commercial since your major in college is marketing and publicity."

Muhamed wrote a letter of homage to his uncle and said that "I saw a car that had a bumper sticker that reminded me of you. It read, EVERYONE DOES BETTER WHEN EVERYONE DOES BETTER. The sticker reminded me of you because you are a self-made man. You forced yourself to do better in order to get better things in life." Muhamed indexed familiarity through appreciation, admiration, and respect.

INDEXING DIALOGIC HISTORY AND INTENT

Endept announced to his friend:

> The reason I write to you today is to tell you something which I saw. It is about a bumper sticker that caught my attention and was about something which you and I disagree. I am sure that you remember our arguments of using cell phones while driving. I know that I still have not been able to convince you …. The sticker I saw said, HANG UP AND DRIVE. I think this is a strong statement and I know you are probably laughing at it already.

This passage indexes dialogic history and intent. Their communicative history encompasses ideological awareness and lays the foundation for this attempt to induce the desired response.

Paulo's awareness of his cousin's beliefs provides context for his written declaration of intent and subsequent urge for his cousin to rethink his ideology. He wrote:

> I am glad that Iraq agreed to let the United Nations send inspectors to see if they have weapons of mass destruction, otherwise, the USA would start a war in Iraq. I know you think war was is the solution, but read this other bumper sticker that was in the picture: *It will be a great day when our schools get all the money they need, and the air force has to hold a bake sale to buy a bomber.*

John stated his intent in his letter through a declaration of agreement:

> I came across a bumper sticker that showed the message "WAR IS COSTLY, Peace is Priceless." I am writing to tell you what the message is conveying. The message is tells that a war must be avoided and only used as last resort, when all solution are gone. I know that you agree with on this point. I am, as you know, a fervent opponent of war.

Serah's statement of intent to her pastor in Brazil reveals her astonishment concerning ideology inconsistent with her own:

> I decided to cover this subject in a letter because I want you to have in my own writing a transcript of some of the "atrocities" that I recently "bumped" into here in Atlanta. My eyes could not believe what I was reading, but it was true. It was the bumper of a car full of radical messages, which advocate several "unchristian" attitudes. However, what really affronted me was the following feminist sticker: FEMINISM IS THE RADICAL NOTION THAT WOMEN ARE PEOPLE.

IDENTIFICATION AND INTENT

When the students wrote letters expressing their ideas about the bumper stickers to the professor who owns the car, the most salient device they use to establish the rhetorical context is a statement of self-identification, which preceded their intent. Endept wrote:

> I am freshman attending .... I usually park next to the recreation area, but yesterday I parked opposite to the student's center. I noticed a blue ford escort with some stickers on its back and later found that it belongs to a professor. I would like to comment on some of these stickers, and ask what that others mean.

Paulo conveyed intent and shifted quickly to identification; however, his concern about identification resides in an assumption about the car owner:

> The English professor showed us your car. He asked us to send you a letter with comments about the car. From a couple of stickers like, Well-behaved women rarely make history, I assume that you are a woman. I could identify most of the points you were trying to make with the bumper stickers, and that shows you are concerned with topics like war, religion, and message with positive comments.

John, like Paulo, focused more on the identity of the car owner, yet John embedded his statement of the car owner's identity in characterization: "I appreciate some of the messages that are on your bumper sticker. Like the one about the cell phone, war & peace. I realize that you are a concerned citizen who is socially aware of today's life."

Serah most blatantly assumed the car owner's identity. She stated in her greeting: "To the President of the Feminist Group." Serah not only assumed that the car owner is a feminist but also chose to address her as president of a feminist group in spite of the fact that no such reference to the car owner occurred in class discussions. She added in a statement of intent:

> The purpose of this letter is to share my thoughts about one specific bumper sticker that is on your car. I understand it is your car and we all as human beings, especially in this country where the free speech is protected, can express ourselves in whatever way we think is the most appropriate. The sticker I am talking about is one that declares, FEMINISM IS THE RADICAL NOTION THAT WOMEN ARE PEOPLE. I personally think this is not a "radical notion" at all.

EVALUATION, SOLICITING RESPONSE, AND IDEOLOGICAL BECOMING

As students indexed evaluations of the bumper stickers, momentum built in response. Methods of conveying evaluation attest to the students' realization that just as speakers of utterances are socially situated, so are respondents. Some evaluations resonated common ideology. Paulo suggested, "I understand the messages you are trying to pass on, and I think they are good messages. Every form of educating people with good messages is valid, and I think it is good you chose your car and the bumper stickers to send messages, even though people may think it makes your car look ugly." He added:

> I understand all the messages you were sending with the stickers, I am not sure what you meant with the Apple stickers. Is it because you think it is cute? On the other hand, perhaps something deeper like, for some reason you are against Microsoft and regular PC's. I would agree with that, I think Macintosh computers are much better, but the problem is they are more expensive.

John exclaimed: "Some of your messages are original. I feel that I can relate to some of them. The way you are putting your messages across is unique and authentic. You are trying to attract as many people as you can, to see your messages." And Muhamed elevated evaluation to appreciation with, "Thank you for putting these words of wisdom on your vehicle for the world to see. You are a brave individual to put your opinions in the public eye. You are an inspiration to all people. Even though I do not put bumper stickers on my car, I am going to find to way to put my options out so everyone can them."

Resonating common ideology through positive evaluation represents only one evaluative stance. Endept began the negative, or counter-commentary, and then Paulo, John, and Serah exemplified Hermans's (1999) reference to Bakhtin's notion of innovation: "It is on the interface between self and other, as opposite positions in a spatialized structure, that innovation emerges" (p. 70). Morris (1994, p. 5) explained, "It is this responsive interaction between self and other, that constitutes the capacity of language to produce new meaning." Bakhtin (1981, pp. 299–300) surmised that "The prose writer makes use of words that are already populated with the social intentions of others and compels them to serve his own intentions, to serve a second master." Endept suggested:

> There were some bad stickers. Some I did not understand and others I do not think I even want to understand. The sticker that said, EVERYONE does good when EVERYONE does good [student's misquote], I thought was the dumbest of all. It is not an eye catching sticker and destroys the whole purpose of being a bumper sticker. I do understand that there is valid meaning behind this but I still do not think that the sticker is good enough to gain any attention.

Revealing a less stringent evaluation, coupled with some advice, Paulo stated:

> Your HANG UP AND DRIVE sticker tells people not to talk on the cellular phone while they are driving. Don't you think people reading the messages on the back of your car while they are driving make the same effect of talking on the phone, distracting them? Maybe you should get a bigger sticker saying: "Only read these messages if the traffic light is red." However, that would make people more curious to read the rest of the stickers; therefore, I do not know what you should do.

What Paulo began, John magnified:

> Your technique has some negative aspects. By transforming your car as a rolling banner on the road, you are causing distractions to other car drivers. This way of sending your messages can cause problems to other commuters. At the same time, a person with a lot of bumper stickers messages is seen as a looser, angry and frustrated. They are usually treated as incompetent individual who could not find another way of demonstrating their position of an issue. Certainly your method is inexpensive but lacks responsibility.

Like Paulo, John offered advice:

I may have some suggestions to you on how to improve your marketing techniques. If you cannot afford renting a banner across the street then you should start a web site to put your messages. It is quite affordable to host a website in a local company. With proper advertising in the major search engines, you will have lot of web surfers that will visit your site.

Rounding out evaluations and moving toward soliciting response, Serah explained, "Those who are against radical feminism, especially Christians like me, do not deny the personhood of women at all. The Biblical vision of womanhood does not make a woman a non-person. Rather, in the entire Bible God affirms the uniqueness of women as co-regents of the human race."

Regardless of the differences in strategies the students used to communicate to someone in their countries and to the car owner, the students ended letters to both parties with expectation, soliciting response and/or offering good wishes.

Endept warmly closed the letter to his friend, "Well I hope that I have made some sense to you. I know that you are never going to agree with me in the near future. Well anyways, I have to go know. I hope to hear from you soon. Convey my regards to everyone and take care."

Serah solicited prayerful assistance from her pastor: "I know we cannot change the whole world, but we can change at least part of the world through the teachings of our Lord Jesus Christ that are written in the Holy Bible. So please help me pray for the owner of this car, because I am going to pray for her also."

Endept closed his letter to the car owner with gratitude and expectation:

Another sticker that made me question the gender of the owner was the one that said, FEMINISM IS THE RADICAL NOTION THAT WOMEN ARE PEOPLE. I could not figure out if the sticker had a sarcastic meaning or a serious meaning to it. I hope you can explain that to me in your reply. I would like to end my letter by thanking you for taking the time for reading this and I hope you can reply as soon as possible.

Muhamed offered sympathy and advice to the car owner: "I think you are a lonely person, probably divorced and with lots of enemies but I still sympathize with you. Therefore, I am suggesting you to seek some professional help. Good luck in your lonely life." Paulo ended his letter by giving advice to the car owner: "Again, It is good that you are sending good messages, but as one classmate said, if you want to sell your car you should take the stickers off."

The final research question links analyses of utterances to ideological becoming, "the process of selectively assimilating the words of others" (Bakhtin, 1981, p. 341). Paramount to the discussion of this question is *selectivity*. At the onset of this study, students walked to the parking lot and selected three bumper stickers. They selected stickers that "spoke" to them, and through their respective selections they learned that "When someone else's ideological discourse is internally persuasive for us and acknowledged by us, entirely different possibilities open up" (Bakhtin, 1981, p. 345). Students drew upon and alluded to their epistemic and affective stances. They synthesized intertextual references to reinforce dialogic histories and evaluated the stickers on the basis of criteria they valued. What Bakhtin described as a utility of the words of other speakers Spellmeyer (1989) considered a journey into the academic world. Taking the next leap into this academic community, three of the five students—John, Serah, and Muhamed—completed the entire portfolio and created their own bumper stickers. John encouraged everyone to "Leave home early, Come home early" and "Eat healthier, Save on medication." Serah suggested "Try Jesus" and "Travel Now." Muhamed announced "Mustang Killer" and "God's gift to imports ... the bottle!" (i.e., nitrous oxide).

DISCUSSION OF FINDINGS

The results of this study suggest that ESOL composition students discover that utterances, others' and their own, are epistemologically informed, ideologically based, politically situated, culturally bound, behaviorally induced and inducing, and affectively perceived. This discovery proves ideologically consistent with Bakhtin (1981):

> The living utterance, having taken meaning and shape at a particular historical moment in a socially specific environment, cannot fail to brush up against thousands of living dialogic threads, woven by socio-ideological consciousness around the given object of an utterance; it cannot fail to become an active participant in social dialogue. After all the utterance arises out of this dialogue as a continuation of it and as rejoinder to it—it does not approach the object from the sidelines. (pp. 276–277)

These students, therefore, selected and interpreted bumper stickers as utterances; cultural artifacts produced in context; derived from social semiotics; which varyingly coalesce, collide with, or locate intermittently on the continua within their own social semiotic repertoires. They subsequently mediated context to forge their responses. Students will, given enough opportunities, enact reciprocal discursive adaptation, applying particular linguistic tools to contextualize utterances to create contextualized responses. When the students in this study responded to the car owner, they enacted one set of strategies: statements of identification and intent, which led them to statements of evaluation. When they responded to someone in their home country, they enacted another set of strategies: statements of familiarity, dialogic history, and intent. They closed their letters in a similar form: solicitation of response. In completing these exercises on bumper stickers, the students demonstrated abilities to evaluate and partic- ipate in the social construction of language and, increasingly, to consider that communicative stances present reciprocally among speaker, listener, author, and interpreter. Students learned too that "intertextuality, like heteroglossia and dialogue, is the natural condition of language interaction and interanimation. Every utterance is created in response to and in anticipation of other utterances, past and future" (Halasek, 1999, p. 65).

PEDAGOGICAL IMPLICATIONS

Students who read utterances dialogically; who hear utterances; who speak rhetorically to texts; who communicate textual salience to others within and outside the academic community, articulating agreement, disagreement, empathy, compassion, and outrage; create additional ways of knowing and ways of being. Consequently, as Blanton (1999) asserted, "Reader-writers with individual responses to public issues speak with certainty about some- thing they own" (p. 135). What they own are ideologies—"an individual's languages, discourse, and rhetoric ... conditioned and defined by complex, fluctuating social relationships" (Halasek, 1999, p. 4).

Bakhtinian theory can help ESOL teachers create learning environ- ments in which both teachers and students appreciate that

> viewing language use as social practice implies ... is always a socially and his- torically situated mode of action, in a dialectical relationship with other fac- ets of "the social" (its social context)—it is socially shaped, but it is also socially shaping, or *constitutive*. (Fairclough, 1995, p. 131)

ESOL students learn, as they increase their skills that "language use is always simultaneously constitutive [of] (i) social identities, (ii) social rela- tions and (iii) systems of knowledge and belief—though with different de- grees of salience in different cases" (Fairclough, 1995, p. 131). Students, then, instantiate "ideological becoming" (Halasek, 1999, p. 109); the stu- dents' selected bumper stickers, reflections about them, compositions, and their subsequently self-created bumper stickers instantiate discur- sively and position them to meander in and about, presenting as author, subject, speaker, audience, and respondent. These ESOL students' aware- ness and demonstration of such interconnected rhetorical stances situate them as introduced to participation in Bakhtin's speech communities, to rhetoricians' calls to approximate the discourse of new discourse commu- nities, and to mediation of academic discourse. Through such introduc- tions, ESOL students herald increased access to second language proficiency and "enter the community of 'knowers'" (Spellmeyer, 1989, p. 274). They become increasingly aware that "Language is not a neutral medium that passes freely and easily into the private property of the speaker's intentions; it is populated—overpopulated—with the intentions of others" (Bakhtin, 1981, p. 294).

REFERENCES

Bakhtin, M. (1981). *The dialogic imagination* (M. Holquist, Ed., C. Emerson & M. Holquist, Trans.). Austin: University of Texas Press.

Bakhtin, M. (1986). *Speech genres and other late essays* (C. Emerson & M. Holquist, Eds., V. McGee, Trans.). Austin: University of Texas Press.

Blanton, L. (1994). Discourse, artifacts, and the Ozarks: Understanding academic literacy. *Journal of Second Language Writing, 3*, 1–16.

Blanton, L. (1999). Classroom instruction and language minority students: On teaching to "smarter" readers and writers. in L. Harklau, K. Losey, & M. Siegal (Eds.), *Generation 1.5 meets college composition: Issues in the teaching of writing to U.S.-educated learners of ESL* (pp. 119–142). Mahwah, NJ: Lawrence Erlbaum Associates.

Bridgeman, B., & Carlson, S. (1983). *Survey of academic writing tasks required of undergraduate foreign students*. Princeton, NJ: Educational Testing Service.

Bruffee, K. (1984). Collaborative learning and the conversation of mankind. *College English, 46*, 635–652.

Bruffee, K. (1986). Social construction, language, and the authority of knowledge. *College English, 48*, 773–790.

Cappelen, H., & Lepore, E. (2002). Indexicality, binding, anaphora and a priori truth. *Analysis, 62*, 271–281.

Elbow, P. (1973). *Writing without teachers*. New York: Oxford University Press.

Elbow, P. (1986). *Embracing contraries: Explorations in learning and teaching*. New York: Oxford University Press.

Emig, J. (1971). *The composting processes of twelfth graders*. Urbana, IL: National Council of Teachers of English.

Fairclough, N. (1995). *Critical discourse analysis: The critical study of language*. London: Longman.

Flower, L., & Hayes, J. R. (1980). The cognition of discovery: Defining a rhetorical problem. *College Composition and Communication, 31*, 21–32.

Flower, L., & Hayes, J. R. (1981). A cognitive process theory of writing. *College Composition and Communication, 32*, 365–387.

Gajdusek, L., & vanDommelen, D. (1993). Literature and critical thinking in the composition classroom. In J. G. Carson & I. Leki (Eds.), *Reading in the composition classroom: Second language perspectives* (pp. 197–217). Boston: Heinle and Heinle.

Glenberg, A., & Robertson, D. (1999). Indexical understanding of instructions. *Discourse Processes, 28*, 1–26.

Hairston, M. (1982). The winds of change: Thomas Kuhn and the revolution in the teaching of writing. *College Composition and Communication, 33*, 76–88.

Halasek, K. (1999). *A pedagogy of possibility: Bakhtinian perspectives on composition.* Carbondale: Southern Illinois University Press.

Hermans, H. J. M. (1999). Dialogical thinking and self-innovation. *Culture and Psychology, 5,* 67–87.

Jacoby, S., & Ochs, E. (1995). Co-construction: An introduction. *Research on Language and Social Interaction, 28,* 171–183.

Lähteenmäki, M. (1998).On meaning and understanding: A dialogical approach. *Dialogism, 1,* 74–91.

Morris, P. (Ed.). (1994). *The Bakhtin reader: Selected writings of Bakhtin, Medvedev, Voloshinov.* London: Arnold.

Ochs, E. (1993). Constructing social identity: A language socialization perspective. *Research on Language and Social Interaction, 26,* 287–306.

Ochs, E. (1996). Linguistic resources for socializing humanity. In J. J Gumperz and S. C. Lveison (Eds.), *Rethinking linguistic relativity* (pp.406–437). Cambridge, England: Cambridge University Press.

Savignon, S., & Sysoyev, P. (2002). Sociocultural strategies for a dialogue of cultures. *Modern Language Journal, 4,* 508–524.

Spack, R. (1988). Initiating ESL students into the academic discourse community: How far should we go? *TESOL Quarterly, 22,* 29–51.

Spellmeyer, K. (1989). A common ground: The essay in the academy. *College English, 51,* 262–276.

Voloshinov, V. (1973). *Marxism and the philosophy of language* (L. Matejka & I. R. Titunik, Trans.). New York: Seminar Press.

Weedon, C. (1987). *Feminist practice and poststructural theory.* New York: Blackwell.

Wertsch, J. V. (1991). *Voices of the mind: A socioculutral approach to mediated action.* Cambridge, MA: Harvard University Press.

Yancy, K. (2001). WPA outcomes statement for first-year composition. *College English, 63,* 321–325.

Zamel, V. (1983). The composing processes of advanced ESL students: Six case studies. *TESOL Quarterly, 17,* 165–187.

Zamel, V. (1989). Questioning academic discourse. In V. Zamel & R Spack (Eds.), *Negotiating academic literacies: Teaching and learning across languages and cultures* (pp. 187–197). Hillsdale, NJ: Lawrence Erlbaum Associates.

Zamel, V., & Spack, R. (1998). *Negotiating academic literacies: Teaching and learning across languages and cultures.* Mahwah, NJ: Lawrence Erlbaum Associates.

Chapter 5

Local Creativity in the Face of Global Domination: Insights of Bakhtin for Teaching English for Dialogic Communication

Angel M. Y. Lin
City University of Hong Kong

Jasmine C. M. Luk
Hong Kong Institute of Education

BAKHTIN IN HIS HISTORICAL CONTEXT: FREEDOM OF CONSCIOUSNESS THROUGH CARNIVAL LAUGHTER

Contemporary readers of Bakhtin may be surprised at his optimism about the possibility of freedom of consciousness, and the possibility of liberation from ideological hegemony of dominant discourses, especially when one notices that Bakhtin was writing, theorizing, and living under one of the most authoritarian regimes in Russian history, when both the everyday world and the intellectual world were dominated by absolute discourses of political ideologies; when heteroglossia in the way he envisioned it seemed most unlikely to happen in his contemporary social, academic, and political scenes; and when his own doctoral thesis and writings were denigrated and prevented from free public circulation by various political and ideological censorships and/or life mishaps. One can perhaps only conclude that it is the extreme material and ideological conditions of monoglossia and public

intellectual closure that had infused this great writer; thinker; and researcher of human discourses, folk literature, and literary genres with the
greatest hope and belief in the invincible human potential to achieve freedom of consciousness, creativity, innovation, and cultural and ideological
change through what he believed to be the inherent dialogic open-
endedness of human utterances. His lifelong fascination with the novel as
an open-ended genre and discursive space for the free juxtaposition and
fruitful dialogic interaction of diverse voices (or social languages, styles,
ideologies, and different consciousnesses); his detailed research of Medi-
eval satirical literature and Russian novels; his exposition of folk humor and
carnival laughter as not merely individual reaction to some isolated "comic"
event but public, collective practices of social and ideological critique; and
his theory of language as dialogic interaction all point to his immense pas-
sion for and belief in the potential liberative power of human agency and local creativity even in the face of absolute ideological domination and official
closure. Bakhtin's greatness cannot be fully appreciated without reading
him in light of his historical and sociopolitical context and in light of how
his theories and analyses provide the greatest hope and insights for others
who find themselves in contexts where ideological and linguistic domination (both explicit and implicit) is an everyday reality with which one must
live and struggle.

GLOBALIZATION, GLOBAL CAPITALISM,
AND THE GLOBAL DOMINATION OF ENGLISH

The late 20th and early 21st centuries have curiously and increasingly witnessed the juxtaposition of the seemingly disparate yet historically intimately
linked processes of global capitalism on the one hand and processes of de-
and neocolonizations on the other. Although often seen in separation, the
historical, cultural, and socioeconomic links of these two sets of processes
render it more instructive to treat them as (analytically different) aspects of a
complex network of interlinked, simultaneously symbiotic and conflictual
processes that attend the new global capitalist, technological, political, social,
cultural, human labor, and semiotic formations. As if Janus-faced, this "complex" (for want of a better name) is paradoxically invested with often-contra-
dictory forces: both de- and neocolonizing energies, globalizing and
localizing tendencies, multiculturalism and national culturalism, transnational organizations, and competing particularisms. In short, the world
seems to have become increasingly intelligible only as highly complex interlinked networks of border-crossing identities, bodies, and capitals as well as
cultural and semiotic formations *without any fixities guaranteed and without a
linear, progressive, universal, teleological history as Hegel or modernism has it*. Capitalist globalization can bring about neocolonization in the form of mega-cor-

porate monopolizing of markets around the world and relentless and borderless exploitation of human physical and cultural/semiotic labor on an even greater scale than in 19th century colonialisms. Communicative globalization can, however, also open up possibilities for transnational solidarities, transcultural–transethnic hybridized identities; erasure of center–periphery/master–slave/civilized–uncivilized binaries; and perhaps even hopes of a global, utopian, intercivilizational alliance against institutionalized suffering (Gandhi, 1998). Capitalist globalization can bring about cultural and ideological homogenization and domination just as it can bring about the particularization of cultures to feed the desires of a growing global tourist industry for the exotic and the multicultural (Robertson, 1995). Given its possibilities for both plenitude and impoverishment, homogenization and proliferation, solidarity and fragmentation, happy dialogic hybridization and ugly unilateral linguistic and ideological domination, understanding and dealing with the consequences of both capitalist globalizing processes and local particularizing practices becomes an important and daunting task.

One entry point for tackling this task is to examine the often tension-filled, conflictual activities attending *English in education* in post/neocolonial contexts, where the domination of English has gained forceful renewed legitimacy when any possible postcolonial critique of English dominance can be powerfully neutralized by the hegemonic discourses of global capitalism. Hong Kong is a case in point for a good illustration of the continuous domination of English in education in the so-called "postcolonial" era. Hong Kong schoolchildren are now expected by the official authorities to emerge from the school with fluency in both English and Putonghua (the national standard Chinese language, which is linguistically related but quite different from most Hong Kong children's own native tongue, Cantonese). For instance, the most recent language education policy document released by the Hong Kong government (Standing Committee on Language Education and Research, 2003) draws heavily on the hegemonic discourses of global capitalism. In the document, English is highlighted side by side with "Chinese," which is taken to mean the standard national Chinese language (as reflected in later parts of the document) rather than the local people's native language, Cantonese. There is a double domination faced by the local people and schoolchildren. Cantonese, the local tongue, can never be expected to be valued—not in education, or in society, albeit always with an invisible taken-for-granted existence in the background. The global language of English and the national language of standard Chinese are placed at the top of the linguistic hierarchy constructed and legitimized through global capitalist discourses. Elsewhere in the policy document, employers' demands are cited as the driving force for improving schoolchildren's "language standards," which refers to proficiencies in English and Putonghua. A labor production driven model

of education is highlighted. The document also calls on universities to ensure the enforcement of a high English language requirement for university
admission: Grade C or above in the General Certicate of Education (GCE)
O-Level English examination or Band 6 in the International English Language Testing System. The consequences of the domination of English in
education might be comprehended by the English-speaking North American readers by imagining the imposition of a GCE O-Level Grade C French
(if not Russian) language requirement for admission to college (no matter
what courses one chooses) in the North American context. The medium of
instruction of all universities in Hong Kong (except the Chinese University
of Hong Kong) has continued to be English, and there is pressure to convert
the Chinese University of Hong Kong into an English-medium university,
where the professional disciplines, such as medicine and computer science,
have already long been taught in English.

What is the relationship between the global domination of English and
the production of the subjectivities of many students in Hong Kong? Cultural studies researcher Stephen Chan, for instance, presented in a seminar
the following perspectives:

Critical stance on the question of Hong Kong subjectivity:

Hong Kong as a community of needs, aspirations and solidarity could not
have taken the form of the dominant culture of modernity we see today without the substantive rule by the British colonizers, especially during the
post-War period.

In conclusion, colonial rule was not simply about political domination but a
persistent rhetoric of colonial dominance that has grown with capitalist modernity itself. This is a situation we may investigate via the case of the global
popular in Hong Kong, asking whether colonialism is in effect a complex
modern regime of culture, a dynamic mechanism of control in which *power is
meant not to prohibit but to produce subjectivity* [italics added]. (Chan, 2002)

If "colonialism is in effect a complex modern regime of culture, a dynamic mechanism of control in which power is meant not to prohibit but to
produce subjectivity" (Chan, 2002), then one should also ask the questions
of whether and how the English-dominant language-in-education policies
and schooling practices are part of that dynamic mechanism of neocolonial
control and what kinds of subjectivities are being produced under that
mechanism. Little work from this perspective has been done so far, and
what follows is a preliminary exploration of the issues from this perspective.
First, from the available data it seems that a deep sense of a "subaltern subjectivity" (Ashcroft, Griffiths, & Tiffin, 1998) is being felt by working-class

schoolchildren located in socioeconomic positions that are not provided with family and community capital for the acquisition of English:

> You want to know why I don't pay attention in English lessons? You really want to know? Okay, here's the reason: NO INTEREST!! It's so boring and difficult and I can never master it. But the society wants you to learn English! If you're no good in English, you're no good at finding a job! (Original spoken in Cantonese by a 14-year-old schoolboy in an informal interview; from Lin, 1999, p. 407)

What this schoolboy is expressing seems to be a deep sense of anger, frustration, and yet almost helpless resignation to the recognition that he is condemned both to a current identity of school failure and a future identity of social failure. The power of the dominance of English in the education system and the society and his own painful vision of himself never being able to master English illustrate well the role played by the English language in a neocolonial, complex, modern capitalist regime of culture that is "meant not to prohibit but to produce subjectivity," in this case, a subaltern subjectivity (Ashcroft et al., 1998) in which the individual perceives him- or herself as without any hope for social mobility. Students' creative, subversive practices in the classrooms (see classroom excerpts, presented later) show us how local classroom participants sometimes resist and contest the production of such subaltern identities by engaging in practices that contribute to the building of alternative counteridentities, perhaps similar to those found in McLaren's (1998) analysis of students' countercultural practices in the inner city schools of North America:

> The major drama of resistance in schools is an effort on the part of students to bring their street-corner culture into the classroom .... it is a fight against the erasure of their street-corner identities .... students resist turning themselves into worker commodities in which their potential is evaluated only as future members of the labor force. *At the same time, however, the images of success manufactured by the dominant culture seem out of reach for most of them* [italics added]. (p. 191)

For the majority of working-class Cantonese-speaking children in Hong Kong, English remains something that is beyond their reach. Unlike their middle-class counterparts, they typically live in a lifeworld where few will (and can) speak or use English for any authentic communicative or sociocultural purposes. To most of them, English is little more than a difficult and boring school subject that, nonetheless, will have important consequences for their life chances. Many of them have an ambivalent, want–hate relationship with English. Although they accept the dominance of English and recognize that English is very important for their future prospects, they also readily believe that they are no good in English; for instance, this is expressed in the words of a working-class adolescent girl (G) to an ethnographic fieldworker (F) in Candlin, Lin, and Lo's (2000) study (p. 33, original utterances in Cantonese):

F: Yes, yes, and you, do you have any aspiration, what do you want
      to do?
G: I want to be a teacher.
F: Teacher (chuckling), Miss Chan (playfully addressing the girl as
      a teacher), it's good to be a teacher, it suits you well. At this
      moment it seems to suit you.
G: Don't know if it will change in the future.
F: You have to be patient, you have to proceed gradually.
G: I have to meet the requirement, my English is poor.

This exchange shows the working-class adolescent girl's lack of confidence in fulfilling her dream of becoming a teacher in the future because of her own self-image as someone with "poor English." Her resigned acceptance of both the importance of English for her future and her poor status in terms of her English ability led to her indication of a lack of confidence in fulfilling her aspiration, despite the fieldworker's encouraging remarks. Such low self-esteem, which is a result of their sense of failure in mastering English, makes English a subject highly imbued with working-class students' want–hate desires. English plays a chief role in constructing these students' subaltern identities and their own (self-limiting) understanding and perception of themselves in relation to others and their subaltern position in the society.

The English-dominant education system seems to have produced an elite bilingual social group whose cultural identities are constructed through their successful investments in an English-medium education, a mastery of the English language, and their familiarity with and membership in English-based modern professional institutions (e.g., the various English-based professional associations of accountants, lawyers, doctors, engineers, and English-mediated professional accreditation mechanisms). At the same time, alongside the production of these English-oriented successful modern professional, cosmopolitan subjectivities, the English-dominant education system also seems to be producing another, much larger group of subalterns, whose own understanding of themselves and their future life trajectories are greatly delimited by a neocolonial, complex capitalist modern regime of culture that seems to have almost stripped them of any possibility of constructing a valuable, legitimate, successful self with other non-English based cultural resources (e.g., mastery of the Chinese language and membership in Chinese cultural institutions, or mastery of Cantonese streetwise tactics and Cantonese popular cultural identities, e.g., through participating in underground Canton-pop bands). The post-1997 years have so far not seen any significant changes in the English-dominant education system and society (see previous discussion in section 2), and the dominance of English in post-1997 Hong Kong seems to be even more steadfastly maintained by a neocolonial, complex modern capitalist regime of culture, now that any public criticism of English linguistic dominance can be powerfully neutralized by the neocolonial globalizing capitalist economic and technological discourses. In Hong Kong, we seem to inhabit a world where increasingly if one does not find oneself an English-conversant, upwardly mobile cosmopolitan, one is very likely to find oneself a limited- or non-English-speaking parochial subaltern located in the lower end strata of the society.

The important question for English language education researchers to ask is: How do English language teaching practices in Hong Kong schools both reflect and enact the ideological domination of English and the labor production driven model of education? What kinds of teaching practices are witnessed that seem to contribute to the reproduction of these global capitalist forces of turning students into worker commodities in which their potential is evaluated only as future bodies of the labor market answering to the dictates of capitalist employers? How do students resist this monoglossia through the penetration of their indigenous popular language, styles, and cultures into the English lesson discourse, thereby hybridizing and dialogizing it and deridingly laughing at it? How do students achieve their dialogic discursive freedom with persistent local creativity and parodic laughter that serves almost as implicit ideological critique of the alienating situation in which they find themselves? In the rest of this chapter, we shall conduct a fine-grained discourse analysis of two excerpts of classroom interactions that were videorecorded in two secondary schools in Hong Kong. Both of them are quite typical of the majority of secondary schools in Hong Kong: The majority of students have come from working-class, Cantonese-speaking communities where English plays few or no communicative and sociocultural roles in their lifeworlds. In the first excerpt, we see how a textbook driven curriculum has constructed English lessons as uncreative parroting sessions for students. In the second excerpt, we see how students insert their local Cantonese jokes and language styles into an English dialogue creation task orchestrated by a liberal native English teacher (recently imported by the Hong Kong government to improve the language standards of local students under the Native English Teacher Scheme) who could, however, have been more familiar with the local languages and cultures to be able to fully capitalize on the students' local linguistic and cultural resources. In the last part of the chapter, we dis-

cuss how insights from Bakhtin can help English language teachers to reflex-
ively analyze and understand the ideological nature of their own teaching
practices, and to appreciate the nature and possibility of dialogic communication, as well as to start thinking about how teachers of English as a second
and foreign language can possibly work on re-creating their practices to
achieve dialogic communication with students, through dialogizing English
with students' local language styles, social languages, and creativity.

PARROTING ENGLISH TEXTBOOK DIALOGUES AND STUDENTS' ACCENTUATION PRACTICES

The intensification of teachers' workload has made many Hong Kong
teachers highly dependent on commercially produced English course-
books in secondary schools in Hong Kong. The main interest of these textbooks is in fulfilling the syllabus requirements of the Education Department (e.g., covering all the functional and structural topics listed in the syllabus). They tend to be reduced in both language and content and to pre-
scribe exercises and tasks that are operations oriented, often requiring the
parroting of second language structural items in mechanical ways (e.g., pronunciation drills of isolated lexical items; prescribed dialogue drills;
decontextualized grammatical exercises; unimaginative/uninteresting reading passages; and superficial, factual, uncritical reading comprehension exercises). These textbooks can bias teachers toward engaging in discourse
practices and activity organization that are geared toward linguistic drills
and not meaning sharing or communication. To get a sense of what such
classroom practices and activities are like, we present a Form 2 (Grade 8)
English lesson excerpt, documented in Lin (1996). The teacher is getting
the students to parrot a textbook dialogue belonging to the service English
register (or social language for service workers; students in Hong Kong
seem to be being implicitly constructed in schools as future service workers
expected to discipline themselves in the voices of service workers); the textbook exercise encourages students to substitute given items (e.g., sweater,
camera) into the set dialogue in a role-play task. The underlined words are
words read aloud from the textbook. A key to transcription terms and conventions is presented in the Appendix.

Excerpt 1

1 T: Well, here, here're three pictures. Mrs Wu is complaining to
         ... the assistant, she's complaining about the.. sweater. Okay,
         let's practice saying the.. dialogue, and then ... I'll explain
         again. Are you ready? Are you ready?
2 B1:   Yeh!

3 T: When we want to say something, want to make a complaint, what do we say first?

4 B2: (eh.. ? ?)

5 T: Excuse me, yes, good. Would you please say after me, let's practise saying this. Excuse me,

6 Ss: Excuse me, [The boy in the back corner next to the researcher said this in a playful exaggerated tone, but this was picked up only by the researcher's camcorder and not the walkman-recorder the teacher was carrying, so, it was probably unavailable to the teacher.]

7 T: I would like to make a complaint.

8 Ss: I would like to (make a complaint). [some students not finishing the last part of the sentence, and different students speaking at different rhythms and paces]

9 T: Please say after me. Excuse me, I would like to make a complaint.

10 Ss: Excuse me, I would like to make a complaint. [different students speaking at different rhythms and paces, finishing at different times]

11 T: Okay, good. Yes, Madam?

12 Ss: Yes, Madam?

13 T: I bought this sweater last week.

14 Ss: I bought this sweater last week. [different students speaking at different rhythms and paces, finishing at different times]

15 T: What's wrong with it?

16 Ss: What's wrong with it?

17 T: I'm afraid it's shrunk.

18 Ss: I'm afraid it's shrunk.

19 T: I only washed it once.

20 Ss: I only washed it once.

21 T: and look at it.

22 Ss: and look at it.

23 T: A child of five couldn't wear it- a-

24 Ss: A child of five couldn't wear it.

25 T: Okay, good, say it again, a child of five couldn't wear it.

This example is not an isolated one; similar operations-oriented classroom practices are commonly found in other classrooms (see Lin, 1996). However, we urge readers to withhold judgement of the teacher. The unimaginative textbook, heavy teaching load, and the lack of professional development opportunities for teachers in Hong Kong must also be considered when we try to understand the origin of operations-oriented, meaning-reduced classroom practices.

Notice how a student (turn 6) resisted this mindless parroting practice by superimposing his playful, ironic accent onto the English dialogue. He was made to repeat after the teacher, but he managed to *populate* this utterance of an "*other*" with his own accent—a playful, ironic accent, an accent which in Bakhtin's terms (Bakhtin, 1994) serves as an implicit social and political commentary on the utterance that he was made to repeat verbatim after the teacher as well as on the situation in which he found himself (i.e., made to parrot the *voice* of an *other*). He has populated the *other*'s utterance with his own *voice* and his own political commentary. This accentuating practice is frequently found in English lessons in Hong Kong, especially when students are made to parrot prescribed English dialogues as a "dialogue practice," which is commonly found in Hong Kong English classrooms, especially in working-class schools.

OPENING UP SPACE FOR CREATING "INDECENT" DIALOGUES AND CARNIVAL LAUGHTER

> There were other parodies in Latin: Parodies of debates, dialogues, chronicles, and so forth. All these forms demanded from their authors a certain degree of learning, sometimes at a high level. All of them brought the echoes of carnival laughter within the walls of monasteries, universities, and schools .... during carnival there is a temporary suspension of all hierarchic distinctions ... Verbal etiquette and discipline are relaxed and indecent words and expressions may be used. (Bakhtin, 1994, p. 203)

The classroom excerpts discussed in this section were taken from a larger pool of data collected from a secondary school in Hong Kong situated in a low socioeconomic area. The class was split into two groups (each having 20 students) for every English lesson. The excerpt happens to be from one of these groups. It is interesting that this group consisted of all boys. According to the teacher (Ms. Berner, a pseudonym), who is a native English-speaking teacher (NET), the pupils in her group were identified to be stronger in English than the other half of the class. This arrangement was made to ensure that the pupils have reached a threshold level of proficiency in English to benefit from the teaching of the NET.

Ms. Berner is an experienced NET in that school. She has a degree in German and French and has ample experience in teaching these two languages. Ms Berner was interested in learning Cantonese, and at the time of the observation she was eager to tell the researcher (Jasmine C. M. Luk) that she was taking a course in Cantonese. She believed that some knowledge in Cantonese would enable her to understand the pupils better and narrow the distance between herself and the pupils.

The class was described by Ms. Berner as her "fun" class. The boys, in her opinion, were lively, responsive, and willing to talk in English but sometimes too talkative, naughty in manner, and imprecise with grammar. The excerpts were taken from what she called an "activity lesson," and it took place in the English room. To create a better English learning environment in schools, the Hong Kong government has granted each secondary school funds for setting up an English corner or an English room. Most of these English rooms are like English learning resource centers; some of them also provide audio–visual equipment, such as computers, tape recorders, and televisions, for self-access learning. After the English room was set up, Ms. Berner proposed that every class should do some English lessons in the English Room so that they would have a better idea of what was available there.

In the double lessons from which the excerpts were taken, Ms. Berner played two games with the students. The activity lesson was conducted by Ms Berner and one male English Language Teaching Assistant (ELTA). ELTAs are native English-speaking pre-university teenage students recruited by certain cultural exchange organizations to assist English teaching in some Hong Kong schools. With the assistance of the ELTA, Ms. Berner was able to conduct the games with a group of about 10 students, all boys, seated around a large table. Such games would be quite difficult to conduct in a normal class of 40 students handled by one teacher.

The first game in the lesson was a simple story composition game. Students took turns putting down on a strip of paper one piece of information, which may be time, the place, the names of one male and one female, and what each of them says. This is a game commonly played among Chinese children, too. Every time, the student puts down only one item, and then he or she folds the paper to cover the information and passes the paper to his or her neighbor, who puts down another piece of information without looking at what comes before. The final product will be a creative story very often with funny characters and an unexpected and nonsensical combination of events. When the activity was conducted the first time, some of the students were reluctant to write anything on the paper even though what was required was only simple words such as a name or a place. After the first-round stories were read aloud by the teacher, the whole group got a good laugh at some of the funny outcomes. When the activity was done the second time, there was an obvious change in the students' behaviors. They became more involved and took the initiative to ask what should be put down next. Some would speak out in English what they intended to write down. Most of the pupils' suggestions were infused with sexual connotations. They usually aroused roars of laughter from the group, and sometimes the teacher too. Therefore, when the second game was introduced, it is by no means exaggerating to say that the group was in high spirits, with their minds filled with sex-related, or what mainstream adults might call "indecent," fun. The following excerpt shows this animated, indecent fun that the students enjoyed through creating dialogues that spring from their adolescent fantasies.

Excerpt 2

The group is looking at a set of nine cartoon pictures with captions underneath each picture. Ms Berner asks the boys to write down what the cartoon characters on the pictures are saying in the form of speech balloons. In this excerpt, she comes to a picture with "babe magnet" as the caption.

1	T:	... [in raised voice] how about? number six, a babe magnet. do you know what a babe magnet is? (.) a babe is a girl. do you know what a magnet is?
2	B:	(Mr Pig)=
3	T:	=a magnet attracts metal, yes? (..) you know //errrm aah
4	B1:	//**ngaa-caat aa, zik-haai?** <*toothbrush, that is?*>] (.)
5	T:	this is (..) a magnet and it //attracts things
6	B2:	//**gung-lei aa?** <*kilometer?*> =
7	Ss:	(to themselves) =**ci-sek** <*a magnet*>, n //and e
8	B2:	//**ngoo, kau-lui aa?** [colloquial Cantonese] <*oh, courting girls?*>
9	T:	yeah, so a babe magnet is someone who //locks woman, (??)
10	B3:	//**kap-jan aa?** <*to attract?*>
11	B4:	yes
12	Leo[1]:	**kau-lui aa?** [Cantonese slang expression] <*courting girls?*>
13	B3:	**kap-jan aa?** <*to attract?*>
14		[Ss laugh]
15	T:	SO cool, very cool, yes ^
16	B:	cool man.
17	T:	English cool, not Chinese cool, very cool, what's he saying then? What's the babe magnet saying?
18	Ss:	Hello ^ [laughs]
19	B:	[in sexy tone] Hi baby ^ [laughs]
20	T:	[imitating the voice of the student, sexy tone] Hi baby ^ [laughs] yeah, a balloon, [in a male voice] Hi, baby ^ [returns to normal voice] okay, write it down, the balloon, [in a male voice] hi, baby? [laughs]

---

[1]It's easy to recognize Leo, as he spoke with a hoarse voice at a relatively higher pitch than the other boys.

21 Bs: **waa!** [an exclamation] **Jay Jay** [seems to be somebody's nickname] (someone seemed to have said Jason)
22 B3:   **kau-lui tin-wong lei gaa-ma:::** <*it's the king/expert in courting girls*>, //**kau-lui tin-wong dou m-zi hai bin-go**? <*you don't even know who's the king/expert in courting girls?*>
23 T: [laughing] //you want to see me later?
24 B3:   Can I love you [Ss laugh]? (..)
25 T: See you in Kowloon Tong?
26   [Ss laugh]
27 B3:   see you in my room?
28 B2:   see you in my bed?
29   [Suddenly students from the other group laugh loudly. Those in Ms Berner's group then join in and laugh even louder.]

It is interesting to notice that the students actively engaged in a negotiation of meaning with the teacher (turns 1–13) and, in a collaborative effort, the students were successful in guessing the meaning of the term *babe magnet* and offered Cantonese expressions for a similar concept: *kau lui* (to court girls, turn 12) and *kau-lui tin-wong* (king/expert in courting girls, turn 22). As soon as they understood the meaning of *babe magnet*, they started to create an imaginary dialogue between the babe magnet and a prospective babe: "Hi baby!" (turn 19). The kind of English discourse on which they drew (e.g., "cool man" in turn 16) appears to be familiar to them through their exposure to adolescent hip hop culture, especially the kind of discourses they come into contact with through basketball magazines; gangster movies; and Black hip-hop culture and songs, which have found a transnational market and circulation even in non-English-speaking societies (Ma, 2002). The everyday lifeworld discourses and social languages of the students situated in Hong Kong were infused into their "English" dialogues in the English lesson, for example, Kowloon Tong is a place in Hong Kong famous for "love hotels." These students managed to have a carnival type of laughter through creating "indecent" English dialogues within the school walls—it is no less significant than the kind of carnival creativity Bakhtin (1994) discussed. Through populating the English language with their own local social languages and voices, they have appropriated English for their own purposes. Unlike students parroting textbook dialogues (see Excerpt 1), they have become owners and authors of the English dialogues that they created through drawing on multiple social languages available to them in English and Cantonese (e.g., Black hip-hop discourses, Hong Kong Cantonese talk show jokes). The teacher's apparent liberal stance (mentioning "Kowloon Tong" herself and thus starting students creating the dialogue in that direction) has helped to create a space for students to engage in such carnival creative work and laughter. Next we look at one more excerpt from the same lesson.

Excerpt 3

This excerpt was taken right after Excerpt 2. The group is looking at a big poster with several pictures on it. Each picture shows two to three people. Ms. Berner assigns one picture to one pair of students and asks them to invent some dialogues between or among those characters depicted in the picture. At the beginning of the excerpt, Ms. Berner is illustrating how to create a dialogue for the characters on one of the pictures. She then invites the students to act out the dialogues.

1	T:	//yeh? I hate garlic, and the other one says we always know who has had garlic for dinner. so look at your picture, and decide who you are going to be, for example, you could be Clinton, and you could be, is that Mr. Jiang [Mr. Jiang is the former President of the People's Republic of China]? (..) what are they saying? what is Mr. Clinton saying? alright, so I'll give you two minutes to think about it.
2	B1:	**mat-shui aa? Daai-lou?** [colloquial] <*who's that? big brother?*>
3	B2:	Ms. Berner, who is he? [ending in an exaggerated rising tone]
4	T:	it doesn't matter who it is.
5	B2:	[in playful tone] **gaa-gi-naang** [In Chiuchauese, a Chinese dialect, meaning *people of our own kind*] [B2 chuckles] [Ss continue talking and joking in Cantonese, unintelligible to an outsider]
6	T:	it doesn't matter
7		{...}
8	T:	you first, you start here, [T sounds a bit angry] come on (..) okay, here, they got a picture of Mr. Jiang and Mr. Clinton, =
9	B1:	=**ngoo! Hak-zai aa**?= <*Oh! "Clink-boy"?*> [Clink-boy is the nickname of Bill Clinton used by HK people]
10	T:	=shaking hands?=
11	B1:	=**Hak-jam-deon aa?** <*"Clink-sleazy-ton"?*> [the nickname of Bill Clinton used in Hong Kong media, referring to his indecent sexual behavior with his female subordinate] [B1 chuckles]
12	T:	so what is Mr. Clinton saying?
13	Leo:	**Kei-wan-si-lei** ("Kate Winsley" [Winslet], the female lead character of "Titanic," but Leo probably means Monica Lewinsky, the female intern of Bill Clinton)
14	Tom:	hello!
15	T:	okay hello, Mr. Jiang, that's not really exciting, okay, hello, Mr. Jiang, what's Mr. Jiang saying? [some are making suggestions in English, inaudible on the tape]

16	Tom:	your hand is very big
17	T:	your head is very big [other boys laugh hearing this]
18	B?:	**zek sau hou-daai** !<*the hand is very big!*> [laughing]
19	T:	[in an amused tone] okay, Mr. Clinton says, hello Mr. Jiang, and Mr. Jiang says, your head is very big (.) [Ss are talking and joking among themselves all along while the T is talking, indistinct while the T is talking] (..) alright, let's have a look at yours, what have you got (.) right, two men whispering and laughing together, what do you think one is saying?
20	B?:	kiss you ^
21	B?:	hello, where are you boy? [Ss laugh]
22	T:	alright, he said [Ss laugh], //shh! shh!
23	B:	//**bin dou aa lei?** <*where are you?*>
24	T:	he says, have a look at this picture, yeah, one man is saying, can I give you a kiss, the other one saying, okay, be quick, yeah? what do you think, they are saying? [many Ss are laughing and chatting, unintelligible on the recorder]
25	B?:	hello, where are you?
26	T:	hello, who- who are //you?
27	B:	//where are you
28	T:	[rising tone over "you," sounds doubtful] where are YOU?
29	B:	yeah! [chuckles]
30	T:	[in a different tone, rising over "are"] hello, where ARE ^ you?
31	Leo:	I'm forty.
32	B1:	where do you come from?
33	T:	I'm what?
34	Leo:	I'm forty. [others laugh]
35	T:	[sounds confused] forty?
36	B?:	[laughs] Chai Wan forty [Chai Wan is a place near the students' school]
37	B?:	**caai ^ waan ^** [anglicized Cantonese of Chai Wan] forty, of Chai Wan
38	T:	[asking another boy sitting on the other side] what have you got over there?

Ms. Berner showed difficulty in making sense of some of the utterances from the pupils. Someone who is not familiar with Hong Kong working-class youth culture would find it difficult to understand some of the students' utterances. The sex scandal in which Mr. Clinton was involved was popularized in Hong Kong media and a hot issue around the time when our classroom audiotaping was conducted in 1999. The sleazy nicknames of

Clinton (turns 9, 11) were widely known in Hong Kong at that time. The name mentioned in turn 11 was coined creatively by changing the middle character, *lam* (literally meaning "a forest"), of the three-word official Chinese translation of *Clinton*, "haak lam deon," into a rhyming counterpart *jam* (literally meaning "sleazy"). With only limited Cantonese, Ms. Berner failed to catch this deriding Cantonese joke made of Clinton's name.

Clinton's sex scandal had given most people the impression that he was a person with strong sexual desires. It could be very natural for boys in Ms. Berner's class to imply masturbation, an act of deriving sexual pleasure often with one's hands. As the picture shows the two men shaking hands, it is highly likely that the image of "hands" had aroused their association with sex.

When we presented the case to a young teacher currently teaching secondary students of similar backgrounds, what she spotted was not the image of "hands" but "head." She told us that many male students coming from working-class backgrounds often joked about the male sex organs, and one such organ involves the use of the Cantonese word for "head." Ms. Berner's mishearing of the pupils' "hand" as "head" (turn 17) might have instigated some more sexual insinuations from the pupils, as evident in their laughter.

The questions "Where are you?" (first appearing in turn 21) and "Where do you come from?" (turn 32), suggested by the pupil(s) in a playful manner, is evidence of their infusing the gang culture and gangster talk in Hong Kong into what can be a most mundane kind of greeting exchange between two people as shown on the picture (turn 19). Asking someone (usually on the first meeting) "Where are you from?" is a way to "state their allegiance" to and membership of triad gangs (Bolton & Hutton, 2002, p. 159). Such a greeting/first-meeting practice of members of the triad societies in Hong Kong often appears in local Cantonese gangster movies. The students' mentioning of "Chai Wan forty" further supports our interpretation. There is a well-known triad gang called "14K" that has branches in different districts. Chai Wan (a pseudonym) is the district in which the school is located, which also means the place where most students resided and hung around. It is also a common pronunciation feature of many Cantonese pupils to mix up *fourteen* and *forty*. Therefore, Leo's "I'm forty" might actually mean "I'm from the 14K."

With the indulgent encouragement of the teacher (partly due to her liberal stance, and partly due to her unfamiliarity with Cantonese slang and so she would not be easily offended), the students occupied this discursive space and populated them with their own meanings, their own preferred social languages and voices, and their own deriding jokes and parodies. It seems perfectly natural for students to make what is alien and boring to them (e.g., greetings between two remote world leaders) into something that is familiar, funny, movielike, or fantasylike. This seems to be an example of carnival laughter and of joking about the name of a powerful world leader, in an otherwise somewhat boring lesson task of learning to parrot the social languages of powerful groups in the society, languages that are remote and alien to them and yet without mastery of which they will become marginalized in the society in their future (see discussion in the previos section). Notice that the teacher's liberal stance (e.g., building on a boy's contribution "kiss you" [turn 20] and suggesting that one man wants to kiss the other man in the picture [turn 24]) also seems to have indulged the boys in creating funny, "indecent" dialogues.

BAKHTIN'S INSIGHTS FOR TEACHING ENGLISH FOR DIALOGIC COMMUNICATION

> Language has been completely taken over, shot through with intentions and accents. For any individual consciousness living in it, language is not an abstract system of normative forms but rather a concrete heteroglot conception of the world. All words have a "taste" of a profession, a genre, a tendency, a party, a particular work, a particular person, a generation, an age group, the day and hour. Each word tastes of the context and contexts in which it has lived its socially charged life; all words and forms are populated by intentions … Language is not a neutral medium that passes freely and easily into the private property of the speaker's intentions; it is populated, overpopulated—with the intentions of others. (Bakhtin, 1981, pp. 273–274)

The students' accentuation and dialogizing practices in the lessons impressed us with the resilience of human agency and creativity, the human need to go beyond monoglossia, that is, the types of social languages imposed on them in school and society, the drive to turn them into future worker commodities, disciplining them in the social languages expected of them in the adult worker world, forcing them to parrot service worker languages (e.g., see Excerpt 1 above), and constituting their voices for them. Even in such a situation, some students did not fail to accentuate the parroted utterances with their own voice and accent, attaching to the prescribed utterances their own implicit social and political commentary and meanings (e.g., the boy using a playful ironic tone when made to repeat the set dialogue in the previous section). The relatively more liberal stance of the English teacher in the Excerpt 2 provided students with a space to slip in their street-corner topics and adolescent sexual fantasies, and to coconstruct their dialogues with the teacher, while populating them with their own preferred social languages and voices.

Bakhtin (1981) differentiated between two kinds of discourses: (a) *authoritative discourse* and (b) *internally persuasive discourse*. *Authoritative discourse* is language or discourse imposed on a person—but for one to really accept, acquire and *own* a language or discourse, it has to become an *internally per-*

suasive discourse, hybridized and populated with one's own voices, styles, meanings, and intentions:

> Both the authority of discourse and its internal persuasiveness may be united in a single word—one that is *simultaneously* authoritative and internally persuasive—despite the profound differences between these two categories of alien discourse. But such unity is rarely a given—it happens more frequently that an individual's becoming, an ideological process, is characterized precisely by a sharp gap between these two categories: in one, the authoritative word (religious, political, moral; the word of a father, of adults and of teachers, etc.) that does not know internal persuasiveness, in the other internally persuasive word that is denied all privilege, backed up by no authority at all, and is frequently not even acknowledged in society (not by public opinion, not by scholarly norms, nor by criticism), not even in the legal code. (Bakhtin, 1981, p. 342)

> Internally persuasive discourse—as opposed to one that is externally authoritative—is, as it is affirmed through assimilation, tightly interwoven with "one's own word." In the everyday rounds of our consciousness, the internally persuasive word is half-ours and half-someone else's. Its creativity and productiveness consist precisely in the fact that such a word awakens new and independent words, that it organizes mass of our words from within, and does not remain in an isolated and static condition. It is not so much interpreted by us as it is further, that is, freely, developed, applied to new material, new conditions; it enters into interanimating relationships with new contexts …. The internally persuasive word is either a contemporary word born in a zone of contact with unresolved contemporaneity, or else it is a word that has been reclaimed for contemporaneity. (Bakhtin, 1981, pp. 345–346)

With Bakhtin's insights on the need for heteroglossia and local creativity even in the face of imposed monoglossia (e.g., imposition of whether global or national languages and certain speaking styles), we suggest laughing with students, cocreating heteroglossic, internally persuasive dialogues of interest to students so that English can become a language populated with students' own voices and become a tool that students can use to construct their own preferred worlds, preferred identities, and preferred voices. Only in this way can English change from an authoritative discourse to an internally persuasive discourse in Bakhtin's (1981) sense. This has to begin with a deeper understanding of the students' preferred worlds, cultures, identities, and voices on the part of the teachers. Teachers can engage themselves in what Bakhtin (1981, 1986, 1990, quoted in Hall, 1999, p. 144) has called the process of *transgredience*, that is, the ability to step outside some existing practices and analyze from a vantage point the sociocultural sources and resources that constitute our own and others' actions. It is through a sensitive understanding of *what* students preferred and why they preferred certain voices and identities that teachers can capitalize on the local resources of students to build bridges between students' world and what is required of them in the school world.

It is therefore also recognized that at some point in the curriculum students need to be provided with access to the social languages preferred and prescribed by school and the mainstream adult society. Care must be taken to prevent school education from simply reproducing the underprivileged lifeworlds of some lower social class students by reinforcing their restrictive discourses. Although we should laugh with students and accommodate heteroglossic voices in the classroom, we may not want language learning activities to be completely unorganized and non-goal-directed. Students need to acquire specific types of communicative competencies in English that will enable them to enhance their life opportunities. We propose explicitly discussing these issues with students and engaging students in a critical discussion of the existence of different social languages and the imposed hierarchy of different social languages in the society. The aim is to create heteroglossia in the classroom and to heteroglossize English and to change English from an authoritative discourse to an internally persuasive discourse to the students, to allow them the space to make English a language of their own by populating it with their own meanings and voices. When students have appropriated English as a communicative tool of their own, it would not be impossible to help them to also master the other social languages of English that they would need to survive and compete in the adult world and in the globalized economy. From this perspective, many of the TESOL canons and pedagogies of teachers of English to speakers of other languages (TESOL) need to be reimagined and reconstituted if the globalization of English is also to mean the dialogization and heteroglossization of English. For example, formal dialogues might not necessarily be taught through a dialogue between two world leaders, and even when such a scenario is used students can be encouraged to think of fun topics in the dialogues of these leaders that may not necessarily be about formal political topics. If students seem to be more interested in some popular cultural issues about popular stars, teachers could capitalize on this interest as a motivating topic to turn some authoritative, formal English into internally persuasive English. Local creativity need not be ad hoc and impromptu. Students could be engaged in systematic and teacher-guided but student-autonomous preparation work. For example, the teacher could create an imaginary context in which students are interviewing one of their favorite soccer stars, such as Beckham (if that is what they enjoy outside school). Students could work in pairs and be assigned different roles. Before role playing the interview, students can access print and electronic media resources to collect relevant information and language they would use in the interview. Students could also be encouraged to critically examine the ways in which popular culture encourages consumerism and how the sport of soccer has become commodified and turned into a global money-making business. Teachers and students can use both their imagination and critical-thinking skills to enrich the learning of English as a language for globalized communication and for interrogating both local and global cultural issues revolving around the differential roles and statuses of different ways of using English in our world. Such critical practices will help students develop critical linguistic awareness about English and about how they can expand their own repertoires of different social languages of English for a plurality of purposes.

REFERENCES

Ashcroft, B., Griffiths, G., & Tiffin, H. (1998). *Key concepts in post-colonial studies*. London: Routledge.

Bakhtin, M. M. (1981). *The dialogic imagination: Four essays by M. M. Bakhtin* (C. Emerson & M. Holquist, Trans.). Austin: University of Texas Press.

Bahktin, M. M. (1986). *Speech genres and other essays* (M. Holquist & C. Emerson, Eds., V. McGee, Trans.). Austin: University of Texas Press.

Bahktin, M. M. (1990). *Art and answerability* (M. Holquist & V. Liapunov, Eds.). Austin: University of Texas Press.

Bakhtin, M. M. (1994). Folk humor and carnival laughter. In P. Morris (Ed.), *The Bakhtin reader* (pp. 194–205). London: Arnold.

Bolton, K., & Hutton, C. (2002). Media mythologies: Legends, "local facts" and triad discourse. In C. Barron, N. Bruce, & D. Nunan (Eds.), *Knowledge and discourse: Towards an ecology of language* (pp. 147–164). London: Longman.

Candlin, C. N., Lin, A. M. Y., & Lo, T.-W. (2000). *The discourse of adolescents in Hong Kong*. Final project report, Department of English and Communication, City University of Hong Kong.

Chan, S. C. K. (2002, December). *Mapping the global popular: An analytical framework for Hong Kong culture*. Paper presented at the Cultural Studies Seminars, Lingnan University, Hong Kong.

Gandhi, L. (1998). *Postcolonial theory: A critical introduction*. Oxford, England: Oxford University Press.

Hall, J. K. (1999). A prosaics of interaction: The development of interactional competence in another language. In E. Hinkel (Ed.), *Culture in second language teaching and learning* (pp. 137–151). Cambridge, England: Cambridge University Press.

Lin, A. M. Y. (1996). *Doing-English-lessons in secondary schools in Hong Kong: A sociocultural and discourse-analytic study*. Unpublished doctoral dissertation, Ontario Institute for Studies in Education, University of Toronto, Ontario, Canada.

Lin, A. M. Y. (1999). Doing-English-lessons in the reproduction or transformation of social worlds? *TESOL Quarterly, 33,* 393–412.

Ma, E. (2002). Emotional energies and subcultural politics in post-97 Hong Kong. *Inter-Asia Cultural Studies, 3,* 187–190.

McLaren, P. (1998). *Life in schools: An introduction to critical pedagogy in the foundations of education.* New York: Longman.
Robertson, R. (1995). Glocalization: Time–space and homogeneity–heterogeneity. In M. Featherstone, S. Lash, & R. Robertson (Eds.), *Global modernities* (pp. 25–44). London: Sage.
Standing Committee on Language Education and Research. (2003). *Action plan to raise language standards in Hong Kong.* Hong Kong: Hong Kong SAR Government.

APPENDIX

Transcription Conventions

Symbols	Meaning
T	The teacher.
B1, B2, …	Different male students in consecutive turns, distinguishable from their voices.
B?	An unidentifiable male student.
Ss	A number or the whole class of students.
faat ming	Transcription of Cantonese utterances followed by free English translation <*To invent*>.
[ ]	Researcher's comments.
(XX)	Uncertain hearing.
(???)	Indecipherable utterances.
.	Falling intonation followed by noticeable pause (as at the end of declarative sentences).
(..)	Short pause.
(…)	Medium pause of up to 5 seconds.
(0.6/7/8,…)	For wait times longer than 5 seconds, the pause will be represented by figures showing the number of seconds involved. Wait times longer than 1 minute will become (1.0), and so on.
,	Continuing intonation.
?	Rising intonation; may or may not be a question.
^	High-pitch utterances, as used when the students anglicize the Cantonese words.
:	Lengthened syllable (usually attached to the vowels); extra colon indicates longer elongation.
–	Self-halting, or abrupt cutoff.
CAPS	Emphatic and strongly stressed utterances.

(continued on next page)

Symbols	Meaning
XXX	Words read aloud from texts, including textbook materials, or students' written works.
=	Contiguous utterances or latching.
//	Overlapping utterances.
\<XXX\>	Utterances made with greater voice volume compared with that of the preceding and following ones.
A-B-C-D	Sounding out the letter names of a word.
{....}	Untranscribed section of the excerpt.

Chapter 6

Metalinguistic Awareness in Dialogue: Bakhtinian Considerations

Hannele Dufva and Riikka Alanen
University of Jyväskylä

In this chapter we report findings from an ongoing research project in which the metalinguistic awareness of a small group of Finnish schoolchildren has been studied since 1998 (for background information, see Sajavaara et al., 1999), with a particular focus on the relationship of metalinguistic awareness and foreign language learning.[1] The longitudinal study covers the children's first 6 years at school, from the ages of 7 to 12. Our theorizing builds on dialogical (Dufva, 2003) and Vygotskian (see Alanen, 2003) frameworks. Here we discuss the ways in which "mother tongue," "foreign language," and "language" are spoken of at school and how these ways of speaking affect the children's metalinguistic awareness. We will argue that children's metalinguistic awareness is multi-voiced and bears traces of many contexts. During early school years, however, the institutional discourse of the school has a particularly powerful influence on children's notions. We argue that the discourses to which the children are exposed mediate a view of language and foreign language learning that not only is strongly literate but also reifies language, that is, sees language in terms of objects. These views are related to formalism in linguistics. In contrast, the dialogical theory would suggest a radically different perspective to

---

[1]Situated metalinguistic awareness and foreign language learning. Funded by the Academy of Finland.

language, to foreign language learning, and to second and foreign language education. Some implications are discussed.

The dialogical theory of language originated in the writings of the Bakhtin Circle (see Brandist, 2002) and its most notable members: Mikhail Bakhtin (1981, 1984, 1986, 1993) and Valentin Voloshinov (1973, 1976), whose contributions we discuss later in this chapter. More recent contributions to dialogical thinking include those of Rommetveit (1992); Marková and Foppa (1990, 1991); Marková, Graumann, and Foppa (1995); Linell (1998); and Lähteenmäki (1998a, 1998b). First we must establish that neither Bakhtin nor the members of the Bakhtin Circle addressed the issue of metalinguistic awareness and only passingly referred to foreign language learning. Our arguments here are thus based on our interpretation of what the dialogical premises would mean in the theorizing of metalinguistic awareness. At the same time, we have also brought in elements from the Vygotskian sociocultural theory of learning and development (Vygotsky, 1987; for different definitions of *sociocultural* and *Vygotskian*, see, e.g., Frawley, 1997; Thorne, 2000; Wertsch, del Río & Alvarez, 1995), and we have found the combination of Bakhtinian and Vygotskian views highly appropriate.

During the past 20 years, there has been a surge of interest in Bakhtin's thinking within the field of second and foreign language research. An interesting early contribution was Courtney Cazden's (1989, 1993) discussion of the similarities between Bakhtin and Dell Hymes as antiformalists and representatives of non-Saussurean linguistics. James Wertsch (1990, 1991, 1998) discussed Bakhtinian ideas, especially the notion of voice, in connection with the sociocultural approach. Wertsch (1991, pp. 12–13) stressed the role of semiotic mediation and communicative practices in understanding human cognition. Claire Kramsch (1995, 2000) has drawn attention to some Bakhtinian aspects in her discussion of language learning as semiotic mediation. Gordon Wells (1999, 2002) has sought to (re)emphasize the role of dialogue as a special type of activity in human learning and has attempted to combine aspects of activity theory, Vygotskian thinking, and dialogism. Wells (2002, p. 44) focused on classroom interaction and criticized its present, antidialogical nature.

Children's metalinguistic awareness has been studied mainly within cognitive frameworks, such as traditional psycholinguistics or Piagetian psychology. However, very few studies have tackled the problem from the point of view of foreign language learning, and none seem to have used dialogical theory as a background. Use of the term *metalinguistic* itself varies considerably (for a survey of research, see Gombert, 1992; for a terminological and theoretical discussion, see, e.g., Bialystok, 2001, pp. 121–134). Seen from the dialogical/Vygotskian point of view, children's metalinguistic awareness is a phenomenon that is not only cognitive (in the traditional meaning of the word) but also a social and interactive phenomenon. Thus, we are duly critical toward the cognitivist view (for a criticism of cognitivism, see Dufva, 1998; Still & Costall, 1991), which often has been the underlying assumption in the earlier studies that have regarded metalinguistic awareness in terms of individual and internal traits or abilities. Instead, we stress the social origin and nature of children's metalinguistic awareness: It is not located in the head and should not be read as processes of the brain. In our theorizing, we aim at combining the social and cognitive viewpoints using the notion of *intersubjectivity* (see Dufva, 2004; Lähteenmäki, 1994; Voloshinov, 1973, 1976; Wertsch, 1985).

Consequently, rather than trying to pin down metalinguistic awareness as a set of internal and individual phenomena, we try to grasp the ways in which it may be present in the interactive situations in which the children are involved. In other words, we investigate children's metalinguistic awareness through "awareness in action" and see it as inherently intertwined with the task at hand. As it is manifested in a particular context of activity, it is also situated in character. Also, we argue that metalinguistic awareness is in most cases acquired through "Others," that is, in social interaction with peers, adults, and teachers. Drawing here also on Vygotskian thinking, we see the role of *mediation* as essential. The development of metalinguistic awareness is mediated through communicative practices in which the participants are engaged in (cf. Rogoff, 1990, 1995).

Inspired by dialogical arguments, we have analyzed metalinguistic awareness in terms of *polyphony*. It is well-known that Bakhtin originally developed the notion of polyphony for the analysis of the novel, but it has also been discussed as a metaphor for the architecture of the mind. The notion of the *multivoiced*, or polyphonic mind has been discussed in various contexts, including language learning and therapeutic discourse (see, e.g., Hermans, 2001; Leiman, 1998; Wertsch, 1991, 1998). Here we argue that children's metalinguistic awareness is necessarily multivoiced because it is acquired in different contexts—family life, language classroom, the media—and is mediated to children in diverse situations involving diverse individuals. By saying that awareness is multivoiced we mean that the children do not have a unified theory of language and of foreign language learning; rather, their awareness consists of various elements and features involving several perspectives—sometimes competing, sometimes disharmonious and contradictory (see also Dufva, 2003). Thus, we do not believe that children construct a "correct" or "true" picture of language bit by bit (which sometimes seems to be the underlying assumption in the cognitivist studies). Instead, they appropriate multiple ways of speaking, ending up with a loose group of subjective theories that concern language, languages, and foreign language learning.

METHOD

To study children's metalinguistic awareness and its relation to their foreign language learning, we used different means of data collection. The methods were basically twofold, reflecting two different conceptualizations: (a) experimental/quantitative and (b) interactional/qualitative. First, we gathered data using standardized tests and measures for childrens' linguistic skills and metalinguistic awareness that were available in the Finnish context or were modifiable to the Finnish context for our purposes. Also, some tasks were planned and designed specifically for our purposes (for more on tasks of foreign language awareness, see Alanen, 2002, and Aro, 2001). Thus, we used part experimental means and part measures of the psychometric tradition.

However, we also paid particular attention to gathering nonexperimental and nontest data. Thus we have, for example, semistructured interview data, documents produced by children, and observational data. Furthermore, most test situations were tape-recorded so that, in addition to the scores gained, we also could study the verbal and nonverbal interaction between the child and the tester. Thus a fairly large amount of data—gained through several techniques and methods—is accessible for analyzing the metalinguistic awareness and its development of these roughly 20 children. The data will illustrate both aspects of the children's awareness of language in general, their mother tongue awareness, and their subsequent foreign language learning process and awareness of it (for preliminary views, see, e.g., Alanen & Dufva, 1999).

Having different kinds of information gives us a certain bird's-eye view of the children's linguistic "mindscape." On the one hand, we have an opportunity to consider how the children develop in terms of *measurable* linguistic achievements (for a discussion of experimental design using phonological working memory tests, see Miettinen, 2003). On the other hand, we will also be able to have a look at the *phenomenal* experience of the children: glimpses of the lifeworld as experienced by children themselves (for an analysis of beliefs, see Aro, 2001). Informed by hermeneutically and phenomenologically oriented views, we believe that children's talk gives us access to such important aspects of "naive" research participants' everyday world that easily escape the scrutiny of experimental design. A third angle is that of analyzing *the interaction* that occurs in classroom, or in interviews or in test situations (for preliminary results of classroom interaction, see, e.g., Hinkkanen & Säde, 2003; Suomela, 2003). In analyzing the classroom data, we used the Bakhtinian concept of utterance (Bakhtin, 1986, p. 99, see also Holquist, 2002, pp. 59–63, and Kramsch, 2000, p. 139).

Thus, it is possible to have three different perspectives to one and the same situation, such as a test of metalinguistic awareness. We can explore a test situation (e.g., our version of the test of metalinguistic awareness based on Blodgett & Cooper, 1987) for the scores that are measured, for the views the child expresses, and as a verbal encounter between the child and the experimenter. The score the child achieves may reflect her awareness of language, but it may also be a manifestation of her ability to express herself, to interact with an adult, and to understand the kind of activity in which they are engaged (cf. Coughlan & Duff, 1994; Markham, 1976; Roebuck, 1998, 2000).

This design also allows us to reflect critically on the methodology of linguistic and psychological sciences. Many earlier studies of children's metalinguistic awareness have tended to focus on experimental methods exclusively and have involved tasks that have very little to do with children's everyday experience. Bronfenbrenner's (1981, p. 17) criticism of developmental psychology observed the artificiality often present in these situations and the potential dangers of generalizing the results: "Developmental psychology, as it now exists, is the science of the strange behaviour of children in strange situations with strange adults for the briefest possible periods of time." It is precisely this point of view we have tried to avoid in our design.

It is our understanding that use of such experimental methods and psychometric means that originated in the positivist research tradition of experimental psychology and psycholinguistics *can* in fact be combined to form the basically phenomenological approach that aims at exploring children's own experiences, beliefs, and conceptualizations (see also Alanen & Dufva, 2001). This combination is not a mismatch but a means to forward theoretical and methodological discussion and a way of teasing out new research questions. Our position—which in a way is between the positivist and hermeneutic philosophies of science—seems to coincide with the dialogical stand, as, for example, Holquist's (1997) interpretation of Bakhtin's views on scientific endeavors indicates (see also Dufva, in press). The triangulation of different methods (which indeed reflect rather different philosophies of science) not only can give insights into understanding their power and scope but also help in analyzing the tacit assumptions present in the research tradition of metalinguistic awareness and the potential contribution of the dialogical theorizing.

RESULTS: HOW CHILDREN SEE LANGUAGE AND FOREIGN LANGUAGE LEARNING

Meta-Linguistic Awareness: Nature Versus Nurture?

The development of metalinguistic awareness has most commonly been regarded in terms of progress influenced by the child's cognitive growth in general and/or his or her acquisition of language in more particular. Children are supposed to become aware (of linguistic entities or properties of language) at a certain age as determined by the stage they have reached in their language acquisition or cognitive development. The role of the social interaction has hardly been touched in the research literature.

Seen dialogically, children's metalinguistic awareness is a complex phenomenon that emerges from the interplay of several factors and contexts. The role of social interaction in both focusing and heightening the child's awareness is important. Much of what the children are aware of is mediated (see also Alanen, 2003), but in order to see what it is that the children are aware of, we need to have a look at the Bakhtinian notion of language, which stresses—in opposition to the Saussurean notion—the elements of variation and change, in other words, *heteroglossia*:

> Thus at any given moment in its historical existence, language is heteroglot from top to bottom; it represents the co-existence of socio-ideological contradictions between the present and the past, … between different socio-ideological groups in the present, between tendencies, schools, circles, and so forth, all given in bodily form. (Bakhtin, 1981, p. 291)

Accepting the dialogical view of language means accepting a view that the child's metalinguistic awareness reflects various social and cultural practices that are present in the interactions in which the children are involved and thus bears traces of the Bakhtinian heteroglossia. According to this view, children are exposed not to an abstract "language" but to various dialects, registers, styles, and, indeed, languages. Children possess knowledge of language that they pick up in various situations, both in their everyday life and at school, both spontaneously and by instruction. This is a very complex chain of influences, and the result cannot easily be seen as pure "learning" or "development" (in the ordinary meaning of "improving" or "increasing in verisimilitude"). In a slightly different manner, we regard the development of metalinguistic awareness at school age as a series of encounters that occur between the common-sense views (of the children) and the professional ones (of the teachers; educationalists; other professionals, and, finally, us as researchers). In studying children's metalinguistic awareness, we cannot hear—to use Bakhtinian terms—not the *voice* of the child as an individual only, but other voices as well. Children have appropriated *alien words* and ways of speaking from "Others." As we have observed, the institutional discourses that are mediated in the practices of mother tongue instruction and foreign language teaching seem to be very strong and therefore they may easily override children's own observations that remain less articulate.

Next, we discuss some examples, aiming at relating the children's remarks to our own observations and theoretical arguments based on dialogical theory. The examples have been taken from interviews, test situations, and classroom interactions. They aim at illustrating how children, when entering school, rewrite their former, often only slightly conscious understanding of language. The initially spontaneous, natural observations about language that precede the school years now start to mix with the views that are expressed in the children's immediate school environment—in textbooks, learning materials, and teacher talk, for example. Thus, the educational context does not simply add to children's metalinguistic awareness but also modifies its quality and replaces some naïve observations with the professional—learned or academic—ones. Note, however, that this does not necessarily mean that metalinguistic awareness becomes deeper or more firmly constructed. Instead, we may find instances showing how the institutional and cultural ways of speaking may be biased, narrow, or misleading.

As an example of this, we discuss how children are made to regard foreign language in terms of written objects to be taught in the classroom by the teacher and to be learned from a book. Our first example comes from a Grade 4 class in English as a foreign language (EFL). The teacher is giving instructions to the class on how to do an exercise in the workbook. She uses both English and Finnish in her instructions; the words in English are printed in boldface type:

| Teacher: | [...] **Ok. now you can do exercise three.** me ehditään just tehdä. sä ehdit kysyä ainaki kolmelta ihmiseltä ((looks at the clock on the wall)). ä jos sä kysyt jotakin tekemistä niin sä voit sanoo siihen alkuun ton **do you** eli **do you watch videos?** katsotko videoita. **do you play football?** pelaatko jalkapalloa [...]. ((the teacher goes on to give a series of sentences in English and their meaning in Finnish)) ja sitten vastaus on jos sä teet sitä nii **yes I do** ja jos et tee nii **no I don't** ja kaikki löytyy tästä kirjasta. |
| Teacher: | [...]*Ok. now you can do exercise three. we have just about time to do this. you'll have time to ask at least three people ((looks at the clock on the wall)). um if you ask about doing something then you can start by starting with this **do you** that is **do you watch videos?** do you watch videos? **do you play football?** do you play football? [...] ((the teacher goes on to give a series of sentences in English and their meaning in Finnish)) and then the answer is if you do it **yes I do** and if you don't **no I don't** and you can find everything in this book.* |

As a whole, the lesson revolves around the textbook and written materials, but it is the final remark of the teacher—"You can find everything in this book"—that summarizes our main argument here. The conceptualization of language that the school mediates to children is strongly associated with books and written language. We develop this argument in more detail later.

Language Is Written

One of the first observations we made when we started collecting data was that children seemed to conceptualize language in terms of *written* language, especially *printed* texts. Among other things, the children identified the units of language with units seen in printed texts, such as words, letters, or sentences. There is much research evidence from earlier studies for the fact that children's awareness of language *is* influenced by written language (see, e.g., Ehri & Wilce, 1980, for an opposite view; however, see Karmiloff-Smith, Grant, Sims, Jones, & Cuckle, 1996, p. 215). We regard the influence of written language as remarkable, and we see it mainly in terms of a cultural filter. The children live in a literate society and are daily exposed to written language everywhere around them. Thus, most of them already have an idea that language is something written. Nevertheless, school is an important mediator. During the first year at school, particular attention is given to learning to read and write, and the practice exercises center around letters, texts, and books. Standard language, strongly related with the written modality, is another important factor. As the children learn to read and write, they also learn to express themselves using the standard forms instead of the dialectal and colloquial ones. The standard language is associated with the written language, and both are associated with correct language. Thus, it is no wonder that children start to think that the "true" language is the written one.

When we asked the first-graders to define some linguistic concepts in a test, more than a half of them gave a definition for *word* that was based on written language, as shown in the following example.

Interviewer:	Entäs, kertosiksää nyt mulle mikä sana on?, mikä on sana?
Jimi:	No se on semmonen että, semmone pieni pätkä, sitä, osaa jostain kirjasta tai taikka semmosesta.
Interviewer:	*Well, could you tell me now what a word is?, what is a word?*
Jimi:	*Well it's kind of like, kind of a small bit, of the, part of some book or something like that.*

Other children described a word as "a long row of letters," or something "people can read." Only one child referred to a *word* as something "people speak with." Similar results have been reported in earlier studies (see, e.g.,

Papandropoulou & Sinclair, 1974). When we observed the same children later, and noted how they spoke about foreign language, we saw the same phenomenon. For example, the children incorrectly understand the English word house as a two-syllable word (*hou* + *se*), which suggests they see the foreign language words through their native writing system and its rules. Also, when talking about English words, the children often use a marked, written language based pronunciation, pronouncing the words letter by letter as if they were reading Finnish.

The written world is available for the child in a very concrete way, in textbooks, learning materials, and the classroom interior—letters written on the blackboard, notices posted on the walls, storybooks available for reading, and so on. But it is also offered to the child as a hidden agenda in teachers' (and other adults') ways of speaking that imply that written forms can be associated with good and correct language use. We thus feel that children's views are only a part of a larger pattern.

We argue, along with Harris (1980), Linell (1982), and Olson (1994), that the practices of the Western societies, being thoroughly literate, have a pervasive effect on the ways of thinking not only of children but of adults and professionals alike. Linell (1982) argued that there is a written language bias present in our culture that narrows our conceptualization of "language" and makes us regard spoken language through the veil of written language. This bias can be seen also in the practices of language education and language assessment. For example, children's linguistic skills are still commonly seen as identical with their abilities in written language, standard language, and/or academic/scholarly language. The bias can be seen in psychological tests of verbal intelligence, which often identify "language" as written language (see, e.g., Olson & Astington, 1990, p. 706). Also, school achievements are often assessed in terms of written language skills only, although it has been shown (see Cummins, 1981) that the interpersonal communicative skills of children should be distinguished from their academic language proficiency, which is strongly associated with literacy skills.

Language Is a School Subject

Another important observation is that children often seem to speak about language as a school subject. Questions about "English," for example, bring answers that regard "language" as a school subject similar to math, as the following example, taken from a Grade 3 interview, suggests:

Interviewer:	Osaaksää selittää millä tavalla (englanti on) erilaista?
Eeva:	Matikassa pitää laskee, ja siinä pitää, niinku, opetella sanat.
Interviewer:	*Can you explain in what way (English is) different?*

Eeva: *In math you've got to calculate, and there [in English]*
                 you've got to, kinda, learn words.

Language (or mother tongue, or English), of course, is a school subject. The problem that might be present in identifying language as something to be learned at school only is that the children may not become aware of language they are exposed to in their everyday lives and the skills they might have acquired there. This seems to be particularly relevant in the case of English as a foreign language. In contemporary Finland, the English language is strongly present. Most children are daily exposed to spoken English, as popular television shows and movies—not dubbed but with subtitles—often are of Anglo-American origin. Written English can be observed in various advertisements, trademarks, magazines, and products of popular culture. Through this exposure most children easily pick up some English words and expressions. However, because children associate "English" very strongly with the school context, they fail to see their everyday skills—often related to popular culture—as relevant in the classroom context. In short, they do not regard their everyday life as a learning environment, and they often fail to realize that they actually know and use some English already. Looking at the ways children talk, one sometimes imagines there are two Englishes: (a) the "proper English" (of the classroom) and (b) the "PlayStation English" (at home), as implied in the following example, taken from a Grade 3 interview:

Sakari: Mullon englanninkielisiä kaikki on
                 englanninkielisiä nuo play station pelit.
Interviewer: No onkos englannista ollu sulle jo jotai hyötyä,
                 ooksää tarvinnu sitä jo jossai?
Sakari: E.
Sakari: *I've got some English-language all of them are*
                 English-language those play station games.
Interviewer: *Well have you found English useful, have you needed it*
                 anywhere yet?
Sakari: *No.*

It is true, however, that the division between English as a school subject and the English of everyday life that is manifest in children's remarks may partly be explained by the context in which the interviews were conducted. As researchers, we interview children at school, and despite our efforts to explain that we are interested in their views, the children still may conceive us as teachers, a view that may be strengthened by the question-and-answer format of the research interview. In other words, the children may be modifying our questions with an unspoken assumption that we are asking something about the school or school-like activities. Perhaps it did not even occur to the boy in the preceding interview excerpt to wonder about the contradiction found in his own responses: The first question was, after all, about the games he plays, and the second—well, clearly it must have been about school?

LANGUAGE IS IN A BOOK

Because "language" is associated with written language and the school context, it is to be found—metaphorically—*in a book*. Of course, textbooks themselves are concrete examples of written language, but it is important to note that their representations of language are often very literate as well. It has been shown that Finnish mother tongue textbooks (Savolainen, 1998, pp. 65–70) represent "language" much in the sense of written language and that, in foreign language classrooms, written texts are the center of attention, with lessons being planned and carried out around them (Pitkänen-Huhta, 2003). As Hinkkanen and Säde (2003) showed in an analysis of our data, the EFL classroom practices involve textbooks and texts in many ways; for example, books are present in teacher's remarks (starting from "open your books" to giving homework) and practices. The following sequence, taken from a Grade 4 EFL classroom, is a small example of teacher talk:

Max:	No mitkä on hanskat. ((to the teacher))
Teacher:	Kattokaapas sanastosta, jos on unohtunu. ((to the class in answer to Max's question))
Max:	*Well what are 'gloves.' ((to the teacher))*
Teacher:	*Why don't you look it up in the vocabulary list, if you've forgotten. ((to the class in answer to Max's question))*

This predominance of books and texts is also seen in children's own remarks. They seem to conceptualize learning as "learning from the book," and they refer to linguistic concepts as something found in the book, as is apparent in the following example, taken from a Grade 4 interview:

Interviewer:	[…] No nyt sitte tämmöne asia ku kertositsää mulle mikä on kertomus?
Emily:	No, kertomus, on sellane et se voi olla jossain kirjassa ja sitte joku lukee sen siitä.
Interviewer:	*[…] Well how about this then could you tell me what a story is?*
Emily:	*Well, a story, is something that can be in some book and then somebody reads it from there.*

Both lessons and homework center on books and literacy. Often this conceptualization connects to the notion that regards "learning" as memorizing chosen contents or items. Thus "mother tongue" may comprise rules of grammar and orthography, whereas "foreign language" may be identified with word equivalence lists, passages to be learned as homework, or grammatical rules to be memorized.

Language Objectified?

One further feature that can be detected in children's remarks and that is related to the features mentioned earlier, is that language—either mother tongue or foreign language—is seen in terms of objects to be learned. These objects may be words to be memorized, as the following examples, from an EFL classroom and a Grade 3 interview, respectively, indicate:

Teacher: TOSI HYVIN muistitte ja täs tuli paljon uusiaki.
                   mä laskin että viime vuonna oli viistoista verbiä.
                   opeteltavia ja tässä oli jo kakskyt yks.
Teacher: *REALLY FINE you remembered these. Also there were
                   many new ones among these. last year we had fifteen
                   verbs to be learned, I counted, and here we had
                   twenty-one already.*

Interviewer: Jaa, miks sää ajattelet että saksa ois vaikeeta?
Matti: No, kun siinä on niin monta, vaikeeta sanaa.
Interviewer: *Uhuh, why do you think German would be difficult?*
Matti: *Well, because it's got so many, difficult words.*

As these examples suggest, language learning is implicitly compared with increasing one's possessions, for example, in terms of the words acquired. Language is seen as quantifiable and measurable. These reifying views, which conceptualize language as a set of items and language learning as memorizing these items, are frequently noted in both children's and teachers' remarks in our data, but similar views are typical of formalistically oriented linguistic frameworks in general. Therefore, many earlier studies have regarded metalinguistic awareness as a capacity to analyze the form and structure of language only and have ignored children's abilities to observe the meaningful and functional aspects of language.

In dialogism, most clearly expressed in Voloshinov's (1976) early work, we find a stand that is quite the opposite to the formalist, reifying view of language. Voloshinov saw that the objectifying view of language originated at the very beginning of modern linguistic thought and was connected with the philological tradition based on the study of dead languages through written documents: "Almost all its (i.e., linguistics) basic categories, its basic approaches and techniques were worked out in the process of reviving those cadavers" (Voloshinov, 1976, p. 71). For the dialogical philosophy of language, Humboldt's (1841) view of language as *energeia* rather than *ergon* is more appropriate.

In our data, the impact of the formalist, reifying view of languages is notable, and much of this has to be due to teaching practices. The fact that language is taken as an object of reflection is fine. But what if language is not only an object of reflection but also is represented as objects—objects like any other material things? Children learn to classify and name linguistic phenomena, and they learn new items of language (e.g., foreign language words) in quantities. But does this accumulating possession of language objects lead to an in-depth knowledge, or an increased awareness? The following example, taken from a Grade 4 interview, seems to show that this may not be the case: Although the girl remembers the word *verb*, she does not seem to have a grasp of its position among the grammatical terms she has acquired, and neither can she think of any possible way to use her knowledge.

Maija:	Tota, että meiän ope kirjotti taululle sitte siihem verbit ja sitt ympyröi sen tai teki siihe semmosen neliön ja sitte.
Interviewer:	Nii.
Maija:	Meiän piti siihe kirjottaa semmosia sanoja mitä oli pitäny opetella kotona, jotka oli verbejä mutku mä en muista mitä ne on.
Maija:	*Well, that our teacher then wrote "verbs" there on the board and then circled it or drew a square there and then.*
Interviewer:	*Yes.*
Maija:	*We had to write there the kinds of words we had had to learn at home, which were verbs but I can't remember what they are.*

Teaching practices put much weight on classification, naming, recognition, and recall of language as objects. Children learn a considerable amount of metalanguage—that is, terms with which to describe language—during the first three grades. They are supposed to be able to talk about nouns, adjectives, verbs, prepositions, pronouns—or even morphemes—and possibly name all the 15 or so cases of the Finnish nominal inflection. These are required knowledge in the assessment and exams. But as our data suggest, although the children may be able to remember the nametags for grammatical categories (and often they fail also in this), they still might have very little idea of what to do with their knowledge.

Language is thus not represented for the children as a potential object of the students' *own* reflection, as a medium for symmetric talk between the teacher and his or her pupils or as a possible object of critical evaluation. In short, language knowledge is not represented as negotiable. The child's own ability of reflection does not come to use and is not enhanced. Active participation is duly replaced with passive reception of knowledge. As Brown, Collins, and Duguid (1989, p. 32) wrote:

> Many methods of didactic education assume a separation between knowing and doing, treating knowledge as an integral, self-sufficient substance, theoretically independent of the situations in which it is learned and used. The primary concern of the schools often seems to be the transfer of this substance, which comprises abstract, decontextualized formal concepts.

The danger is that something precisely like this happens when children are taught language and about language. They begin to see language in terms of *real* objects, and visualize them primarily as written entities such as "words," "letters," "sentences," or "grammar rules." And although a true appropriation of concepts to analyze language would be extremely useful, we are afraid that the pedagogical dialogue is often missing. In our pedagogical views, we refer especially to the ideas discussed by Leo van Lier (1996) and to the still-scarce but increasing literature that attempts to bridge dialogism to language-learning studies or classroom research (see, e.g., Dysthe, 1996, 2000, Morgan & Cain, 2000).

DISCUSSION

In discussing our examples in the framework of dialogism, we have tried to tackle a problem inherent to studying children's metalinguistic awareness. We have argued that children do not only necessarily become *more conscious* of language but that they also, and perhaps more interestingly, become *aware of the ways of speaking about language* that are typical to the school, to their language community, to professional discourses of linguistics and education, and perhaps to the intellectual European tradition as a whole. This may mean that children may become less conscious of such aspects of language that are not salient in institutional discourses. An example of this would be the ability to analyze the properties of spoken language. Thus, the child's growing understanding of language cannot be regarded in terms of straightforward progress. The notion of accumulative or additive language learning—whether in regard to the mother tongue or to foreign language—may not be most appropriate in describing the development of awareness. The process cannot be seen in terms of linear development that starts from zero, adds certain features or elements, and has an endpoint when adult (i.e., complete, correct, or scholarly) understanding is achieved. Indeed, this would be one of the fallacies present in the general developmentalism that is typical of education in general (for a critical discussion of educational psychology, see Howley, Spatig, & Howley, 1999).

In Bakhtinian terms, metalinguistic awareness develops through socialization into discourses of the environment and appropriation of its concepts. As Bakhtin (1981, p. 345, note 31) put it, "one's own discourse is gradually and slowly wrought out of others' words that have been acknowledged and assimilated." Thus, all that we say "is filled with others' words, varying degrees of otherness or varying degrees of 'our-own-ness,' varying degrees of awareness and detachment" (Bakhtin, 1986, p. 89). This holds at both the linguistic and metalinguistic levels, and although children are exposed to linguistic and metalinguistic diversity in their daily lives, the hegemonic discourse of the school undoubtedly creates an asymmetrical situation. A child's everyday observations do not add to his or her metalinguistic awareness unless they are certified by the teacher or some other authority, and thus they remain less conscious and less articulate. Although different voices echo in metalinguistic awareness, some are weaker than others.

It is our view that the dialogical thinking could make an important contribution to the philosophy of language education and its practices In discussions of language policies, curricula, and textbook production, the notion of "language" itself should be seriously reconsidered. Here we are reminded of many other critical approaches—critical pedagogy and critical language awareness, for example—which aim at exploring such issues as power, asymmetry, and ideology in the context of language education. As we see it, rethinking language and children's metalinguistic awareness on a dialogical basis could have important consequences for the practices of language pedagogy and language assessment. As long as the core concept— "language"—is borrowed from the formalist and literate tradition of linguistics only, we will continue to see the child's linguistic abilities in terms of analytical skills that focus on language form only and perhaps even only on written language form.

Voloshinov (1976, p. 81) described how linguistic and pedagogical practices may reify the system of language and regard "living languages as if they are dead or alien." Language, then, will be tossed like a ball from generation to generation. This is what actually still seems to happen in education. In contrast, Voloshinov (1976, p. 81) argued that language should be learned by entering "the stream of verbal communication." This suggests that language education is ideally a dialogical process in which talking about language and negotiating the concepts is important and in which children's own observations, experiences, and everyday knowledge as brought into the classroom. Our last example, taken from a Grade 4 interview, summarizes some of the things we see as important. The boy, Rauli, who had just been interviewed, was about to leave the room when he suddenly turned around and faced the interviewer:

Rauli: Ja vielä yks kysymys.
Interviewer: No.
Rauli: Mikä on daktylogrammi?
Interviewer: En tiijä muuten mikä on daktylogrammi. Onko se
                    tota. Mikä se on. Mikä on daktylogrammi?
Rauli: Sormenjälki.
Interviewer: Ai jaa sillon niin hieno nimi kato. En ois tienny
                    tota.
Rauli: Se on sivistyssana.
Rauli: *And one more question.*
Interviewer: *Yes.*
Rauli: *What is a dactylogram?*
Inteviewer: *I really don't know what a dactylogram is. Is it well,*
                    what is it, what is a dactylogram?
Rauli: *A finger print.*
Intreviewer: *Oh I see it's got a fancy name I see. I wouldn't have*
                    known that.
Rauli: *It is a learned word.*

This example shows that Rauli is good at certain skills of conversation and interaction: He turns the tables and assumes the role of the interrogator. The test-taker turns into a tester, and a piece of real conversation occurs in which the boy teaches the adult and shows his vocabulary expertise. This is what we think should happen at school: the children bringing in the expertise they have gained in their everyday lives. Thus, language education should be dialogical in all senses of the word, encouraging learners to find out things about language by way of observation and reflection and by noticing patterns and engaging learners as coparticipants in talking about language.

REFERENCES

Alanen, R. (2002, December). *Language transfer and metalinguistic awareness: perceived distance revisited.* Paper presented at AILA '02 (International Association of Applied Linguistics) Conference, Singapore.

Alanen, R. (2003). A sociocultural approach to young language learners' beliefs about foreign language learning. In P. Kalaja & A.M.F. Barcelos (Eds.), *New approaches to research on beliefs about SLA* (pp. 55–86). Dordrecht, The Netherlands: Kluwer Academic.

Alanen, R., & Dufva, H. (1999, March). *Children's socio-cognitive knowledge of L1 and L2.* Paper presented at TESOL '99, New York.

Alanen, R., & Dufva, H. (2001). Tutkija ja tutkittava: Bahtin, Vygotski ja kokeellinen tutkimusasetelma [Researcher and her subjects: Bakhtin, Vygotsky, and experimental research]. In H. Sulkala & L. Nissilä (Eds.), *XXVII Kielitieteen päivät Oulussa 19.-20.5. 2000* (pp. 25–33). Oulu, Finland: University of Oulu.

Aro, M. (2001). *Kolmasluokkalaisten käsityksiä englannin ja suomen kielistä* [Third-graders' beliefs about English and Finnish]. Unpublished master's thesis, University of Jyväskylä.

Bakhtin, M. M. (1981). *The dialogic imagination.* Austin: University of Texas Press.

Bakhtin, M. M. (1984). *Problems of Dostoevsky's poetics.* Minneapolis: University of Minneapolis Press.

Bakhtin, M. M. (1986). *Speech genres and other late essays.* Austin: University of Texas Press.

Bakhtin, M. M. (1993). *Toward a philosophy of the act.* Austin: University of Texas Press.

Bialystok, E. (2001). *Bilingualism in development: Language, literacy, and cognition.* Cambridge, England: Cambridge University Press.

Blodgett, E. G., & Cooper, E. B. (1987). *Analysis of the language of learning: The practical test of metalinguistics.* East Moline, IL: LinguiSystems.

Brandist, C. (2002). *The Bakhtin Circle: Philosophy, culture and politics.* London: Pluto.

Bronfenbrenner, U. (1981). *The ecology of human development: Experiments by nature and design.* Cambridge, MA: Harvard University Press.

Brown, J. S., Collins, A., & Duguid, P. (1989). Situated cognition and the culture of learning. *Educational researcher, 18*, 32–42.

Cazden, C. (1989). Contributions of the Bakhtin Circle to "Communicative competence." *Applied Linguistics, 10*, 116–127.

Cazden, C. (1993). Vygotsky, Hymes and Bakhtin: From word to utterance and voice. In E. A. Forman, N. Minick, & C. A. Stone (Eds.), *Contexts for learning* (pp. 197–213). New York: Oxford University Press.

Coughlan, P., & Duff, P. A. (1994). Same task, different activities: Analysis of SLA tasks from an activity theory perspective. In J. Lantolf & G. Appel (Eds.), *Vygotskian approaches to second language research* (pp. 173–193). Norwood, NJ.: Ablex.

Cummins, J. (1981). Empirical and theoretical underpinnings of bilingual education. *Journal of Education, 163*, 16–19.

Dufva, H. (1998). From "psycholinguistics" to a dialogical psychology of language: Aspects of the inner discourses. In M. Lähteenmäki & H. Dufva (Eds.), *Dialogues on Bakhtin: Interdisciplinary readings* (pp. 87–104). Jyväskylä, Finland: Centre for Applied Language Studies.

Dufva, H. (2003). Beliefs in dialogue: A Bakhtinian view. In P. Kalaja & A. M. F. Barcelos (Eds.), *New approaches to beliefs in SLA* (pp. 131–151). Dordrecht, The Netherlands: Kluwer Academic.

Dufva, H. (2004). The contribution of the Bakhtin Circle to the psychology of language. In M. Nenonen (Ed.), *Proceedings of the 30th Finnish Conference of Linguistics* (pp. 21–26). Joensuu, Finland, University of Joensuu.

Dufva (in press). Culture, language and thinking: Whorf, Bakhtin, Merleau-Ponty and situated embodiment. In F. Bostad, C. Brandist, L. S. Evensen, & H.C. Faber (Eds.), *Thinking culture dialogically* New York: Macmillan.

Dysthe, O. (1996). The multivoiced classroom: Interactions in writing and classroom discourse. *Written Communication, 13*, 385–425.

Dysthe, O. (2000). The teacher's role in the multivoiced classroom. In K. Sjöholm & A. Ostern (Eds.), *Perspectives on language and communication in multilingual education* (pp. 55–72). Åbo Akademi, Finland: Turku.

Ehri, L., & Wilce, L. S. (1980). The influence of orthography on readers' conceptualization of the phonemic structure of words. *Applied Psycholinguistics, 1*, 371–385.

Frawley, W. (1997). *Vygotsky and cognitive science: Language and the unification of the social and computational mind.* Cambridge, MA: Harvard University Press.

Gombert, J. É. (1992). *Metalinguistic development.* New York: Harvester/Wheatsheaf.

Harris, R. (1980). *The language makers.* Oxford, England: Duckworth.

Hermans, H. J. M. (2001). The dialogical self: Toward a theory of personal and cultural positioning, *Culture and Psychology, 7*, 243–281.

Hinkkanen, H.-M., & Säde, A.-L. (2003). *Puhutaanko kielestä vai kielellä? Tapaustutkimus englannin kielen tunnilla käytetyn kielen kohteista, sisällöistä ja merkityksistä* [Do we speak about a language or in a language? A case study about the goals, contents and meanings in the language used in an EFL class]. Unpublished master's thesis, Department of Teacher Education, University of Jyväskylä.

Holquist, M. (1997). Bakhtin and beautiful science: The paradox of cultural relativity revisited. In M. Macovski (Ed.), *Dialogue and critical discourse* (pp. 215–236). New York: Oxford University Press.

Holquist, M. (2002). *Dialogism* (2nd ed.). New York: Routledge.

Howley, A., Spatig, L., & Howley, C. (1999). Developmentalism deconstructed. In J. L. Kincheloe, S. S. Steinberg, & L.E. Villaverde (Eds.), *Rethinking intelligence: Confronting psychological assumptions about teaching and learning* (pp. 27–52). New York: Routledge.

Humboldt, W. von (1841). Über die Verschiedenheit des menschlichen Sprachbaues und ihren Einfluss auf die geistige Entwicklung des Menschengeschlechts. *Gesammelte Werke, VI.* Berlin: Carl Brandes.

Karmiloff-Smith, A., Grant, J., Sims, K., Jones, M.-C., & Cuckle, P. (1996). Rethinking metalinguistic awareness: Representing and accessing knowledge about what counts as a "word," *Cognition, 58*, 197–219.

Kramsch, C. (1995). Rhetorical approaches to understanding. In T. Miller (Ed.), *Functional approaches to written text: Classroom applications* [Special issue]. TESOL-France The Journal 2/2, 61–78.

Kramsch, C. (2000). Social discursive constructions of self in L2 learning. In J. P. Lantolf (Ed.), *Sociocultural theory and second language learning* (pp. 133–153). Oxford, England: Oxford University Press.

Lähteenmäki, M. (1994). Consciousness as a social and dialogical phenomenon. *Finlance, 14*, 1–21.

Lähteenmäki, M. (1998a). On dynamics and stability: Saussure, Voloshinov, and Bakhtin. In M. Lähteenmäki & H. Dufva (Eds.), *Dialogues on Bakhtin: Interdisciplinary readings* (pp. 51–69). Jyväskylä: Centre for Applied Language Studies.

Lähteenmäki, M. (1998b). On meaning and understanding: A dialogical approach. *Dialogism, 1*, 74–91.

Leiman, M. (1998). Words as intersubjective mediators in psychotherapeutic discourse: The presence of hidden voices in patient utterances. In M. Lähteenmäki & H. Dufva (Eds.), *Dialogues on Bakhtin: Interdisciplinary readings* (pp. 105–116). Jyväskylä, Finland: Centre for Applied Language Studies.

Linell, P. (1982). *The written language bias in linguistics.* Linköping, Sweden: University of Linköping Press.

Linell, P. (1998). *Approaching dialogue: Talk, interaction and contexts in dialogical perspectives.* Amsterdam: John Benjamins.

Markham, E. (1976). Children's difficulty with word-referent differentiation. *Child Development, 47,* 742–749.

Marková, I., & Foppa, K. (Eds.). (1990). *The dynamics of dialogue.* New York: Harvester Wheatsheaf.

Marková, I., & Foppa, K. (Eds.). (1991). *Asymmetries in dialogue.* Hertfordshire, England: Harvester Wheatsheaf.

Marková, I., Graumann, C., & Foppa, K. (Eds.). (1995). *Mutualities in dialogue.* Cambridge, England: Cambridge University Press.

Miettinen, H. (2003). *Nonword repetition and L2 knowledge.* Unpublished master's thesis, Department of Languages, University of Jyväskylä.

Morgan, C., & Cain, A. (2000). *Foreign language and culture learning from a dialogic perspective.* Clevedon, England: Multilingual Matters.

Olson, D. (1994). *The world on paper.* Cambridge, England: Cambridge University Press.

Olson, D. R., & Astington, J. W. (1990). Talking about text: How literacy contributes to thought. *Journal of Pragmatics, 14,* 705–721.

Papandropoulou, I., & Sinclair, H. (1974). What is a word? Experimental study of children's ideas on grammar. *Human Development, 17,* 241–258.

Pitkänen-Huhta, A. (2003). *Texts and interaction: Literacy practices in the EFL classroom.* Jyväskylä Studies in Languages 55, University of Jyväskylä.

Roebuck, R. (1998). *Reading and recall in L1 and L2: A sociocultural approach.* Stamford, CT: Ablex.

Roebuck, R. (2000). Subjects speak out: How learners position themselves in a psycholinguistic task. In J. P. Lantolf (Ed.), *Sociocultural theory and second language learning* (pp. 79–95). Oxford, England: Oxford University Press.

Rogoff, B. (1990). *Apprenticeship in thinking: Cognitive development in social context.* New York: Oxford University Press.

Rogoff, B. (1995). Observing sociocultural activity on three planes: Participatory appropriation, guided participation, and apprenticeship. In J. V. Wertsch, P. del Río, & A. Alvarez (Eds.), *Sociocultural studies of mind* (pp. 139–164). Cambridge, England: Cambridge University Press.

Rommetveit, R. (1992). Outlines of a dialogically based social–cognitive approach to human cognition and communication. In A. H. Wold (Ed.), *The dialogical alternative: Towards a theory of language and mind* (pp. 19–44). Oslo, Norway: Scandinavian University Press.

Sajavaara, K., Alanen, R., Dufva, H., Mäntylä, K., Pääkkönen, M., & Saarela, S. (1999). Children's metalinguistic awareness in L1 and L2: A socio-cognitive perspective. In P. Pietilä & O.-P. Salo (Eds.), *Multiple languages–multiple perspectives: Texts on language teaching and linguistic research* (pp. 218–227). Jyväskylä, Finland: AFinLA.

Savolainen, K. (1998). *Kieli ja sen käyttäjä äidinkielen oppikirjasarjan tuottamana* [Language and its user as produced by the mother tongue textbooks]. Kasvatustieteellisiä julkaisuja 43, University of Joensuu.

Still, A., & Costall, A. (Eds.). (1991). *Against cognitivism: Alternative formulations for cognitive psychology.* New York: Harvester Wheatsheaf.

Suomela, S. (2003). Elekieltä: Opettajan eleet, ilmeet ja katse englanninkielisessä opetuskeskustelussa [Gesture language: The teacher's gestures, facial expressions and gaze in English-language educational discourse]. Unpublished master's thesis, Department of Teacher Education, University of Jyväskylä.

Thorne, S. L. (2000). Second language acquisition theory and the truth(s) about relativity. In J. P. Lantolf (Ed.), *Sociocultural theory and second language learning* (pp. 219–243). Oxford, England: Oxford University Press.

van Lier, L. (1996). *Interaction in the language curriculum: Awareness, autonomy and authenticity.* London: Longman.

Voloshinov, V. N. (1973). *Marxism and the philosophy of language.* New York & London: Academic.

Voloshinov, V. N. (1976). *Freudianism: A Marxist critique.* New York: Academic.

Vygotsky, L. S. (1987). *The collected works of L. S. Vygotsky: Volume 1.* In R. W. Rieber & A. S. Carton, Eds., N. Minick, Trans.). New York: Plenum.

Wells, G. (1999). *Dialogic inquiry. Toward a sociocultural practice and theory of education.* Cambridge, England: Cambridge University Press.

Wells, G. (2002). The role of dialogue in activity theory. *Mind, Culture, and Activity, 9,* 43–66.

Wertsch, J. V. (1985). *Vygotsky and the social formation of mind.* Cambridge, MA: Harvard University Press.

Wertsch, J. V. (1990). Dialogue and dialogism in a socio-cultural approach to mind. In I. Marková & K. Foppa (Eds.), *The dynamics of dialogue* (pp. 62–82). New York: Harvester Wheatsheaf.

Wertsch, J. V. (1991). *Voices of the mind: A sociocultural approach to mediated action.* Cambridge, MA: Harvard University Press.

Wertsch, J. V. (1998). *Mind as action.* New York: Oxford University Press.

Wertsch, J. V., del Río, P., & Alvarez, A. (1995). Sociocultural studies: History, action, and mediation. In J. V. Wertsch, P. del Río, & A. Alvarez (Eds.), *Sociocultural studies of mind* (pp. 1–34). Cambridge, England: Cambridge University Press.

Chapter 7

"Uh Uh No Hapana": Intersubjectivity, Meaning, and the Self

Elizabeth Platt
Florida State University

Steven Thorne (2000) has suggested the need for a shift in second language aquisition from "an understanding of language learned as context-independent lexical and grammatical meaning ... to an acknowledgment of the relative and context-contingent nature of language-in-use" (p. 230). Long dominated by frameworks that view second and foreign language learning with the assumption of linguistic autonomy and only a marginal acknowledgment of context, the field has recently seen the emergence of new approaches rooted in culture-based theories. These approaches differ at many levels from those assuming either transmission communication models (i.e., Jakobson, 1973; Weaver & Shannon, 1949), autonomous linguistics (i.e., Chomsky, 1965, 1986), or an interactionist view (Gass, Mackey, & Pica, 1998; Long, 1996).

One promising way to understand early-stage foreign language learning is by means of the sociohistorical view taken in this volume. Although largely concerned with literary genre, the writings of Mikhail Bakhtin and Valentin Voloshinov provide a legitimate point of departure for the analysis of nonliterary genres as well. The task I describe in this chapter is one such genre, in which two early second language learners, Majidah and Florentine[1] participated in a two-way information task in Swahili. The socio-historic view of the task performance affords an analysis of utterances in

[1]"Majidah" and "Florentine" are pseudonyms, although each name is one commonly used in their respective countries of origin, Malaysia and Romania.

context in terms of the setting, the interlocutors' perspectives, their constructed meanings, and the transformations of thought emerging from their encounter. Such an analysis is crucial if we as second language/foreign language teachers hope to understand and re-create those moments in classrooms where learners may truly *engage* with each other and the language (Platt & Brooks, 2002).

The questions I address in this chapter pertain to how the two novices (Majidah and Florentine) achieved intersubjectivity and constructed meaning in their incipient knowledge of Swahili, and how Majidah, heretofore believing herself a poor language learner, came to see herself as a good one. Stories of self-acknowledged successful language-learning encounters, although they do not provide quantitative evidence of morphological or lexical items mastered, nonetheless offer rich insights into how learners breathe life into a new language and make it their own.

THEORETICAL FRAMEWORK

Dialogism

Associated with the writings of Kant, and a disciple of Russian Formalism early in his career, Bakhtin later became more closely allied with Marxist thought and its concerns with the historical and social world (Holquist, 1981, 1990).[2] Through several iterations of their ideas Bakhtin, Voloshinov,[3] and others established *dialogism* as the central tenet of their work: "To be means to communicate dialogically. When the dialog is finished, all is finished. ... One voice alone concludes nothing and decides nothing, Two voices is the minimum for life, the minimum for existence" (Bakhtin, 1984, p. 213). Their view of language and linguistics eschewed monologism/idealism and a focus on the human being as deracinated from his or her sociohistorical context. According to Bakhtin (1984), "On the basis of philosophical monologism genuine interaction of consciousnesses is impossible, and therefore genuine dialog is also impossible. In essence, idealism knows only a single form of cognitive interaction between consciousnesses" (p. 66). In challenging a biologically deterministic position *vis á vis* the human being, Voloshinov (1976) lamented the "fear of history" entailed in the writings of Freud and others who attributed all drives and motivations to biological, sexual man and backgrounded his

---

[2]Bakhtin later was exiled during the height of the Stalin era with the repudiation of Marxism (Klagas, 2001). Because intellectuals needed to protect themselves from the excesses of this period, they could not always express their views openly.
[3]Voloshinov, strongly dedicated to Marxism, was an important contributing member of the Bakhtin Circle. Although speculation abounds about whether Bakhtin, and not Volosinov, authored works attributed to the latter, writings produced by circle members were probably inspired by lively discussion of various topics in multivoiced dialogic encounters (Brandist, n.d.).

social nature. He noted a motif threading its way through various periods of intellectual history during which are assumed the *"supreme power and wisdom of Nature"* (biological drives) "and the *impotence of history with its much ado about nothing"* (p. 11).

For Bakhtin (1990), the *function* of language—for communication, artistic expression, or cognition—was the legitimate object of study, and thus discourse should be the unit of analysis rather than formal features of language studied for their own sake. In dialogic relationships, ideas become renewed only insofar as they encounter other, *foreign*, ideas: "It is in the point of contact of these voice-consciousnesses that the idea is born and has its life" (Bakhtin, 1990, pp. 71–72). "Like the word, the idea wants to be heard, understood and answered by other voices from other positions" (Bakhtin, 1990, p. 72). Bakhtin (1990) also wrote of "double-directed words, words which contain as an integral part of themselves a relationship toward another person's utterance" (p. 154). Tzvetan Todorov, translating and interpreting Bakhtin and Voloshinov in the present day, wrote that the "most important feature of the utterance, or at least the most neglected, is its *dialogism"* and that all discourse is "in dialogue with prior discourses on the same subject, as well as with discourses yet to come." The single voice is not heard outside the "complex choir of other voices already in place" (Todorov, 1984, p. x). This metaphor of the interconnectedness of voices, although they do not always sing the same notes, precisely captures the essence of the discourse constructed by Florentine and Majidah as they performed the information gap task.

In this chapter I focus on intersubjectivity, meaning, and the self as explicated in the writings of Bakhtin, Voloshinov, and other adherents of a sociohistorical perspective on human language. I argue that in Majidah's and Florentine's attempts to achieve and maintain intersubjectivity with respect to the problem-solving task, each struggled successfully to be understood using their rudimentary knowledge of the new language. This occurred despite differences in their respective beliefs about both language-learning approaches and procedures to solve problems. Moreover, Majidah claimed the task to be the catalyst that prompted an altered view of herself as a language learner. Data in support of these two claims rest firmly on a dialogic view of the problem-solving task in which Majidah and Florentine were engaged.

Intersubjectivity

Intersubjectivity, a term that refers to mutual understanding being created in social contexts, is a major component of dialogism.[4] Language is an "in-be-

---

[4]The concept of intersubjectivity has also been referred to as *attunement* (Rommetviet, 1974) and a *constitutive structuring* (Manjali, 2001).

tween phenomenon" (Manjali, 2001, p. 1), and "*I* can actualize itself in discourse only by relying upon *we*" (Voloshinov, 1973, p. 251). Intersubjectivity was a term used by Kant, who attempted to capture the relationship between the individual and his or her social world; communication is the means by which the *self* enters into a dialectic with the contents of the knowledge of the *other* (Manjali, 2001). The self–other (I–thou) relation is crucial to an understanding of dialogism, and the notion that intersubjectivity is established on occasions when interlocutors enter "temporarily shared social world(s)" (Rommetviet, 1974, p. 29). Voloshinov (1973) wrote that to play the part of the other in discourse, "he or she must also understand clearly the position of the other participants" (p. 257). As will be shown in the examples portrayed in the RESULTS section, Florentine and Majidah each constructed the position of the other, both literally and metaphorically.

Under the local conditions created when intersubjectivity is achieved, *ellipsis* may freely occur. For example, in Clarke and Wilkes-Gibbs's (1992) tangram experiments, after participants had agreed on detailed descriptions for each of 12 tangram figures in early rounds, they began to elide portions of those descriptions, omitting more and more information until, by the last round, only a word or two was necessary to describe each figure. In their study, the procedures were proscribed and systematic, and only one speaker controlled access to the tangram pictures. I discuss instances of both ellipsis and *prolepsis* in connection with the current information gap task (Doughty & Pica, 1986; Pica, Kanagy, & Falodun, 1993). Prolepsis also advances intersubjectivity by "trigger(ing) anticipatory comprehension, … what is made known will necessarily transcend what is said" (Rommetviet, 1974, p. 88). In the process of prolepsis, the speaker must make inferences from tacit information, reaching beyond the concrete data (Spina, 1996). Although he did not use the same term, Voloshinov (1976) alluded to prolepsis: "Verbal discourse … arises out of an extraverbal pragmatic situation and maintains the closest possible connection with that situation. Moreover, such discourse is directly informed by life itself and cannot be divorced from life without losing its import" (p. 98). As will be seen, the extraverbal situation obtaining between the interlocutors in the present study was highly relevant to task accomplishment. Their personal language-learning histories, learning preferences, and stances toward languages in general exerted a powerful influence on the way they participated in the problem-solving task.

Meaning

Understanding requires more than one perspective, and utterances *mean* only in the context of a dialogue that "interanimates different voices and different perspectives" (Wegerif & Mercer, 1997, p. 2). According to Voloshinov

(1976), "The concrete utterance (not the linguistic abstraction) is born, lives, and dies in the process of social interaction between the participants of the utterance. Its form and meaning are determined basically by the form and character of this interaction" (p. 105). The context-dependent character of meaning also entails much more than the sum of the spoken words:

> Articulated words are impregnated with assumed and unarticulated qualities. What are called "understanding" and "evaluation" of an utterance (agreement or disagreement) always encompass the extraverbal pragmatic situation together with the verbal discourse proper. Life, therefore, does not affect an utterance from without; it penetrates and exerts an influence on an utterance from within. (Voloshinov, 1976, p. 106)

"Meaning for Bakhtin is never fixed or exhausted in a single interpretation, because the language is dialogical, with heteroglot meanings reacting upon one another" (Heartfield, n.d.). With reference to the talk produced around the problem-solving task in this study, meanings were in a state of flux, and signs arose "only on inter-individual territory" (Voloshinov, 1973, p. 12). Evidence of the within-ness of many of Florentine's and Majidah's utterances is clearly illustrated.

Problem-Solving (Information Gap) Genre.   Not only is word meaning of importance in a dialogic account, but so is the nature of the larger discourse unit, or genre. When learners know a language well, they know how to participate in everyday cultural routines (see Hall, 1993, and M. H. Goodwin, 1990, for accounts of how richly textured oral practices are instantiated among members of in-groups). Yet, when no pre-established utterance types are available as working models, such as when foreign language learners are facing a complex pedagogical task, opportunities for communicative creativity emerge, with the strategies used being constrained only by the personal and cultural histories of the learners (di Pietro, 1987). "The structure of the utterance, just like that of expressible experience, is a *social structure*" (Voloshinov, 1973, p. 112).

Voloshinov mentioned several oral genres: the talk of production in the workplace, business talk, everyday conversation, and ideological talk or propaganda. Although the information gap task bears resemblance to both workplace talk and everyday conversation, it appears to be its own genre. First, although in conversations turn-taking and other listener-sensitive conventions are observed (see Sacks, Schegloff, & Jefferson, 1974; Schegloff & Sacks, 1984), in a problem-solving episode they need not be. Problem solution takes precedence over politeness, and some of the talk is characterized by talk to the self, akin to private speech (Platt & Brooks,

1994).[5] Second, whereas in a formal work setting an established set of steps or procedures may be followed, an information gap task is informal, lending itself to less organized guesswork. Finally, although conversations are not necessarily characterized by explicit goals, the agreed-on aim of the information gap genre is problem resolution.

Intonation.   As will be seen, intonation was one of the nonlinguistic resources used in the dialogic activity between Florentine and Majidah. Bakhtin (1990) wrote that a word, when spoken, is given an intonational contour that reflects the speaker's attitude toward it: "The word does not merely designate an object as a present-on-hand entity, but also expresses by its intonation my valuative attitude toward the object, toward what is desirable or undesirable in doing so" (pp. 32–33).

Elinor Ochs (1992) argued that talk also indexes and reinforces broader cultural values and meanings through both "the referential content of a word, phrase, or clause, or through some linguistic feature that has no reference" (p. 338). Intonation is one such feature. In writing about a study of indexicality and gender in Japanese society, Ochs described how affect was directly indexed, and gender indirectly indexed, by means of two different particles, *ze* and *wa*: "Softness and hesitancy are expected constituents of female comportment, and forcefulness is part of local conceptions of being male … the direct indexing of affect evokes gender identities or gender voices of participants as well" (Ochs, 1990, p. 295). Although no generalization from the Japanese case is being attempted, it is possible that certain intonation patterns, too, may index certain stances, such as the utterance-final rising intonation pattern discussed in this chapter. For the female speaker, this pattern tends to weaken or mitigate the force of an utterance (Lakoff, 1975), although such generalizations about the linguistic features of female speech have been contested (e.g., Romaine, 1999).

The Self

As we have already seen, the self–other relationship in a dialogic view of human interaction is crucial to understanding the discourse. As Voloshinov (1976) wrote, "Outside society, and consequently outside objective socioeconomic conditions, there is no such thing as a human being. *Only as part of a social whole, only in and through a social class, does the human person become historically real and culturally productive*" (p. 15).

In child development, the formation of the human being occurs as the child appropriates social speech, intrapsychological forms reflecting pre-

---

[5]Bakhtin would say that, although directed to the self, there is nonetheless addressivity in this genre; the "Other" within being the addressee (Holquist, 1990).

cedents of an interpsychological nature (Wertsch & Stone, 1985). The self comes to fruition as a result of dialogic encounters during one's language socialization in the early years, and it is continuously renegotiated through the life span. Di Pietro (1987) wrote that "To speak is to be human, and to learn how to speak a new language is to find new ways in which to express that same humanity" (p. 12). By learning a new language and becoming increasingly aware of the subtle cultural shaping that occurs when taking on more functions in it, the individual creates a new self (see Pavlenko & Lantolf, 2000, for particularly powerful accounts of this re-enculturation process by highly proficient second language writers).

A sense of struggle is present in how the self comes to respond to and appropriate the voices of others; an utterance produced by an individual is viewed as imbued with those other voices:

> In the makeup of almost every utterance spoken by a social person—from a brief response in a casual dialogue to major verbal-ideological works ... a significant number of words can be identified that are implicitly or explicitly admitted as someone else's, and that are transmitted by a variety of different means. Within the arena of almost every utterance an intense interaction and struggle between one's own and another's word is being waged, a process in which they oppose or dialogically interanimate each other. (Bakhtin, 1981, p. 354)

Long and repeated associations with the voices of their respective home and community environments, as well as other subsequent experiences, have already shaped the selves participating in any dialogic encounter. Bakhtin (1981) discussed the kinds and origins of the voices that pervade the consciousness of participants in dialogic activity, most notably the powerful effects of the authoritative voice. These "voices of the fathers" (Bakhtin, 1981, p. 342) arise from several sources: those of higher social status within a linguistic group, Revealed Knowledge in a religious text, repressive foreign or domestic governmental authority. Participants in dialogic activity index the authoritative voice in different ways, from open rebellion to tacit, unquestioning acceptance. A different voice is that of "internally persuasive discourse," whose "creativity and productivity consist precisely in the fact that such a word awakens new and independent words, that it organizes masses of words from within, and does not remain in an isolated and static condition." (Bakhtin, 1981, p. 345). Within the individual self, then, a tension exists among the various discourses claiming attention, a struggle, as in the study reported in this chapter, over the hegemony of different "available verbal and ideological points of view" (Bakhtin, 1981, p. 346).

Summary

In the next section I present data in which the participants brought to the task very different perspectives on language, different procedural preferences, and different goals for accomplishment. I discuss evidence that the two struggled to establish, and then to maintain, intersubjectivity and that despite their meager lexicon in Swahili, they mutually constructed meanings using various linguistic and nonlinguistic strategies. Finally, I explain how Majidah, with Florentine's implicit encouragement, eventually came to recognize herself anew as a good language learner. Thus, selves may be defined one way when they come in the door, another way when they leave. It is clear that when one has successfully negotiated a challenging task in a language he or she hardly knows, and subsequently believes in him or herself as a good learner, something of value has been learned. Thus, it is necessary to study what has happened in the encounter that brought about this breakthrough and might be repeated at another time. As indicated earlier, the following two questions guided the data analysis: (a) how did Majidah and Florentine establish meaning with their meager knowledge of Swahili? and (b) how did they come to construe their language-learning selves?

METHODOLOGY

Task Background

As a part of a graduate course in second language education, I taught a short unit on East African geography in the Swahili language through various approaches and small-group practice activities. The purpose of this unit was for students to reflect on their own and their classmates' language-learning processes by recording cognitive strategies for understanding and remembering the language, feelings during instruction, obser- vations of classmates, enabling and inhibiting factors in the instruction, and insights about the language itself. Each also responded to a survey about preferred modal styles (visual–spatial, verbal, musical, mathematical–logical, interpersonal, intrapersonal, kinesthetic) and cognitive styles (field dependence, concreteness, sequentiality, tolerance of ambiguity, and flexibility). The importance of such reflection can not be overstated; becoming learners themselves in settings being promoted for second and foreign language learning, they should be better able to understand and empathize with their own future students. Furthermore, if we assume that language learning most effectively takes place in rich social milieus, then we must help students engage metacognitive as well as cognitive and linguistic processes. A focus on the self-as-learner in the wider context of a partner or partners and the whole class challenges each person to acknowledge that his or her reality is not necessarily shared.

Task Description

At the end of the course, a few students volunteered to assist in a research project; Majidah and Florentine were two of these. They were assigned a two-way information gap task, a communicative pedagogical activity designed to test interlocutors' ability to use a target language to create a convergent graphic representation out of two different ones. Two different maps of East Africa, with their information about tribes, mountains, lakes, national boundaries, and towns are shown in Fig. 7.1A and 7.1B.[6]

Each person had one of two versions of the map, with some features labeled on both maps, some on only one version, and some absent from both.

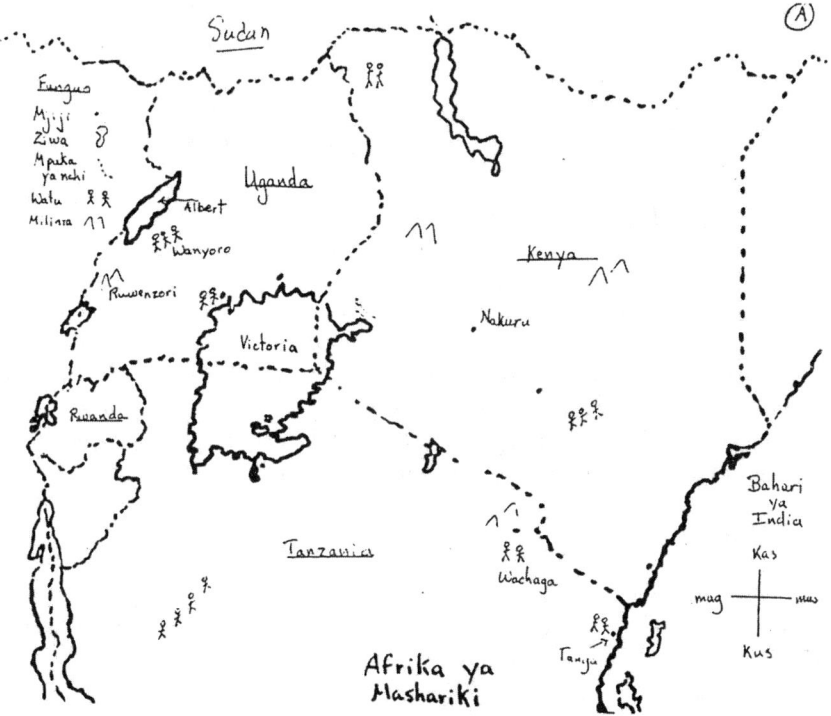

FIG. 7.1A.   Map of East Africa.

---

[6]These are the same materials described in Platt and Brooks (1994).

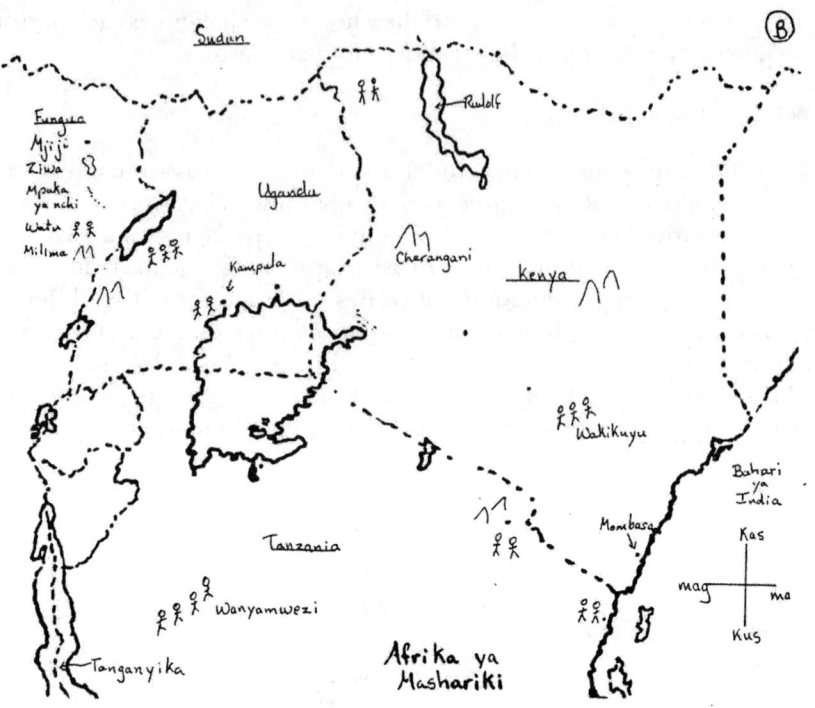

FIG. 7.1B.   Map of East Africa.

Although such tasks are contrived and artificial, they are typical of foreign language classroom activities. Both participants took the task seriously, complied with the overall goals, and used the target language as much as possible. During the task, Florentine and Majidah were seated at right angles to each other, with a box placed between them, but they were able to see each other's faces and upper torsos and some hand gestures.

Data Sources

Three sources of data were used in the analysis of this task: (a) information about each participant, (b) a transcript of the videotape of the task performance, and (c) recorded commentary from each participant on viewing the videotape several months later.

Personal Information.   As claimed earlier, the formation of the self is a sociohistorical process through which the individual gradually learns to function in an increasing number of speech genres and functions as he or she grows. One's secondary socialization in the community and school further shape the individual's beliefs about, and uses of, the language(s) spoken in those settings. The personal language-learning histories gleaned from the students' journals, as well as the style preferences survey, enabled both them as reflective learners/teachers and me as the researcher to understand in greater depth the cognitive and affective processes underlying their unique second langauge learning experiences. Reported next are data from the journals and surveys; interviews with Majidah and Florentine; and a few of my own observations of these young people, informed by my knowledge of the cultural, political, and ideological forces in their respective backgrounds. The participants' learning preferences and beliefs could be identified in the way they executed the task and in the way they discussed it afterward.

A native of Malaysia, Majidah learned English almost as early as she learned her native Malay, as her parents both were English teachers. Her mother's mother tongue is Javanese, a language Majidah often heard while growing up but did not speak because she was teased by extended family members who expected her to speak the language perfectly. Such expectations are common in this multilingual society, where ethnic identity is fostered in large part by home language maintenance. Majidah had also studied French and Koranic Arabic. Thus, because Swahili, like Malay, had borrowed extensively from Arabic, she was more motivated to learn the language for its own sake than some of her classmates. A conservative Moslem, teacher of the children at the local mosque, and student of Koranic Arabic, she believed strongly in the authority of the text, a fact that became concrete at the beginning of her task performance

Of her experience with Swahili, Majidah reported that she felt less competent than some of her classmates; in her journal she wrote of frustration by not being given word-for-word translations of each utterance. On the informal measure of cognitive style she acknowledged being both concrete and sequential and "not at all able" to tolerate ambiguity. She reported requiring context and feeling "desperation," when she got lost during Swahili classes. Furthermore, she said she wanted to write down whatever she heard so that she could memorize the vocabulary and was frustrated when that prohibition was made during one or two of the lessons. She found the greatest barrier to learning within herself: Her need for exact translation interfered with her ability to learn more effectively. Of interpersonal qualities she acknowledged ambivalence toward leadership but pleasure in social interaction. She also reported being comfortable working alone, and her journal entries suggested an ability to be introspective and analytical as well. Finally, she said she enjoyed map work; had a good sense of direction, and favored spatial, visual, and kinesthetic learning.

Florentine's early foreign language learning experiences in Romania were quite dominated by a grammar-translation approach, but he knew

Italian and was highly proficient in spoken and written English on his arrival in the United States. He reported that his English had improved in a college literature course when he had had to use the language more as a tool than as an object of study. During his first semester in the graduate program his class had one communicative lesson in Swahili, which he seemed to enjoy and understand, but when asked to teach a bit of Romanian a few weeks later, his lesson was of the typical grammar-translation type. At the time, he said he could never teach Romanian to beginning students whose language he could not speak, and only after 2 years did he finally agree to try teaching Romanian communicatively. This conservative approach to new tasks and avoidance of risk was manifested often in his performance of the task to be described. I had often surmised that his reluctance to take risks arose from his ability to survive as a student and professional in Romanian life during a time of highly authoritarian and capricious policies, bizarre and inconsistent expectations, social upheaval, and repression.

Florentine said that his attitude toward learning Swahili was good, even though it was a language he would not use, and he benefited from reflecting on his experience and that of his classmates. He claimed strengths as a learner only in verbal–linguistic and interpersonal modes, among them leadership. He also expressed a preference for visual information and said he needed context, but not necessarily sequential order. He reported being able to learn from a wide range of approaches, from grammar translation to TPR (Total Physical Response). Strategies he used included those he had used learning other languages: rote memorization, word association, and a near-futile search for cognates. He benefited from small-group work because he was not put "on the spot," and he liked the lessons that were both "cognitively challenging" and "reinforcing" in terms of vocabulary.

Transcription and Analysis.   The second source of data is the transcription of the task itself. This task has been analyzed using a transcription of all speech and other accompanying activity relevant to a descriptive and interpretative view of the processes involved.[7] To manage the analysis of the data, I identified 32 subtasks, each consisting of an initiation by one person identifying a map feature to be located, the intervening discussion, and the last thing said before the next initiation of a feature. Table 7.1 specifies who

---

[7]The transcription conventions are as follows. The unit of analysis is the turn, and within a turn each separate utterance occurs on a new line. Information about manual gestures, direction of gaze, facial expressions, head movements, posture, and body orientation is enclosed in parentheses. Special transcription symbols used are a carat word finally or question mark phrase finally for rising intonation: a period for falling intonation, hyphens to indicate false starts, and commas for brief pauses. A double colon after a vowel indicates lengthening. Tabbing on one line over to the point under a word in the previous line is used to indicate where one speaker overlaps the other. When a new Swahili word appears, it is presented in italics in the text.

TABLE 7.1
Performance of Florentine and Majidah on task

Initiator	Initiation	Ask	Tell	S/yes	S/no	Fail
Florentine	16	11	5	8	6	2
Majidah	16	11	5	5	3	8
Total	32	22	10	14	9	10

initiated each new feature and whether he or she asked for (Ask) or gave (Tell) new information. A successful outcome, regardless of its correctness, is labeled *S/yes*. *S/no* means that the hearer understood the request but did not have the requested information. *Fail* means there was no successful conclusion to the interchange (i.e., giving up, not understanding, rethinking the initiating utterance).

The table illustrates that, of the equally shared turns, the asking strategy predominated. (A telling strategy is more efficient, because it does not yield as many negative responses.) In contrast to a coincidence in turn-taking and strategy choice, however, is the apparent success of Florentine's initiations and the failure of Majdah's. This can be explained by examining the data; Majidah simply assisted Florentine more than he did her. Nonetheless, Majidah came through the experience declaring herself to be a "good language learner." Hence, one needs to understand what dialogic processes caused her to attribute this powerful realization to her modest performance on this little task.[8]

The analysis of the data portrayed in this chapter attempts to capture both the words and the nonverbal behavior of the two participants in as much detail as possible.[9] Conversation analysis uses a rigorous ethnographic method (Schegloff, Ochs, & Thompson, 1996) to explain the structure of conversations (Sacks, Schegloff, & Jefferson, 1974), capturing in nuanced detail all aspects of both speech—and, more recently, with the use of videotaping—nonlinguistic components of communication as well (C. Goodwin, 1996). Gestures have emerged as relevant in the study of narrative (McNeill, 1992, 2000); they are embodied cognition, the "material carriers of thinking" (McNeill & Duncan, 2000, p. 155; attributed to Vygotsky). In second language learning research (McCafferty, 1998; McCafferty & Ahmed, 2000; Stamm, 2004), gestures are claimed to provide parallel support to cognition as well as communication, thus enhancing second lan-

---

[8]I use the term *realize*, because a multilingual person like Majidah would certainly be considered a *gifted* language learner in the eyes of most monolingual Americans.

[9]Admittedly, not all conventions of a conversation–analytic approach have been used here.

guage learning. Conversation analysis, according to C. Goodwin (1996); M. H. Goodwin (1990); Ochs, Gonzalez, and Jacoby (1996), and others, does not privilege an encapsulated, independently functioning linguistic system but attends to the *extraverbal* conditions of the situation as well.

> In life, verbal discourse is clearly not self-sufficient. It arises out of an extraverbal pragmatic situation and maintains the closest possible connection with that situation. Moreover, such discourse is directly informed by life itself and cannot be divorced from life without losing its import. (Voloshinov, 1976, p. 98)

Post Hoc Interviews. A third source of evidence offered in this chapter is the participants' commentary while viewing the videotape of themselves several months after the original event. Jerome Bruner raised important issues concerning the methods and goals of current psychological research, challenging the notion that research pariticpants' stated intents, feelings, and beliefs are less relevant than their actions. Accordingly, he proposed asking them to explain the thinking behind their actions. "Saying and doing represent a functionally inseparable unit in a culturally oriented psychology" (Bruner, 1990, p. 19). His views resonate with those of Voloshinov, who opposed privileging the biological aspect of man, minimizing the role of consciousness, and viewing history and culture as deriving from nature alone. Rather than objectifying Majidah and Florentine in this research, I enlisted them as coinvestigators, learning that each attributed to the other a greater knowledge of the target language as well as other positive qualities as learners. This observation instantiates what Bakhtin called the *excessive look* and what Holquist (1990, p. 35) described as a *surplus of seeing*. "I author a unified version of the event of our joint existence from my unique place in it by means of combining the things I see which are different from (in addition to) those you see, and the things you see which are different from (in addition to) that difference (Holquist, 1990, p. 37). The information gap task was structured in just this way: Each person had information the other lacked. But each also constructed a picture of what the other knew about Swahili, their abilities to lead, their preferences for moving about the map, and so on.

Wishing to learn more about the participants' respective utterances, recollections of thoughts during the task, and the turning point that led to Majidah's second language learning breakthrough, we three viewed the tape together. This collaborative *a posteriori* focus on the task provided a new chapter in the narrative of each task participant's language learning and a new data source for what Bruner (1990) called *plausible interpretations* of the research issues. If Majidah's claim of being a good language learner is to be believed, then what learners identify as milestone events in their learning histories must be examined carefully to determine what specific elements made them successful.

RESULTS

In this section I present several kinds of evidence to exemplify the three main concepts introduced earlier: (a) establishing intersubjectivity, (b) constructing meaning, and (c) rediscovering the self. As discussed previously, the evidence comes from Majidah's and Florentine's personal data, from the transcripts of task performance, and from post hoc interviews held while they viewed that performance.

Establishing Intersubjectivity

Overall, the task in which Majidah and Florentine were engaged proceeded quite well, but in several cases their dialogic activity was characterized by struggle because of different orientations and expectations. Despite their overall achievement of intersubjectivity, asymmetries arose over procedural matters, which is made clear in the first subtask. Despite the fact that they knew what sort of task this was, they were still unclear how much information they could assume the other person had. In the examples below, F represents Florentine, M represents Majidah, and E represents Elizabeth, the researcher.

Example 1: Subtask A

45	F:	(looks at map kabila ^ uh magharibi ru-, ziwa Rudolf *tribe west lake Rudolf* (looks at E, no expression at first as if waiting for a reaction, then gradually breaks into a kind of conspiratorial smile, laughs)
46	M:	kabila *tribe* (spoken with high pitch, strong stress on second syllable, looks in notes for 15 sec., smiles, waves hand in dismissive gesture twice)
47		unatoka wapi? *You come from where* (inaudble) (hand out to side, palm up, long pause)
48	F:	tribe (glances at E) tribe
49	M:	it's a tribe (mumbling, nods as in ok, right hand out)
50	F:	Kenya ^
51	M:	Kenya ok.
52	F:	Kenya uh ziwa Rudolf ^ *Kenya lake Rudolf*
53	M:	ziwa Rudolf (looking through notes) um (right hand still up)

54   hapana ziwa Rudolf *no lake Rudolf* (shakes head)
55 F: um kaskazini *north*
56 M: uh kaskazini -ah Kenya ⌃
57 F: kaskazini Kenya
58 M: ok (writes)
59   uh

Florentine's rising intonation on *kabila* in turn 45 indicates that he was asking for the name of a tribe. But, as indicated in turn 46 by her hand-waving and palm-up gestures, her strong stress on *kabila*, and her search through the notes, Majidah was confused by his utterance. According to her remarks on viewing the video, Florentine did not establish a point of reference; he had neither provided the name of the country, Kenya, nor realized she might have lacked Lake Rudolf on her map (unless he was just playing, as his smile suggested). Furthermore, he had used the word for *"tribe"* rather than the word *watu*, for *"people."* She mentioned on viewing the video that although *kabila* is a word borrowed from Arabic into Malay, she nonetheless sought the word in her notes, perhaps thinking it unlikely that Florentine, without the same background, would know this word. Her question in turn 47, *unatoka nini,* *"What do you come from?"* (meaning "Where are you?") was assembled from her class notes, and Florentine's nonresponse reflected that he did not understand it, instead addressing in English her first remark before providing the location (turns 48–50). Having been given the information she sought, Majidah was able to label a new feature on her map (turns 52–59).

They continued in Swahili, maintaining mutual understanding through Subtask B, after which Majidah took over, as shown in Subtask C, Example 2.

Example 2: Subtask C

66 M: um um mashariki uh kusini ⌃ *south east*
67 F: mashariki kusini ⌃
68 M: Nakuru
69 F: mmm (looking at map)
70 M: kab- mji huu ni nini,[10] uh *town this is what* (consulting notes;
            scratches head, hand in air)
71 F: (looks at M) uh
72 M: ku- mash- mashariki kusini *east south* (large gesture - right
            hand goes down and right in the air)

_____

[10]The target word for *"town," mji,* is variously pronounced throughout the data. Attention to the interesting errors made, however, is beyond the scope of this chapter.

73	F:	mashariki kusini?
74	M:	m hm Nakuru
75		kabi- uh
76	F:	Nakuru no
		hapana
		(both look at their maps for 9 secs)

In this case, rising intonation in turn 66 indicated Majidah's way of offering information, thus confusing Florentine throughout the exchange. She probably assumed her elliptical statement would indicate to him that he should begin at Lake Rudolf and look southeast. Adding to the confusion was her question in turn 70, which was infelicitous because she already knew that the town was Nakuru. But this, the only sentence in her notes to approximate her desire to tell him the name of the city near Lake Rudolf, was stated as a question. Thus, at the end Florentine indicated he did not have Nakuru (turn 76), still thinking he was being asked for information. Their comments on this apparent impasse while viewing the video were as follows:

M: You used just the words. I had the whole sentence.
F: If you go over four or five words, you've lost me.
M: Shut up!

Majidah's use of her notes to compose sentences clearly contributed to Florentine's refusal to understand and respond. Her teasing response on hearing his admission revealed her belief that his Swahili was better than hers, that any problems were errors of reception or production on her part. She continued, "He knows best! I always see him as knowing a lot more than me. Don't tell this in class!" Although her last remark was made partly in jest, it was clear she wanted to maintain face in the presence of her peers.

In the ensuing three subtasks the two maintained the adjacency pattern that Majidah had begun to establish in Subtask C, identifying in turn Mombasa, Tanga, and the Chagga tribe in Tanzania. Beginning with the feature named at the end of each subtask, and following a circular path around the map, they were able to elide previously mentioned information, thus building intersubjectivity.

Majidah and Florentine did not always comprehend each other or bring a subtask to fruition, but they nonetheless remained with the task, struggling not only with features that were not clearly marked but also with the discourse itself. Part of the struggle emerged from the way Majidah provided information, as in Subtasks Q and R.

Example 3: Subtask Q

175 M: uh mlima kusini magharibi ziwa Albert ^ *uh mountain*
           south west lake Albert? (F shakes his head no)
           milima ^ (she is telling him she has this)
176 F: mm milima ^
177   hapana *no*

Example 4: Subtask R

178 F: milima *mountain* (looking around his map)
179 M: (pause) Ruwenzori (points pencil to self)
           (F is looking at his map; does not see her gesture or seem to
           hear her)

Having in Subtask P identified the Wanyoro tribe in the vicinity of Lake
Albert in Uganda, Majidah proceeded to tell Florentine about the mountains nearby (turn 175). However, her utterance-final rising intonation pattern may have caused Florentine to believe she was requesting information,
and he denied having the mountains in question (turn 177). His repeating
milima in turn 178, however, was accompanied by his search for a mountain
elsewhere, thus breaking the adjacency pattern they had followed successfully earlier. Asked later why he did not accept Majidah naming these
mountains (turn 179), he said, "It wasn't her turn. She changed the pattern." So whereas Majidah thought they were following a strategy of moving
from one location to an adjacent one, Florentine claimed they were obeying
the conventions of turn-taking; in other words, rules of participation at this
time were contested. Despite the fact that there were occasional breaches of
that pattern (as when he took four turns in a row, in Subtasks T throughW),
he appeared confident of his interpretation of the videotaped evidence and
did not mention the more subtle intonation pattern.

Whether the two different understandings of the procedures undermined intersubjectivity or simply reflected the differences in the way each
conceptualized the task parameters, the pair continued to work through it.
The talk in Subtask Z, when the Ruwenzori Mountains were finally identified, illustrates the fruits of their cooperative efforts.

Example 5: Subtask Z

219 F: milima uh kusini kusini magharibi ziwa Albert ^ *mountains uh*
           south southwest lake Albert (looks over the box at Majidah)
220 M: uh kusini mashariki? *Southeast*
           o magharibi? *Or west*

221 F: kusini magharibi ziwa Albert *southwest lake Albert*
222 M: kusini magharibi Albert ^ (very softly)
          (right palm holding pencil, turned up)
223 F: huh no? (quietly)
224 M: kabila? *Tribe?*
225 F: uh uh
226   milima *mountains* (looks over, rubs hands)
227 M: Ruwenzori
228 F: how do you spell that?
229 M: R-u-w-e-n z-o-r-i (writes)
230 F: Ruwen -r-i

Possibly Majidah's close questioning of Florentine's utterance (turns 220, 222, and 224) could be because she thought she had already identified these mountains for him earlier. Nonetheless, they succeeded in bringing closure to the subtask and adding to the convergent set of map features.

Constructing Meaning

Majidah and Florentine came to the task knowing only a few words and phrases of the target language. To compensate, they relied on several other resources: names printed on the map and in the key, English, gestures and body orientation, private speech and private gestures, intonation patterns, and map features and direction words strung together without function words. Subtask I illustrates the use of gestures both to communicate and to orient oneself.

Example 6: Subtask I

124 M: uh mbili *two*
          kabila (waves hands to her left and right, then right hand to
          left and right)
          kabila na nini?[11] *Tribe and what*
          (waves one hand, laughs, gasps)
          (F & M look at each other and laugh quietly)
          Oh God!
125 F: (puts up right palm facing M, requesting her to stop or wait)
126 M: uh

The interesting point to be made about this brief subtask is Majidah's excessive use of gestures. The first gesture in turn 124 was ambiguous, for it

---

[11]The word for "*is*" is *ni*, which is probably what she meant. Small words such as *na* and *ni* are easily confused in early Swahili learning.

functioned both to orient herself and possibly to communicate where this tribe was in relation to Kampala, where they had been in Subtask H. However, Florentine later said he was attending not to her gesture but to his next move. Majidah later admitted "I was trying to show him, but I may have confused him even more." His gesture in turn 125, is clear, reducing her to "uh" in turn 126. This is one of the several ways in which the within-ness of Florentine and Majidah's communication is realized.

As portrayed in Subtask K, however, Florentine's controlling of Majidah's efforts had a purpose that was not immediately apparent to her. In this task they were still trying to figure out what feature was located to the north of Lake Victoria.[12] Majidah had also been using her notes to find the correct Swahili phrases she had written down in class. However, after Subtask K, her use of notes ended.

Example 7: Subtask K

136 M: (inaudible) (shakes head, then pushes pencil into the air)
          kaskazini Victoria *north Victoria*
          mjini? *town*

137 F: hey hold on. I don't think that, I don't have a name for
          Victoria. We know that for sure.

138 M: you don't know Victoria?

139 F: the big one in the center (gesture, palms out, shrugs)
          ok um

140 M: kaskazini Victoria.

141 F: kaskazini Victoria ^

142 M: uh huh
          nini? *what*
          wait (looks at notes)

143 F: mjí ni mjí ^ *city is city*

144 M: town

145 F: m hm

146 M: mjiji ni nini *town is what*
          (giggles out of control, puts hand to mouth, and rolls toward
          the table)

147 F: (smiles with M)

148 M: confused (stupid?)

149 F: (laughs with M)

During turns 136 through 139 they revisited Lake Victoria, already named earlier, using English to reorient themselves to a known point. Hav-

---

[12]This area of the map produced considerable difficulty because there were three cities and a tribe shown between the two maps, and only Kampala was labeled.

ing done so, Majidah said "north Victoria" (turn 140), started to ask a question with *nini*, in 142, and then in 146 put together the phrase *mjiji ni nini*, causing her to lose control. After this moment of levity (146–149) there was no resolution to the task. Although Majidah said during the debriefing that she was laughing because the phrase sounded funny (all the /i/ sounds in a row), Florentine said he was laughing because he did not know what she was talking about.

> F: I considered myself having less knowledge. It's like the blind leading the blind.
> M: oh yeah
> E: Are you surprised to hear him say he's confused too?
> M: m hm. I knew from the beginning he was confident, not nervous.
> F: I wasn't nervous. What did I have to lose?
> M: But I was a poor language learner!

Yet after Subtask K, Majidah discontinued her use of notes, question forms, and self-orienting gestures, an important milestone in the progress of this task. She may have realized that reading phrases from her notes was not a strategy that Florentine accepted. She may also have begun to feel more comfortable with the map and her knowledge of the four direction words in Swahili.

Construction of meaning in this dialogic activity also meant relying implicitly on a number of precedents: their respective educational and language-learning backgrounds, individual learning preferences, and cultural values. As seen earlier, for Majidah, her language-learning self was at stake, but for Florentine there was a task to be done as expeditiously as possible. Two very different beliefs about language and language learning have been manifested in the examples from the transcript and conversations presented thus far. For Majidah, a language was a system of rules and lexical items that was to be written down and memorized for future use. Swahili was interesting because of its numerous Arabic borrowings, also an important feature of her native Malay. Florentine had come to think of the language as a tool for getting things done, holding few expectations about using it correctly, whatever language it was. Majidah's use of forms he did not understand inhibited his ability to proceed and, rather than ask her or check his own notes, he simply said *hapana*, gestured her to stop, or went silent. Yet his tacit insistence on using the language in a communicative manner probably was the breakthrough Majidah needed in order for her to break free of her need to speak "proper Swahili." Thus, the struggle in which these two intrepid language learners was engaged was ideological as well as cultural and stylistic.

As Florentine and Majidah navigated about the map, they skillfully used previously labeled information and the adjacency strategy, indicating the context-dependent nature of the information gap task. It is clear that cumulative experiences and information helped alleviate difficulties that arose. In Subtask Y they used as points of reference the city of Mombasa, established in Subtask D; the Wachanga[13] tribe, established in Subtask F; and the Wakikuyu tribe, established in Subtask X, to ask about a mountain to the south (Kilimanjaro). However, despite the fact that they almost established that neither one's map had the feature, they were not able to actually express this.

Example 8: Subtask Y

206 F: eh Mombasa ^ mjí Mombasa ^ *city Mombasa*
         eh kusini Wakikuyu. *South Wakikuyu*
207 M: m hm
208 F: kusini Wakikuyu mjí Mombasa.
209 M: kusini Waki- (mji?) Mombasa (repeating)
210 F: (inaud)
211 M: uh milima Wachanga ^ *mountain Wachanga*
212 F: Wachanga ^
213 M: karibu Wachanga ^ *near Wachanga*
214 F: (wiggles pencil, looks at map)
         Wachanga.
215 M: milima *mountains*
216 F: m hm
217   milima milima Wachanga ^ (his pencil is suspended over his
         map; after a six- sec pause he sniffs, straightens up very tall,
         looks down at map)
218 M: karibu Wachanga *near Wachanga*
         (neither speaks for 12 secs)

In turn 211, Florentine labeled the mountain *Wachanga* but, having taken account of the information already provided, Majidah correctly noted in turn 213 that the mountain was not named Wachanga[13] but was near the tribe of that name. In turn 216, Florentine appeared to agree, although nonetheless he continued to associate the name of the tribe with the mountain (turn 217). The two appeared to be at an impasse at this point. On viewing the tape, she said, "We don't have the structures for small talk, so it's like if we don't have it, we pause." In this case it is clear that they had experienced limitations with the problem-solving genre as well. "Thought

---

[13]The correct pronunciation of the tribe name is *Wachagga*, not *Wachanga*.

is not merely expressed in words; it comes into existence through them"
(Vygotsky, 1986, p. 125).

Redefining the Self

Majidah's coming to see herself as a good language learner does not seem
possible as we examine some of the previous subtasks. Florentine did not
accept her long utterances, did not always respond to her initiations, and
sometimes simply stopped talking. However, in viewing the videotape, all
three of us found Subtask CC to be the probable turning point. Here
Majidah succeeded in asserting herself in several ways despite Florentine's
attempts to deflect her from her goal.

Example 9: Subtask CC

256	M:	kusini ziwa Victoria *south lake Victoria*
257	F:	kusini ziwa Victoria ^
258	M:	mjiji? *town*
259	F:	kusini uh kusini magharibi ^ *south west*
260	M:	uh uh (strongly)
		kusini (hand in front of face) *south*
261	F:	kabila Wanyamwe- *tribe Wanyamwe-*
262	M:	uh uh
		no hapana *no*
		mjiji kusini ziwa Victoria. *Town south lake Victoria*
263	F:	kusini ziwa Victoria.
264	M:	m hm
265	F:	mjí *town* (looks up at camera, no expression)
266	M:	in Tanzania
267	F:	uh hapana
268	M:	hapana? (surprise expressed)
269	F:	m hm
		...	
274	F:	hapana hapana
		mjí kusini ziwa Victoria hapana. *Town south lake Victoria no*

The first instance of this change is indicated in turn 256, when Majidah
said "kusini ziwa Victoria" as a statement with falling, as opposed to her
usual rising, intonation. In this case she may have wanted to avoid sounding
tentative as she had implied in earlier subtasks. Also, in turns 256 and 258
she provided more complete information than usual, although Florentine
was still not sure if she was asking or preparing to tell him. When he asked in
turn 259 if it was southwest, she answered "uh uh" strongly. And when he

further tried in turn 261 to move to a tribe south of the Lake Victoria, she interrupted in 262 with three negations, "uh uh no hapana!", reasserting that she was looking for the town south of the lake. She provided the final bit of information in turn 266 in English: "in Tanzania." The subtask was successfully concluded when they ascertained that he did not have the information she sought (turn 274).

It is quite clear that the authoritative voice had been a very strong one for Majidah as we read her personal language-learning history, her learning preferences, her assemblages from the notes during the early part of the task, and her occasionally droll comments on viewing the video. A Moslem upbringing, strict expectations about proper use of community languages in the home environment, and a preference for order and nonambiguity in learning settings—any of these could have empowered that authoritative voice within Majidah. If her words are to be believed, she truly saw herself in a new way after doing the task, and she maintained that belief over the several months between the task performance and the debriefing. This is a case of Holquist's (1990) "surplus of seeing." The "Other" within Majidah was able to make the new Majidah-cum-good-language-learner possible. The "Other" outside of Majidah, Florentine, also saw her in quite a different way than she saw herself. Although outwardly resisting his comments about her superior Swahili, they nonetheless confirmed her newfound belief in her ability to learn languages and her willingness to take risks despite making mistakes.

Florentine's performance on this task was played out very much in accord with the preferences he had expressed earlier as gleaned from his personal language-learning history and learning preferences inventory, and his language-learning self was not contested during this task. He did mention at one point long after doing the task that the experience was "humbling" and reminded him when he taught his own students how difficult those early struggles with a new language could be. This was, of course, my original intention by having the students grapple with a new language in a communicative content-based setting. Florentine also seemed quite free of the authoritative voice, possibly allowing the internally persuasive voice to guide him as he did the task. He had certainly come a long way from his early days as a grammar-translation advocate. Yet a lesser investment in learning Swahili and in the information gap task prevented his making the activity more the language-learning experience Majidah apparently sought. It may have been his desire simply to complete the task successfully, to reduce the cognitive load, or to avoid risk, that curtailed his efforts.

DISCUSSION AND CONCLUSIONS

A dialogic account of learner task performance should reflect how the participants struggled to establish and maintain intersubjectivity with respect to the language, each other, and the underlying goals and procedures of the task. The data have indicated ways in which this struggle was manifested. First, the participants shared a common goal—namely, to finish the task as assigned— even though they were not equally motivated to learn Swahili for its own sake. Second, intersubjectivity was maintained at a global level, despite lack of mutual understanding from time to time (not always singing the same notes). Florentine's earliest utterances did not make sense to Majidah; the two evidently did not share the same assumptions about how much information might be available on both maps. And Majidah's frequent use of prepackaged utterances was simply not acceptable to Florentine, as he did not recall having learned to use them in class, nor had he brought his notes along to work with. Majidah's intonation patterns probably further confused him. Intonation, according to Todorov (1984), is "the sound expression of social evaluation" (p. 46). Majidah's rising intonation, suggesting tentativeness or the avoidance of forcefulness, was problematic for Florentine because for the most part he used rising intonation to mean asking. Majidah, being unsure of herself, was more ambiguous. Wanting to appear self-assured and in control, Florentine used gestures, most notably the "halt" gesture mentioned in the discussion of Example 6, Subtask I. Intonation and gestures, then, indirectly indexed stance and possibly gender as well (Lakoff, 1975).

Third, unlike the participants in Clarke and Wilkes-Gibbs's (1992) tangram experiments, Majidah and Florentine negotiated the procedures as they went along. The "temporarily shared world" that Majidah and Florentine created was characterized by both successful and unsuccessful attempts at ellipsis. During their dialogic encounter their *differences* contributed to the building up of understanding, as Holquist (1990) claimed. Dialogism reconciles opposites, and it was clearly the case, according to their self-reported cognitive preferences, that these two were really quite different in the way they preferred to function in this task. Sometimes their reliance on previously established context worked (Subtasks D, E, F, Z); sometimes did not (Subtasks A, C, Q, R, Y). These differences could be attributed to their opposing orientations to the task (leader vs. follower; adjacency vs. random strategy, nonadherence to strict turn-taking) and their presentational styles (rising intonation as statement and question, natural vs. contrived utterances). The struggle over these ways of approaching the task contributed to the problematic nature of some of the subtasks but also represented the "asymmetries and tensions of communication" (Linell, 2000, p. 23). Prolepsis pertains to what is tacit, examples of which included Majidah's deference to Florentine as the acknowledged task leader, their mutual positive attributions, and his disallowing utterances of "more than four or five words."

Fourth, although both Majidah and Florentine had participated in many of the same kinds of oral genre in the English language, and each clearly was able to function in a great many routinized oral practices of their own communities, they were unaccustomed to performing an information gap task. Thus, Majidah and Florentine had to negotiate the shape of this genre for themselves, each at different times placing certain expectations on how the dialogic activity should be accomplished, either following the implicit rules of conversations or of problem solving. Bakhtin wrote that oral genres become conventionalized, so it follows that if an activity is not conventional, then a part of the problem is that the task participants had no such conventions to fall back on, as acknowledged by Majidah, who said, "We didn't have the structures for small talk," in which case they might resort to English, or simply stop talking.

Fifth, in addition to constructing convergent maps, Majidah and Florentine were simultaneously creating a picture of what the other knew or could do: the information on the map, their respective knowledge of Swahili (and other related languages), their abilities to lead, their preferences for proceeding in the task. That their beliefs about each other were not always congruent with those of their respective selves was of interest in these data, as each reported a modest view of his or her own abilities and attributed greater knowledge or ability to the other person. Thus, the relation between the two selves was the connecting link that enabled the two to complete the task as assigned.

Finally, whether intended or not, Florentine pushed the encounter in a more spontaneous direction, and during this brief encounter the participants both acquired and surrendered their freedom. After all, really talking with someone is not about looking in one's notes and saying something "properly." In reaching intersubjectivity with respect to how to use the language, they "pushed the edges of the code, making the language their own" (Lantolf, 1993, p. 229). For Majidah, the successful completion of the task in collaboration with Florentine, the subtle pressure on her to use the language communicatively, and her finally taking control during Subtask CC ("uh uh no hapana," turn 262) resulted in a true breakthrough.

> It was kinda crazy. It [Learning of Swahili] gave me a good feeling, apart from [having mastered] English at an early age, that I could actually learn to speak another language .... I gained confidence in myself as a language learner, everything happening at the same time. If I have a purpose for learning a language, like I have for learning Arabic now, I'd really push for it.[14]

I have now documented the gradual processes by which Majdiah and Florentine successfully solved the information gap task and by which

---

[14]Three years after this task was performed, Majidah reaffirmed this conviction, telling me of her renewed efforts to use Javanese despite making mistakes, and of her sustained commitment to learning Arabic.

Majidah came to see herself a good language learner. Stories of second and foreign language learning with such happy endings need to be told and studied in detail so that we teachers can better learn how to provide opportunities for learners to truly *engage* with the language, making it their own.

ACKNOWLEDGMENTS

An earlier version of this study was reported at the 1999 conference of the American Association of Applied Linguistics. Its title was "Hapana All the Time: Beginning Language Learners Face Their Personal Demons."

REFERENCES

Bakhtin, M. M. (1981). *The dialogic imagination: Four essays.* Austin: University of Texas Press.
Bakhtin, M. M. (1984). *Problems of Dostoevsky's poetics* (C. Emerson, Trans.). Minneapolis: University of Minnesota Press.
Bakhtin, M. M. (1990). *Art and answerability: Early philosophical essays* (M. Holquist & V. Liapunov, Eds., V. Liapunov & K. Brostrom, Trans.). Austin: University of Texas Press.
Brandist, C. (no date). Internet encyclopedia of philosophy. Retrieved September 28, 2003. From http://www.utm.edu/research/iep/b/bakhtin.htm
Bruner, J. (1990). *Acts of meaning.* Cambridge, MA: Harvard University Press.
Chomsky, N. (1965). *Aspects of the theory of syntax.* Cambridge, MA: MIT Press.
Chomsky, N. (1986). *Knowledge of language.* New York: Praeger.
Clarke, H. H., & Wilkes-Gibbs, D. (1992). Referring as a collaborative process. In H. H. Clarke (Ed.), *Arenas of language use.* Chicago: University of Chicago Press.
di Pietro, R. (1987). *Strategic interaction: Learning languages through scenarios.* Cambridge, England: Cambridge University Press.
Doughty, C., & Pica, T. (1986). Information gap tasks: Do they facilitate second language acquisition? *TESOL Quarterly, 20,* 305–325.
Gass, S. M., Mackey, A., & Pica, T. (1998). The role of input and interaction in second language acquisition: Introduction to the special issue. *Modern Language Journal, 82,* 299–307.
Goodwin, C. (1996). Transparent vision. In E. Ochs, E. A. Schegloff, & S. Thompson (Eds.), *Interaction and grammar* (pp. 370–404). New York: Cambridge University Press.
Goodwin, M. H. (1990). *He said–she said: Talk as social organization among Black children.* Bloomington: Indiana University Press.
Hall, J. K. (1993). *Tengo una bomba:* The paralinguistic and linguistic conventions of the oral practice *chismeando. Research on Language and Social Interaction, 26,* 55–83.
Heartfield, J. (no date). Retrieved September 28, 2003, from http://www.heartfield.demon.co.uk/structure.htm
Holquist, M. (1981). Introduction. In M. Holquist (Ed.), *The dialogic imagination: Four essays by M. M. Bakhtin* (pp. xv–xxxiii). Austin: University of Texas Press.
Holquist, M. (1990). *Dialogism: Bakhtin and his world.* London: Routledge.

Jakobson, R. (1973). *Main trends in the science of language.* London: Allen & Unwin.

Klagas, M. (2001). *Mikhail Bakhtin.* Retrieved August 17, 2003, from http://www.colorado.edu/english/engl2012klages/bakhtin.html

Lakoff, R. (1975). *Language and woman's place.* New York: Harper & Row.

Lantolf, J. (1993). Sociocultural theory and the second language classroom: The lesson of strategic interaction. In J. Alatis (Ed.), *Strategic interaction and language acquisition: Theory, practice, and research* (pp. 220–233). Washington, DC: Georgetown University Press.

Linell, P. (2000). What is dialogism? Retrieved August 14, 2003, from www.tema.liu.se/tema-k/personal/ perli/what_is_dialogism-rtf.rtf

Long, M. H. (1996). The role of the linguistic environment in SLA. In W. C. Ritchie & T. K. Bhatia (Eds.),. *Handbook of second language acquisition.* San Diego, CA: Academic.

Manjali, F. (2001). *Dialogics or the dynamics of intersubjectivity.* Retrieved August 13, 2003, from http://www.revue-texto.net/inedits/manjali_dialogics.html

McCafferty, S. G. (1998). Nonverbal expression and L2 private speech. *Applied Linguistics, 19,* 73–96.

McCafferty S. G., & Ahmed, M. K. (2000). The appropriation of gestures of the abstract by L2 learners. In J. P. Lantolf (Ed.), *Sociocultural theory and second language learning* (pp. 199–218) Oxford, England: Oxford University Press.

McNeill, D. (1992). *Hand and mind: What gestures reveal about thought.* Chicago: University of Chicago Press.

McNeill, D. (Ed.). (2000). *Language and gesture.* Cambridge, England: Cambridge University Press.

McNeill, D., & Duncan, S. D. (2000). Growth points in thinking-for-speaking. In D. McNeill (Ed.), *Language and gesture* (pp. 141–161). Cambridge, England: Cambridge University Press.

Ochs, E. (1990). Indexicality and socialization. In J. Stigler, G. Herdt, & R. Shweder (Eds.), *Cultural psychology: Essays on comparative human development* (pp. 287–308). Cambridge, England: Cambridge University Press.

Ochs, E. (1992). Indexing gender. In A. Duranti & C. Goodwin (Eds.), *Rethinking context: Language as an interactive phenomenon* (pp. 325358). New York: Cambridge University Press.

Ochs, E., Gonzalez, P., & Jacoby, S. (1996). "When I come down I'm in the domain state": Grammar and graphic representation in the interpretive activity of physicists. In E. Ochs, E. A. Schegloff, & S. A. Thompson (Eds.), *Interaction and grammar* (pp. 328–369). New York: Cambridge University Press.

Pavlenko, A., & Lantolf, J. P. (2000). Second language learning as participation and the(re)construction of selves. In J. P. Lantolf (Ed.), *Sociocultural theory and second language learning* (pp. 155–178). Oxford, England: Oxford University Press.

Pica, T., Kanagy, R., & Falodun, J. (1993). Choosing and using communication tasks for second language instruction and research. In G. Crookes & S. Gass (Eds.), *Tasks and language learning: Integrating theory and practice* (pp. 9–34). Clevedon, England: Multilingual Matters.

Platt, E. J. & Brooks, F. B. (1994). The "acquisition-rich" environment revisited. *Modern Language Journal, 78,* 497–511.

Platt, E. J., & Brooks, F. B. (2002). Task engagement: A turning point in foreign language development? *Language Learning, 52,* 365–400.

Romaine, S. (1999). *Communicating gender.* Mahwah, NJ: Lawrence Erlbaum Associates.

Rommetviet, R. (1974). *On message structure: A framework for the study of language and communication.* New York: Wiley.

Sacks, H., Schegloff, E. A., & Jefferson, G. (1974). A simplest systematics for the organization of turn-taking in conversation. *Language, 50,* 696–735.

Schegloff, E. A., Ochs, E., & Thompson, S. A. (1996). Introduction. In E. Ochs, E. A. Schegloff, & S. Thompson (Eds.), *Interaction and grammar* (pp. 1–51). New York: Cambridge University Press.

Schegloff, E. A., & Sacks, H. (1984). Opening up closings. In J. Baugh & J. Scherzer (Eds.), *Language in use: Readings in sociolinguistics.* Englewood Cliffs, NJ: Prentice Hall.

Spina, S. U. (1996). *Prolepsis.* Retrieved August 14, 2003, from http://lchc.ucsd.edu/mca/mail/smcamail.1996_01.dir/0209.html

Stamm, G. (2004). Changes in patterns of thinking with second language acquisition. Unpublished doctoral dissertation, University of Chicago.

Thorne, S. (2000). Second language acquisition theory and the truth(s) about relativity. In J. P. Lantolf (Ed.), *Sociocultural theory and second language learning* (pp. 219–243). New York: Oxford University Press.

Todorov, T. (1984). *Mikhail Bakhtin: The dialogical principle.* (W. Godzich, Trans.). Minneapolis: University of Minnesota Press.

Voloshinov, V. N. (1973). Discourse in life and discourse in poetry. In *Marxism and the philosophy of language* (L. Matejka & I. R. Titunik, Trans.). Cambridge, MA: Harvard University Press.

Voloshinov, V. N. (1976). *Freudianism: A Marxist critique* (I. R. Titunik, Trans., N. H. Bruss, Ed.). New York: Academic.

Vygotsky, L. S. (1986). *Thought and language* (A. Kozulin, Trans.). Cambridge, MA: MIT Press. (Original work published 1934)

Weaver, W., & Shannon, C. E. (1949). *The mathematical theory of communication.* Urbana: University of Illinois Press.

Wegerif, R., & Mercer, N. (1997). A dialogical framework for investigating talk. In R. Wegerif & P. Scrimshaw (Eds.), *Computers and talk in the primary classroom* (pp. 49–65). Clevedon, England: Multilingual Matters.

Wertsch, J. V., & Stone, C. A. (1985). The concept of internalization in Vygotsky's account of the genesis of higher mental functions. In J. V. Wertsch (Ed.), *Culture, communication, & cognition: Vygoskian perspectives* (pp. 162–179). New York: Cambridge University Press.

Chapter 8

Authoring the Self in a Non-Native Language: A Dialogic Approach to Agency and Subjectivity

Gergana Vitanova
University of Central Florida

> *To be means to communicate. Absolute death (not being) is the state of being unheard, unrecognized, unremembered. (Bakhtin, 1984, p. 287)*
>
> *I cannot live when I cannot speak. Yazyk eto zhizn'. (Language is life.)*
>
> —*Vera, adult immigrant*

These two excerpts—the first from Mikhail Bakhtin, a Russian philosopher of language, and the second from a 51-year-old immigrant struggling to forge a meaningful life in a non-native language—closely parallel each other. Vera, a journalist in Russia, who later became a kitchen manager in the United States, has articulated a belief that mirrors Bakhtin's own. Throughout his career, Bakhtin was preoccupied with the themes of selves authoring their signifying spaces and voices embedded in discourse. Some of these voices were dominant and loud, while others were subdued and weak. In communist Russia, he could not overtly argue for a social theory of the self. Thus, Bakhtin turned to the novel and to the analysis of complex relationships between authors and heroes, between utterances themselves as a metaphor for human existence. Although philosophers, anthropologists, and psychologists have increasingly used Bakhtin's notions of

149

dialogue and subjectivity, his ideas remain largely unexplored by second language researchers. The Russian thinker, in whose framework people acquire awareness in their native language, and to whom selves are always located "on the threshold" (Bakhtin, 1984, p. 147), wasn't explicitly concerned with issues of education, nor was he overtly interested in second language acquisition. What insights, then, could Bakhtin offer to our understanding of adult immigrants, who themselves are on the threshold, entering new linguistic and social landscapes? How do they author themselves in a complex interplay of discourses? How can an ordinary second language speaker enact agency, and what is the nature of agency? To address these complex questions, I turn to the writings of Mikhail Bakhtin and his philosophy of language and self. My discussion pivots on the three interrelated concepts of voice, consciousness, and answerability, as these can be traced in the lived experiences of three East European immigrants.

THEORETICAL UNDERPINNINGS

Reviewing research on language and agency, Ahearn (2001) noted "the recent agentive turn" in social sciences and suggested that it has transpired not only because of postmodern critiques within the academy but also because questions about agency are "central to contemporary political and theoretical debates" (p. 109). Ahearn outlined current approaches to agency (e.g., agency as free will, agency as resistance, or the absence of agency), and concluded that scholars should approach this term with caution. Its definition, she reflected, is made difficult by questions that theories of agency have left largely unanswered. For example, one question, related to the very location of agency, asks whether it is individual, collective, intentional, or conscious. Summarizing the research on agency in applied linguistics, Pennycook (2001) expressed a concern highly reminiscent of Ahearn's:

> The challenge is to find a way to theorize human agency within structures of power and to theorize ways in which we think, act, and behave that on the one hand acknowledge our locations within social, cultural, economic, ideological, discursive frameworks but on the other hand allows us at least some possibility of freedom of action and change. (p. 120)

That language scholars have found this concept challenging is hardly surprising considering that the nature of self has been problematic for philosophers and social scientists to define. In second language acquisition, the term *agency* has emerged only recently, and its elusive nature has been accented by the varied theoretical perspectives that second language researchers have employed in exploring this subject. Some (notably, Peirce, 1995; McKay & Wong, 1996; also see Pavlenko, 2001a) have embraced a feminist poststructuralist framework showing how second language learners take up different subject positions in different discourses. For example, in her pioneering article, Peirce (1995) challenged the grand theories in second language acquisition, particularly the traditional understanding of motivation. Building on Bourdieu and Passerou's (1977) notion of cultural capital, she instead forwards *language investment* as a central concept in her analysis of agency, which was later adopted and extended by McKay and Wong (1996) in their own study of high school immigrant students. Lantolf and Pavlenko (2001) take a slightly different perspective. Drawing on activity theory, they stressed the socio-historic nature of agency and claimed that agency is a relationship, mediated between learners and their communities of practice. Their argument that agency is both individual and co-constructed is akin to Bakhtin's view of the self as a unique human being and, at the same time, a dialogic phenomenon. These tendencies in viewing second language learners and the nature of language learning itself have reflected the theoretical undercurrents in sociology, cultural studies, and psychology in general. My goal here is not to provide a detailed review of the different approaches to agency to date—a task that could easily require a book. Instead, I will sketch two dominant schools of thought in the larger context of social sciences that have implicitly and explicitly influenced second language research. Then I focus on Bakhtin's conceptualization of language, self, and authoring and show how these could be illustrated through excerpts of Eastern European immigrants' narratives.

A quick assessment of current theories of the self shows a movement away from positivist discourses. Davies (2000) aptly juxtaposed the concept of self in two major schools of thought: humanistic and poststructuralist theories. In humanism, the individual possesses a unified identity and is capable of making choices based on rational thought. Citing Benson, Davies wrote that humanist scholars see agentive acts as purely individual. Similarly, Taylor (1989) portrayed the distinctly modern selves as characterized by disengaged freedom (in other words, people are no longer perceived as part of some great cosmic world order, as they were in earlier traditional approaches) and by their self-defining nature. Cushman (1990) has summarized this notion of the modern self as self-contained individualism, wherein freedom is equated with self-autonomy. In contrast, in a powerful reaction against modernism, postmodernist thought has depicted the subject as completely decentered and identities as no longer essential (Hall, 1996). In their effort to deconstruct the self, poststructuralists reject the very term *identity*. Instead, they introduce the concept of *subjectivity*, which is constituted through different discourses in which the person is positioned at different times.

Poststructuralism, by its very nature, is a movement averse to neat definitions, and the large scope of disciplines to which it has been extended—for example, literary theory, psychoanalysis, and the social sciences—makes the task of capturing its essence particularly challenging. Regardless of their multiple theoretical foci, poststructuralists still share some common perspectives. Whereas the positivist self is distinguished by a unified, coherent, and rational identity, the nature of the postmodern subject is irrevocably fragmented and contradictory. While the modern self is free to make choices, in a poststructuralist view of agency, choices are "more akin to 'forced choices'" (Davies, 2000, p. 60). In this model, the subject loses its "disengaged freedom" along with the possibility to self-define: "One can only ever be what the various discourses make possible, and one's being shifts with the various discourses through which one is spoken into existence" (Davies, p. 57).

The use of passive voice above is not accidental; it stresses the subject's impossibility to author her/himself. As becomes evident in prominent poststructuralist works (Barthes, 1977; Derrida, 1976) texts exhibit one of the most critiqued tenets of the model: the death of the author. For instance, in his famous book *Of Grammatology*, Derrida (1976) noted that "there is nothing outside the text" (p. 158). If, according to humanists, individuals are self-contained agents, capable of making purposeful, rational choices, then in poststructuralist theory, as Davies (2000) observed, agency is "fundamentally illusory" (p. 60). And yet Davies, building on feminist writers such as de Lauretis or Cixous, does not irrevocably deny the subject a possibility for agency. The type of agency she described, however, is fundamentally different from its positivist counterpart. In it, the subject can move between discourses; reflect on how they position him or her; and can negotiate, modify, or even resist them in the process of experiencing one's subjectivity. It is clear that the concept of agency does not liberate the self from its discursive constitution but stems from the self's ability to create new opportunities in establishing one's voice. Thus, Davies cogently defined *agency* as

> a sense of oneself as one who can go beyond the given meaning in any one discourse and forge something new, through a combination of previously unrelated discourses, through the invention of words and concepts that capture a shift in consciousness that is beginning to occur, or through imaging not what *is*, but what *might be*. (p. 67)

Davies' understanding resonates with Bakhtin's hopeful micro-sociology of everyday life, in which selves are never finalized. Furthermore, the creative nature of agency in Davies' definition strikingly resembles Bakhtin's notion of everyday creativity. Indeed, Bakhtin's focus on voice, authorship, and carnival as a form of resistance has prompted postmodernists to explore the links between the Russian thinker's theories and the poststructuralist condition (e.g., Kujundzic, 1997). Bakhtin and poststructuralists share some similar assumptions—for example, the centrality of discourse, discourse as a source of asymmetric power and a struggle of voices—but they also differ in a significant manner. Whereas in poststructuralism the subject is fragmented, and the focus is on larger social and cultural organizations, selfhood in a Bakhtinian sense is underlied by something uniquely human, something inherent only to the individual her or himself: a voice carrying a distinct emotional–volitional tone. While in poststructuralism discourses position individuals, in Bakhtin's framework *"individuals actively use speech genres to orient themselves in their relationships and interactions"*[1] (Burkitt, 1998, p. 165). And yet this focus on the individual by Bakhtin is by no means analogous to the individualism conceived by humanists, as the Bakhtinian self is never whole without the defining presence of the Other. In this chapter, I suggest that Bakhtin's dialogic philosophy of human consciousness and his emphasis on active, creative answerability can help bridge the larger domains of social activity and individual ways of authoring subjectivities.

Voice, Consciousness, and Answerability

In articulating his view of an active, responsible, and languaged self, Bakhtin has drawn on an extensive range of themes in the domains of ethics, linguistics, philosophy, literary criticism, aesthetics, and psychology. Thus, an analysis of Bakhtin's theories could be a daunting and hardly linear task. In this section, I will look at these concepts in his work that apply to this chapter and that best illuminate Bakhtin's understanding of the subject as an author of his/her discursive existence.

The very concept of human existence is, to Bakhtin, intimately linked to having a voice. "To be means to communicate," he wrote in his work on Dostoevsky (Bakhtin, 1984, p. 287). In the modernist lingo, language is a transparent medium that serves to express inner thoughts, emotions, and ideas. To Bakhtin, however, language is not merely a tool for understanding the self and its extralinguistic surroundings; rather, it is the prerequisite for consciousness itself. That Bakhtin firmly locates the very possibility for being and living in language is evident throughout his work. Moving beyond the aesthetic relationships between the characters in Dostoevsky's novels, Bakhtin (1984) pointed out the link between human beings' struggle for voice and their capacity for creativity and growth: "As long as a person is alive he lives by the fact that he is not yet finalized, that he has not yet uttered his ultimate word" (p. 59). This nexus between one's existence and the ability to author her/his words is essential in understanding the Bakhtinian subject. It is in this sense of unfinalizability—in the continuous dialogic practice of responding to and addressing others—that the potential for human agency is realized and hope for the future is created.

---

[1]It is important to note in this context that Bakhtin's notion of speech genre is comparable to the notion of discourse as used by modern social scientists.

Although Bakhtin is not unique in suggesting that the subject's formation lies in language practices (e.g., linguistic determinists believed that language shapes our perception of the world, and postmodernists claim that the self is constituted by discourses), two central concepts make Bakhtin's philosophy distinct: the concepts of dialogue and answerability. Voices are always entangled in dialogic relationships with others: "To be means to be for another, and through the other, for oneself. A person has no internal sovereign territory, he is wholly and always on the boundary; looking inside himself, he looks *into the eyes of another with the eyes of another* or *with the eyes of another*" (Bakhtin, 1984, p. 287). In Bakhtin's work, dialogue is not a mere verbal exchange between interlocutors; it is a complex model of the world that stresses interconnectedness and the permeability of symbolic and physical boundaries (Gardiner, 2000). Human action and life itself are synonymous with dialogue in this epistemology:

> Dialogue here is not the threshold to action, it is the action itself. It is not a means for revealing, for bringing to the surface the already ready-made character of a person: no, in dialogue a person not only shows himself outwardly, but he becomes for the first time what he is. (Bakhtin, 1984, p. 252)

Dialogue, in a Bakhtinian sense, is a socially embedded, meaning-making process. It is impossible to voice oneself without appropriating others' words. In this theory of language, linguistic forms have already been used in a variety of settings, and language users have to make them their own, to populate them with their own accents. As Hicks (2000) suggested, it is this appropriation of discourses and making one's own that comes to denote an important aspect of agency:

> Agency entails the ability to take the words of others and accent them in one's unique way. Moreover, response entails the ability to read the particulars of a situation and its discourses and engage with those particulars in ethically specific ways. (p. 240)

Active engagement with one's situation is embedded in a central concept in Bakhtin's notion of authoring : *otvetstvennost'*. *Otvestvennost'* (translated as "answerability/responsibility") invokes the need of dialogues between selves who act to answer others' actions. In this sense, dialogue is perceived as a form of answering to others' concrete or generalized voices and thus their axiological positions. As Clark and Holquist (1984) summarized, "What the self is answerable to is the social environment; what the self is answerable for is the authorship of its responses" (p. 9). In this sense of authoring, Bakhtin (1993) viewed one's whole life as a complicated *postupok* (act) and the self as a responsible human being putting her/his signature beneath his/her actions. According to Morson and Emerson's (1990) interpretation of Bakhtin's philosophy of the act, "What defines an act is not primarily its content or its mode of realization, but rather the degree and kind of personal responsibility one assumes for it" (p. 69). *Otvestvennost'* is critical in this conceptualization of the human act because it is exactly where the uniqueness of each individual originates. In answering the world around them, selves imbue their responses with unrepeatable intonations, and through these emotional–volitional tones—a vital component of voice—they impart new meanings. The distinctiveness and creativity of each response underlie the act of life authoring as answerability.

THE NARRATIVE AS A FORM OF AUTHORSHIP

Personal narratives have established their presence across disciplines. Scholars in cultural psychology (Bruner, 1990; Mishler, 1986), anthropology (Holland, Lachicotte, Skinner, & Cain, 1998), and education (Wortham, 2001) have pointed out the relationship between narrativity and human consciousness. Recently, second language acquisition researchers have taken up this call. For instance, Pavlenko and Lantolf (2000; see also Pavlenko, 2001a, 2001b) examined the formation of identity through the memoirs of successful bilingual individuals. Here, building on Bakhtin, I suggest that we can view narratives as zones of dialogic constructions and an essential form of authorship.

Analyzing Bakhtin's conception of authorship, Holquist (1986) wrote, "That anyone who speaks thereby *creates* is arguably the most radical implication of Bakhtin's thought and the root concern that unifies his translinguistics" (p. 67). In extrapolating the complex relationship between authors and narrators of written texts Bakhtin, according to Holquist has endowed the ordinary, prosaic speaker with the right to author his/her own voice: "We are all creators; a speaker is to his utterance what an author is his text" (p. 67). The author in Bakhtin, however, is not the modernist monologic subject. In contrast, Bakhtin argued that narrative consciousness is never a single consciousness. In this sense, the very creation of narratives is a polyphonic meaning-making process. When subjects speak, they are not describing events or referring to other subjects; neither are they are simply recounting what took place at a given moment of their lives. Instead, they enter into an active dialogue with these concrete others of whom they speak or a generalized other—somebody who is not necessarily physically in attendance but whose presence is palpable in the narrator's emotional–volitional tone (Bakhtin, 1993).

Bakhtin (1981) emphasized the active nature of language and the speaker; to him, "Every word is directed toward an *answer* and cannot escape the profound influence of the answering word that it anticipates" (p. 280). Any utterance forms a relation to other utterances; any viewpoint stands in relation to the viewpoint of another. Narrative spaces, in this view, become the intertextual ground for contesting others' voices, re-accentuating their utterances with new meaning, and re-interpreting the self through another. Through challenging others' discursive practices, narratives may also become zones for agentive possibility. Wortham (2001) has articulated a similar stance about the transformative power of personal narratives:

> Autobiographical narratives might construct or transform the self in part because, in a telling the story, the narrator adopts a certain interactional position … In other words, autobiographical narratives may give meaning and direction to narrators' lives and place them in characteristic relations with other people, not only as narrators represent themselves in characteristic ways but also as they enact characteristic positions while they tell their stories. (p. 9)

I have found this particular value of narratives and meaning-making of the self to be critical. By evaluating and naming the world around them, the participants in this study have claimed their voices and signed their own acts of authoring.

THE NARRATIVE EXAMPLES

To illustrate these Bakhtinian concepts, I have drawn on narrative discourse examples from East European immigrants. The narratives, collected over the course of 2 years through in-depth semistructured and unstructured interviews, were part of a larger inquiry about the lived experiences of eight men and women who lived in a Midwestern city in the United States (Vitanova, 2002). In this chapter, however, discourse excerpts from only five of the participants are considered. The interviews were primarily conducted in English, but the participants frequently code-switched. Translations from Russian are indicated in the transcripts.

All participants were highly educated. Vera, a 51-year-old woman from Russia, who used to work as a Spanish teacher and later journalist in her hometown, became "a kitchen manager" in the United States. Toward the end of the study, Vera established her own catering business. Sylvia and Boris (a husband and wife) were in their late 40s in the beginning of the project and came from Ukraine. Boris, who was an architect in Ukraine, was employed as a construction worker in the United States. In her home country, Sylvia was a communications engineer, but in the United States she worked initially as a fitting room helper at a discount department store, and currently as a clerk at a bank office. Natalia and Dmitri (also a couple) were in their mid-20s. In Ukraine, Natalia was studying finance, and Dmitri had just earned a degree in computer science. Here they became part-time students continuing their university education while working as servers at a restaurant. When I met the participants, they had all been in the country for about 6 months. Although they had all studied some English in high school or college, this instruction had been highly unsystematic, and none of them were fluent in the second language.

The Languaged Self: When One's Voice Is in the Second Language

> I am conscious of myself and become myself only while revealing myself for an-other, through another, and with the help of another. (Bakhtin, 1984, p. 287)

Bakhtin was interested in the seemingly small lives of ordinary people, whose lives were on the threshold and whose voices were in crises. What bigger crisis, then, can the speaking subject endure than the crisis of losing one's voice? When the participants in this project arrived in the United States, they lost the ability to "reveal" themselves to others in their first language. Because of their lack of English, they also lost the status of intelligentsia, in which they took pride in their home countries. For example, in the new setting, Boris, a highly qualified worker, took a job as a construction worker. Vera, who took pride in using her native language with precision as a journalist, got employed as a kitchen manager. She commented that she felt like a child in "the kindergarten" because she couldn't speak English well; then she quickly corrected herself, saying that children in the kindergarten spoke better than she did. The narratives of the participants reveal that not only was the loss of voice a painful experience for all of them, but they also were cognizant of the social implications. Language is the force that molded their social standing and the relations with native speakers of English at the workplace, as Vera suggested:[2]

> Do you know / sometimes they stay and they are talking in their native language / and I cannot understand because they talk very very fast / and I don't know about / what they are talking / and they ask me something / I cannot answer them because I don't know about what they talk. And / they are looking / "Mm …" / do you know? *Nu / tyajelo* … It's very hard.

In this excerpt, Vera is looking at herself through the eyes of her English-speaking co-workers, and her emotional–volitional tone (Bakhtin, 1993) clearly reveals her response to the image she sees projected onto her: the position of a silent foreigner who cannot understand and, thus, cannot answer.

The awareness of language as a central positioning factor is expressed by all other participants. Another narrative example comes from Natalia and Dmitri, who, on coming to the United States, started working as servers in a

---

[2]See the Appendix for a legend of transcription symbols.

restaurant to support themselves through school. In the following excerpt, they are describing a situation in which the music at the restaurant was loud and Dmitri couldn't hear what a client was saying:

Dimitri (D):	I served a couple mmm and they asked me about something. And I can't understand I couldn't understand and he told me that "Please call somebody who understands English." And Natalia followed me and==
Natalia (N):	I followed him and the man just "Excuse me" and called me and he just==
D:	And Natalia couldn't understand==
N:	No no! You didn't hear it! It was too noisy because it was a band over there and it's not that [Dmitri] didn't understand.
D:	But people ... I don't know people heard our accents and they==
N:	Just (raising her voice) "Wow! Just nobody nobody can speak English in this restaurant!" Just it was (lowers her voice) ...

This excerpt not only serves a referential purpose (describing a discursive episode) but also, by engaging others' words, it conveys the speakers' evaluative responses. Voices, to Bakhtin, are essentially worldviews, and in this case Natalia's and Dmitri's overlapping voices clash with the voice of a third presence. Using a strategy Bakhtin would call *double-voicing*, Natalia incorporates someone else's discourse. At first glance, it might seem that she is merely repeating what the client said. To Bakhtin, however, an author or narrator, when telling a story, by investing the words with her/his own evaluations, always orients the information in a novel way toward the world. In this case, as Natalia incorporates the client's discourse in her own words, she is re-accenting it with her angry emotional–volitional tone and thus with her active evaluative stance.

To Bakhtin, one's emotional–volitional tone (a complex of one's feelings, desires, and moral evaluations) is a key aspect of authoring selves because it makes one's responses to ordinary social realities unique and inherently moral. The emotional–volitional tone is not a vague, abstract category; rather, it is born in particular relational contexts and constructed by a particular discursive situation. "Everything that is actually experienced is experienced as something given and as something-yet-to-be-determined, is intonated, has an emotional-volitional tone, and enters into an effective relationship to me within the unity of the ongoing event encompassing us," asserted Bakhtin (1993, p. 33). Similar to Natalia's, Sylvia's excerpt below reveals that emotional experiences, as ongoing events, are discursive and created in the process of relating to another:

> Today, for example, the head of [an institution] called us / and she was looking for my daughter / my older daughter Lydia. And we speak / we spoke to each other. And I told her that Lydia is not available [...] And then she / told me / many information. But I understood 50%. And I ... after it / I called Lydia in her office and [told] her about it. And she called back the head of [the institution]. And the head was very surprised: "Why do you call me? I just told with your mother!" It's a shame!

In this case, lacking the linguistic resources in the second language, Sylvia cannot enter into a relationship with the other speaker. Similar to Vera, she is looking at herself through the eyes of another, and this encounter produces a powerful emotion.

These and other instances illustrate that human consciousness is shaped by language use and that it is a border, rather than a singular phenomenon. Boris, for example, reflecting on his new social position, unfolded several blueprints of buildings and pointed to them, saying that he still had the knowledge and skill of an architect, but without language, his expertise remained invisible to the world:

> (Translation) I will say it in Russian. I know my profession. But I don't know the language, so I can't show that I can do it. To show that you know, you need to speak.

The loss of language affects not only the participants' professional worlds but all spheres of existence, including their perception of culture, and they demonstrated a keen awareness of that. Boris, for instance, reflected on his family's immigrant journey:

> (Translation) And so we came here. We knew a little of what awaited us, but, nevertheless, reality surpassed our expectations. In the good and the bad sense. America is a very diverse country. It is not black or white. It contains the whole color spectrum. You should (it is your responsibility) to understand life (in this country). Without knowing the language, you don't know anything, you cannot understand how people communicate with each other, their relations.

Boris' statement exemplifies Bakhtin's notion of the dialogic nature of selves. To Bakhtin, one becomes a subject only by participating in dialogue. There is nothing more frightening than not being understood, heard, and answered by another, yet this is exactly what happened to these immigrants. At the same time, Boris alluded to a sense of responsibility toward the Other in this new country—a responsibility for understanding their *zhizn'* (life). *Zhizn'*—this all-encompassing Russian word for human existence—is not restricted to the individual him/herself, as evident from the preceding excerpt. Life, larger than the person, as Boris defined it, in a very Bakhtinian way, is synonymous with how people relate to each other. The understanding of life, according to Boris' own words, is possible only through and in language.

Acts of Authoring: Creative Answerability

According to Bakhtin (1986), "The better a person understands the degree to which he is externally determined ... the closer to home he comes to understanding and exercising his real freedom" (p. 139). This statement accentuates the role of reflexivity in understanding the self as a social being and actor. The participants' ability to analyze their contexts and to interpret their new sociolinguistic realities establishes a necessary foundation for agency. Bakhtin called the process of interpreting our worlds *responsive understanding*, and this process is both dialogical and creative. Creativity, to Bakhtin, is never an abstract entity; born out of necessity, it is always a response to a specific problem in a specific life situation. For the younger Natalia and Dmitri, responding to their immigrant realities entailed continuing their formal education in an American university in their original fields of study. The older immigrants, however, realized that they would not be able to obtain the occupations they previously held, and in this context, Sylvia's and Vera's experiences provide examples of the everyday creativity to which Bakhtin was referring.

Sylvia said of herself and her husband, "We came with open eyes," meaning that they knew they had to abandon an important aspect of their identities. Nevertheless, they could not be ready for everything in the new context, and their acts had to be active responses to what was directed toward them. Sylvia, as all other participants, saw English as a prerequisite for the possibility of authoring her personhood in the second language country, and her everyday acts were intimately connected to the use of the second language and to other language users. For example, when she was offered a job as a babysitter, Sylvia declined because it would not provide her with the opportunity to interact in English. Instead, she became a dressing room helper in a discount department store where she could communicate with customers. Her new social position demanded the appropriation of new professional discourses, which in Sylvia's case coincided with the acquisition of English itself. For instance, she gradually incorporated vocabulary specific to her new work settings: *wide skirts, open-neck sweaters, the floor* (indicating the whole store), and phrases like *"It's cute,"* which she felt the

customers required of her. Moreover, she started purposefully experimenting with the new discourse by interacting with customers:

> Interesting moment. I didn't know how I can say when they return after try-
> ing on. I need to ask them "Do you keep these goods?" or "Do you take?" or
> "It suits?" "It fits?" I didn't know. I tried all of them.

In authoring her immigrant existence, Sylvia was preoccupied with the
acquisition of new "professional skills." For example, about her goal for the
future, she stressed: "I hope that I would be able to learn English because I
have basic English in Ukraine. Mm I I wasn't afraid of this. I was scared
more mmm getting professional skills especially computer skills, communications with Americans and mm American traditions." Sylvia started taking basic computer courses at a community college to get familiar not only
with the major software programs but also to improve her English technical
vocabulary. One day, she mentioned that she was preparing to apply for a
job at a large bank as an office assistant, and as she asked for some help with
her resume, she surprised me by saying that, instead of an engineer, she was
going to present herself as a "technician":

> Resume. Very difficult. It's very diplomatic because I was explained—very
> strange! I was explained that I don't have to show to show my education be-
> cause when they saw my application my resume with my university degree
> with my work experience they they begin to afraid ... They don't understand
> why the people with education try to get a job in low position.

In this excerpt, Sylvia engages in a dialogue with the voices of two different invisible, but palpable, audiences. On the one hand, she invoked the
voices of more experienced (as she saw them), immigrants, and her own
voice ultimately agreed with them. On the other hand, Sylvia actively anticipated the semantic positions of her potential American employers, and
thus she oriented her position toward them. In responding to her new social
reality, Sylvia found that she had to abandon her former discourse of engineer so that she could gain access to new discourses.
    In re-authoring her lived world, Vera's acts revealed her own creativity.
Having just arrived in the United States and started a job as a kitchen manager, the former journalist expressed how uncharacteristic this new position was to her:

> The name of my job is kitchen manager. *Eto nemnozhko smeshno* (this is a little
> funny) because I never think ... I never thought in Russia I can work as a
> kitchen manager.

In Russia, Vera enjoyed a network of friends and colleagues, and the opportunity to meet and speak with a number of different people was what she liked most about her journalist job. In the United States, Vera found herself in a very different situation: Instead of the precise grammar and diction she expertly used in her native language, she was groping for lexical items and making "grammar errors" in English all the time. (Even as she spoke in the preceding excerpt, Vera was attempting to correct her verb tenses.) After work, she immersed herself in the grammar volumes she had brought from Russia, and she would carefully do the exercises at the end of each chapter. For months, to Vera, authoring her second language voice meant perfecting the grammar through going to evening in English as a second language classes and reading her grammar books. From a traditional second language acquisition view, Vera was the epitome of the good language learner (Rubin, 1975). Already fluent in one foreign language (Spanish), she possessed an impressive repertoire of learning styles and strategies. She frequently applied her highly developed metacognitive and metalinguistic strategies to the learning of English vocabulary. And yet, toward the end of the study, Vera's narrative discourse suggests that it is not through the acquisition of formal English grammar or memorizing lexical items that she had re-created her lived world (Holland & Skinner, 1997). Rather, it was through establishing dialogic relations with others, as she herself suggested:

> Now I receive satisfaction from my job and I will not change it. It's nice and many people call for me and they say "Oh we'll do the wedding or graduation" and we do it and we create our new meals and it's interesting! Do you know it's like ... *protses sozidaniya* (a process of creation).

This statement, which contrasts with Vera's initial sense of displacement, reveals that her satisfaction with the new job stems from the possibility of entering meaningful relations with others, being recognized and validated by others as an expert. It also reveals that this immigrant woman, a wordsmith in her native language, has found an unexpected way to re-author her creative verbal energy through experimenting with recipes and ingredients in her new job:

> And now / *ya podpisalas' na ochen' horoshyi Amerikanskiy zhurnal* (I subscribed to a very good American journal / very nice American magazine / *Cooking Light* / and I look on the recipe in this / magazine / and I change something / and I mix one Russian recipe / or one recipe what I know / and this recipe / and sometimes [...] *I potom / ya dayu komu-to pobrobovat' / esli ochen' nravitsya / ya nachinayu gotovit' eto blyudo. Ponimaesh? Eto poluchaetsya neproizvol'no / nu ya poluchayu s etogo udavol'stvie. I ya ne zhaleyu!* No! (And then, I give it to some-

body to try. If he/she likes it, I start preparing this dish. Do you understand? This is not random, but I enjoy it. I don't regret it! No!)

Like Sylvia's, Vera's re-authoring process involved the assimilation of new professional discourses. For example, Vera abandoned the course in English as a second language because as she pointed out, it was teaching her words she would never use in real life, and she would never have to write a five-paragraph essay. Instead, in preparing for a future career as an independent caterer, she decided to take a business course, in which she was acquiring terms such as *payroll*. She also subscribed to American magazines such as *Cooking Light* and started reading cookbooks in English so she could enrich her professional vocabulary. Toward the end of the study, Vera had acquired so much expertise in the food industry area that she and another Russian woman were able to open their own catering business. When speaking about her communication in English with American clients, Vera's voice is confident:

> And I know that if I need something I can go and talk. Maybe my English is not so fine but the people understand about what we are talking and I understand them. Maybe I don't understand all the words but I understand the sense about what we talk.

English remains an essential ingredient in re-authoring the self, but as Bakhtin (1986) would put it, Vera had abandoned the realm of pure, abstract linguistics (1986) and had started to view her language acquisition as dialogic, as a process that is located not within herself and her linguistic knowledge but on the border between the self and the Other. In this view, *understanding*, as Bakhtin emphasized, and as Vera stresses herself, repeating the word four times, is what matters in the creation of a speaking subject.

Resistance as an Act of Agency

Although necessary, understanding is only one facet of becoming a responsible, speaking subject. A speaking subject is also someone who can contest others' voices and can resist them in a voice of one's own. The immigrants' dialogic relations with others were not always enjoyable. Sometimes, they found they had to use their voices to answer in ways that challenged the unequal power between themselves and others. In one case, for example, Vera worked very hard to organize a party for an American co-worker. Before the party, as Vera put it, the woman was "very nice" to her. After the party, however, she consistently ignored Vera and wouldn't even answer her greetings. The party was a success, so Vera had no doubts it had something to do with her caterer skills. Instead, she was certain that the other woman, once she didn't need Vera's expertise any longer, was ignoring her as a foreigner, someone who is not worthy of attention. Vera had commented several times that she had seen *eto prenebrejenie* (this disparaging attitude) directed toward foreigners at work. In this particular case, Vera refused to remain silent, and she confronted the woman directly at a work-related social gathering:

Vera:	And / last year / on this party / [we] are sitting in front of each mm other. [Face to face.] And she said, "Oh Vera, hi!" I say, "I am sorry Judy. I won't say you hi." She said, "What is the matter?" I say, "What is the matter? It's very strange that you will say me hi. This is the first time in the year. All the year / each day / we see each other every day / but you never say me hi. I don't know why. You think you are more intelligent? I don't think it. And all the people / they are quiet and look on me ...
Gergana:	Were they Russians or Americans?
Vera:	Only Americans! I only Russian. I only one Russian. They look on me / and I say==She said / she was red like / my cup (points to the cup she is holding) / she said me, "What is the matter?" I say, "I don't know what is the matter. If you think / that you are very nice person and / you are / your level is very high / and you is very intelligent / I don't think it." Then I say, "You think only you have high education / I have the same. You have one university (one college degree) / I have two...

In her direct interaction with the person and in this narrative discourse, Vera was able to author her meaning and actively resist in her second language voice. Moreover, she was using English to confront the very others who disregarded her for being a second language speaker and a foreigner. The significance of this fact is not lost on Vera herself, who pointed out that she was the "only foreigner" there. She had appropriated the Other's own words, her native language, but this was no mere memorization or reproduction of linguistic forms. Instead, Vera had imbued the native words and grammatical patterns of these others with her own intentions.

Resistance, however, doesn't necessarily require a direct confrontation with the Other. In a narrativized world, resistance can take on elements of carnivalesque discourses where laughter becomes an act of resistance itself. When using indirect discourse in narratives, one does not merely report another's words. Instead, the self enters a dialogic space in which s/he critically evaluates and responds to others' utterances. Once, as Vera was cooking for an American client, she was struck by his arrogance toward her

Russian co-workers and herself. The client, who had briefly traveled in Russia, used an obscene Russian word. Vera asked him not to mention it in front of her female colleagues. The client, however, who had already had a couple of drinks, would not be silenced, and he wanted to share his opinion of the Russians:

> He said, "OK OK but they [Russians] drink many times in the day." [I said to him] "I am sorry / what are you doing now? You talk with me and you drink and drink and drink." He said me "Ah it's true. But I have the party today." But why drink now? Drink when your / guests come. And / when the party / when the party finished / he cannot say no one word (imitates his slurred speech and laughs).

As Vera imitated his face, his intonation, and his slurred speech, her whole being was laughing at this man and the irony of the situation: Here she was, working in this wealthy neighborhood for a client who, being drunk himself, was making judgments of people he didn't know and whom he stereotyped.

To Bakhtin (1984), laughter can have a profound social significance as it is "directed toward something higher—toward a shift of authorities and truths, a shift of world orders" (p. 126). Laughter and irony, with their liberating, transformative powers, become acts of resistance themselves toward oppressive utterances. "*Smeh—eto ne svoboda, a osvobojdenie* (Laughter is not freedom but the process of becoming free," Averintsev (1992, p. 8) pointed out in his analysis of Bakhtin. The other participants also engaged in carnivalesque acts of laughter and sarcasm. For instance, as Boris imitated his American boss' slow tone and his exaggerated facial expression when addressing him, "Wha:t do you wa:nt? **Wha:t** do you want?", he was laughing both at the other man and himself for his imperfect English pronunciation that caused misunderstanding. He also laughed when he mentioned that some of his White American co-workers were calling the newly hired Mexican immigrants "monkeys," although his voice was not happy.

Dmitri and Natalia also used laughter and irony in responding to how Americans positioned them as foreigners, as "the other" in everyday discursive situations:

Dimitri: People [tell us] "you have **charm** accent" (sarcastic tone).
Natalia: Yeah, "Don't lose it" (imitates the other's intonation).
Both: (Laugh).

In yet another example, Dmitri commented on how "the people in the Midwest" were always asking where he was from, and he considered replying that he was from Mars. He said he hadn't done this yet, but he had told someone he was a KGB agent in an attempt to shock the person. In these and other examples, the participants' voices challenge, contest, and resist the more authoritative voices of others and the ways they are being positioned by them.

CONCLUSION

The participants' narrative discourse illuminates a Bakhitian framework of subjectivity, which is embedded in unique answerability and has underlying emotional–volitional tones. Becoming an author would be impossible without language in this framework. It is in one's native language, Bakhtin would argue, that humans are first able to achieve awareness. To be a person is synonymous with having a voice, being heard, addressed, and responded to. Even though Bakhtin was not writing about second language learners or their immigrant settings, his words are not alien to these contexts. The stories of these immigrants illustrate what happens when subjects suddenly find themselves silent and when the positions assigned to them are unfamiliar. It was the lack of language resources that positioned them in these new, uncharacteristic situations, and it was through discursive practices with others and through everyday acts of creativity that they re-established their voices.

A traditional second language theorist may focus on the interlanguage development of these participants and observe that the two-year study suggests fossilization in the area of grammar. A traditional second language acquisition researcher may also comment on cultural differences and on the social distance between Vera, Sylvia, and Boris, on the one hand, and the native speakers of English, on the other hand, that impeded their acquisition of English, or even that, once Vera, Sylvia, and Boris found that they could function in their second language milieu, they lost motivation to perfect their accents and their linguistic structures. A poststructuralist would disagree and would rightly point to the invisible power structures that lock subjects into social positions. In articulating a micro-sociolinguistics of everyday life—with a focus on the ordinary people and their ordinary acts—Bakhtin's writings allow us to take an approach to agency not only for second language users but also for all individuals who have been placed in disempowering subject positions. Bakhtin's philosophy of the speaking self as an author, who is always in a process of creative answerability, allows disempowered human beings to transcend their subject positions. The participants in this study engaged in acts that were creative and that exemplified responsive understanding of their social surroundings. For example, in performing their own architectonics of answerability (Clark & Holquist, 1984) they abandoned professional discourses to appropriate new ones. In their concrete and narrativized worlds, they entered dialogic relations in which they evaluated others' semantic positions and responded with viewpoints of their own. In no case, however, were these responses random acts. Instead, they involved what Bakhtin (1981) termed *active understanding*: a process in which one establishes "a series of complex relationships, consonances and dissonances with the word and enriches it with new elements" (p. 282). In their acts of authoring, these subjects also resisted monologic, oppressive discourses of others by challenging them in these others' own language or by using strategies of resistance, subverting power relations in carnivalesque ways.

"*Yazyk eto zhizn*" (Language is life), said Vera, and she equated the inability to use words with death. Much earlier, Bakthin himself was preoccupied with the presence of words in one's life. Indeed, to him, human existence was defined by language. What sets Bakhtin's language philosophy of language apart from other linguistic theories, however, is that he proposed a framework in the center of which we find the conscious self and in which the source of consciousness is embodied in the voices surrounding us. Thus, in articulating a type of micro-sociolinguistics that bridges the social with what makes the individual unrepeatable, Bakhtin could help us achieve the precarious balance for which Pennycook (2001) called. This micro-sociolinguistics is also hopeful in that it views the person as a creative process, an author who is continuously re-creating her/his lived world.

APPENDIX

Transcription Symbols

/ indicates a pause	italic text indicates foreign language segments
boldfaced text indicates an emphasis	==indicates rapid turn-taking with some overlap
[...] indicates deleted text	

REFERENCES

Ahearn, L. (2001). Language and agency. *Annual Review of Anthropology, 30,* 109–137.

Averintsev, C. C. (1992). Bahtin, smeh, hristiyanskaya kul'tura [Bakhtin, laughter, Christian culture]. In L. A. Gogotishvili & P. S. Gurevich (Eds.), *M. M. Bahtin kak filosof* (pp. 7–19). Moscow: Nauka.

Bakhtin, M. (1981). *The dialogic imagination: Four essays by M. Bakhtin* (M. Holquist, Trans.). Austin: University of Texas Press.

Bakhtin, M. (1984). *Problems of Dostoevsky's poetics* (C. Emerson, Trans.). Minneapolis: University of Minnesota Press.

Bakhtin, M. (1986). *Speech genres and other late essays* (V. W. McGee, Trans.). Austin: University of Texas Press.

Bakhtin, M. (1993). *Toward a philosophy of the act* (V. Liapunov, Trans.). Austin: University of Texas Press.

Barthes, R. (1977). *Image music text.* (S. Heath, Trans.). New York: Hill & Wang.

Bourdieu, P., & Passerou, J. (1977). *Reproduction in education, society, and culture.* Beverly Hills, CA: Sage.

Bruner, J. (1990). *Acts of meaning.* Cambridge, MA: Harvard University Press.

Burkitt, I. (1998). The death and rebirth of the author: The Bakhtinian circle and Bourdieu on individuality, language, and revolution. In M. M. Bell & M. Gardiner (Eds.), *Bakhtin and the human sciences: No last words* (pp. 163–180). Thousand Oaks, CA: Sage.

Clark, C., & Holquist, M. (1984). *Mikhail Bakhtin: Life and works.* Cambridge, MA: Harvard University Press.

Cushman, P. (1990). Why the self is empty. *American Psychologist, 45,* 599–611.

Davies, B. (2000). *A body of writing: 1990–1999.* Walnut Creek, CA: AltaMira.

Derrida, J. (1976). *Of grammatology* (G. Spivak, Trans.). Baltimore: Johns Hopkins University Press.

Gardiner, M. E. (2000). *The critiques of everyday life.* London: Routledge.

Hall, S. (1996). Who needs identity? In S. Hall & G. du Paul (Eds.), *Questions of cultural identity* (pp. 1–17). London: Sage.

Hicks, D. (2000). Self and other in Bakhtin's early philosophical essays: Prelude to a theory of prose consciousness. *Mind, Culture, and Activity, 7,* 227–242.

Holland, D., Lachicotte, W., Skinner, D., & Cain, C. (1998). *Identity and agency in cultural worlds.* Cambridge, MA: Harvard University Press.

Holland, D., & Skinner, D. (1997). The co-development of identity, agency, and lived worlds. In J. Tudge, M. J. Shanahan, & J. Valsiner (Eds.), *Comparisons in human development* (pp. 193–221). Cambridge, England: Cambridge University Press.

Holquist, M. (1986). Answering as dialogue: Mikhail Bakhtin's translinguistics. In G. S. Morson (Ed.), *Bakhtin: Essays and dialogues on his work* (pp. 59–71). Chicago: University of Chicago Press.

Kujundzic, D. (1997). *The returns of history. Russian Nietzscheans after modernity.* Albany: State University of New York Press.

Lantolf, J., & Pavlenko, A. (2001). (S)econd (L)anguage (A)ctivity theory: Understanding second language learners as people. In M. P. Breen (Ed.), *Learner contributions to language learning: New directions in research* (pp. 141–202). London: Longman.

McKay, S. L., & Wong, C. S. (1996). Multiple discourses, multiple identities: Investment and agency in second-language learning among Chinese adolescent immigrant students. *Harvard Educational Review, 66,* 577–608.

Mishler, E. (1986). *Research interviewing: Context and narrative.* Cambridge, MA: Harvard University Press.

Morson, G. S., & Emerson, C. (1990). *Mikhail Bakhtin: Creation of a prosaic.* Stanford, CA: Stanford University Press.

Pavlenko, A. (2001a). "How am I to become a woman in an American vein?": Transformations of gender performance in second language learning. In A. Pavlenko, A. Blackledge, I. Piller, & M. Teutsch-Dwyer (Eds.), *Multilingualism, second language learning, and gender* (pp. 133–174). New York: Mouton de Gruyter.

Pavlenko, A. (2001b). Language learning memoirs as a gendered genre. *Applied Linguistics, 22,* 213–240.

Pavlenko, A., & Lantolf, J. (2000). Second language learning as participation and (re)construction of selves. In J. P. Lantolf (Ed.), *Sociocultural theory and language learning* (pp. 155–177). Oxford, England: Oxford University Press.

Peirce, B. N. (1995). Social identity, investment, and language learning. *TESOL Quarterly, 29,* 9–31.

Pennycook, A. (2001). *Critical applied linguistics: A critical introduction.* Mahwah, NJ: Lawrence Erlbaum Associates.

Rubin, J. (1975). What the "good language learner" can teach us. *TESOL Quarterly, 9,* 41–51.

Taylor, C. (1989). *Sources of the self: The making of the modern identity.* Cambridge, MA: Harvard University Press: Cambridge, Mass.

Vitanova, G. (2002). *Gender and agency practices in a second language.* Unpublished doctoral dissertation, University of Cincinnati.

Wortham, S. (2001). *Narratives in action: A strategy for research and analysis.* New York: Teachers College Press.

PART II

IMPLICATIONS FOR THEORY AND PRACTICE

Chapter 9

Language, Culture, and Self:
The Bakhtin–Vygotsky Encounter

Ludmila Marchenkova
The Ohio State University

The theory of dialogue elaborated by Mikhail Bakhtin is of great interest to second language research and practice. It focuses on cultural and interpersonal dimensions of language and examines discourses that are formed by multiple voices. Grounded in a philosophical aspiration for dialogic polyphony, it can help us see the relations among languages and cultures in a different light from the traditional approaches in second language learning (SLL) scholarship. These traditional approaches emerged at the time of the Chomskian revolution in linguistics in the 1960s, simultaneously with the transition in psychology from behavioral to cognitivist theories. SLL research in its early phase was likewise interested in the linguistic properties of learner language; that is, many researchers were preoccupied with the acquisition of second language grammar. The traditional interest of linguistics has always been concentrated on the universal principles, grammatical structures and modeling at the level of an individual sentence. Accordingly, the linguistic approach in SLL seeks to describe the language that learners acquire and to explain its structure. Psycholinguistics, by contrast, focuses on how a new language is acquired and attempts to explore the internal processes that the learner undergoes and the strategies he or she uses in acquiring the new language. The SLL researchers who came from the psycholinguistic perspective from the beginning were interested in describing and analyzing such phenomena as interlanguage and the mental processes associated with its functioning (Corder, 1967; Selinker, 1972). In both linguistic and psycholinguistic approaches the social, cultural, and discursive contexts in which language learning takes place are not acknowledged as important factors, even though they may be recognized as potential variables that can either help or hinder the development of a purely internal knowledge of language by an individual.

The focus on the individual learner was first challenged by proponents of the sociolinguistic approach. The emergence of the sociolinguistic perspective in SLL research was the result of global sociopolitical and economic changes. However, the ideas about language that inspired sociolinguists in the 1960s and 1970s had already been formulated earlier in the 20th century by such scientists as Franz Boaz, Edward Sapir, Georg Herbert Mead, Benjamin Lee Whorf, Lev Vygotsky, and Mikhail Bakhtin. The basic tenet of these scholars' views is that language is always immersed in a social and cultural context, and its central function is to serve as a medium of communication. As the influence of the view grew, scholarly interest began to shift from the individual learner and his or her internal mental activities to interaction and communication among learners. Language increasingly came to be viewed as inextricably linked to relations of power and to their change in society. Thus, the 1990s were characterized by an emergence of new approaches, such as critical (Pennycook, 1990), ideological (Pennycook, 1994; Phillipson, 1992; Rampton, 1995; Tollefson, 1995), sociocultural (Lantolf, 1994; Lantolf & Appel, 1994), ecological (van Lier, 1996; see also in Kramsch, 2000), and identity studies (Peirce, 1995; McKay & Wong, 1996). Despite the fact that social and interactional studies are a rapidly growing area in SLL research, many observers are convinced that there is still tension between acknowledging the role of social and discursive components of language use and learning, on the one hand, and the predominant role of the individual cognition in research interest, on the other hand (Firth & Wagner, 1997, 1998; Hall, 1995, 1997; Rampton, 1995, 1997).

In the polemic launched by *The Modern Language Journal,* Firth and Wagner (1997) proposed "a reconceptualization" of second language acquisition research to "enlarge the ontological and empirical parameters of the field" (p. 285). They called for a "significantly enhanced awareness of the contextual and interactional dimensions of language use" (p. 285) and for understanding language "not only [as] a cognitive phenomenon, the product of the individual's brain" but also as "fundamentally a social phenomenon, acquired and used interactively, in a variety of contexts for myriad practical purposes" (p. 296). In response to this proposal, I believe that Bakhtin's ideas can expand the conceptual basis of SLL. Bakhtin's theories allow us to address the problems of language, culture, and self on a fundamental philosophical level, which is what "enlarging the ontological and empirical parameters of the field" presumably means. At the same time, the discussion of these theories in the context of SLL concerns hardly needs to be purely philosophical. Rather, the basic concepts of Bakhtin's philosophy should be interpreted in such a light that it becomes clear how they are relevant to our field.

In seeking ways to apply Bakhtin's concepts to language pedagogy, however, one must realize that pedagogical concerns were not a part of his academic and intellectual interests and that Bakhtin didn't leave behind an explicit theory of learning. His theory of language and literature is not by itself a pedagogy, but it can doubtless be useful for articulating a theory of learning language and culture. It needs to be linked with pedagogical concerns, and Lev Vygotsky's (1978, 1986) theory of cognitive development can provide such a link.

Although unique each in their own way, the legacies of Bakhtin and Vygotsky are compatible and can be used in conjunction with each other. Working in different areas—literary and cultural theory and developmental psychology, respectively—the two scholars shared many basic intuitions and developed parallel approaches to language and culture. Their theories appear to be mutually complementary and together give a broader and more complete conception of human interaction in learning. Furthermore, for both scholars dialogue is the main factor in the formation of the self. If a common ground were established between Bakhtin and Vygotsky's theories, it would transcend disciplinary boundaries by supplementing Bakhtin's philosophical and linguistic insights with Vygotsky's pedagogical approach. Just as Vygotsky's ideas have become influential in education and have already been adopted by second language researchers (Lantolf, 1994, 2000; Lantolf & Appel, 1994), Bakhtin's ideas can likewise influence the debate on pedagogy in general and second language pedagogy in particular. Caryl Emerson (1986, 1997), who advocates studying both scholars in parallel, has predicted, for example, that in the 21st century Bakhtin's legacy will have a great impact on educational theory and practice (Emerson, 1997, pp. 274–276).

The goal of this chapter is thus to build parallels between Bakhtin's theory of dialogue and Vygotsky's psychological theory. Furthermore, the focus is on three main areas within Bakhtin's theory: (a) language, (b) culture, and (c) the formation of the self. In what follows, I synthesize Bakhtin's and Vygotsky's ideas on language and examine how they applied the dialogic principle to language use, investigate how they conceived the learning of culture and the development of intercultural understanding, outline their views on the formation of the self and the role of the other in this process, and connect this discussion to the second language context. One of the key concepts in the analyses I present is *understanding*. Readers should bear in mind that, for Bakhtin, understanding among human beings is the culminating moment for the sake of which dialogue exists, with all elements of its complex and dynamic structure. This has a direct bearing on SLL. The purpose of teaching second and foreign languages is to make communication among people and cultures possible. As teachers, we are privileged to participate in creating global understanding. Our classes are miniature copies of the contemporary world. In fact, they are more than reflections of this world and its multilingual and multicultural relations; they are a part of this real world and therefore, as teachers, we do not merely prepare our students for functioning in real world situations but already live and function in a real world situation every class session.

LANGUAGE AND DIALOGUE

There seems to be a common conceptual ground between Bakhtin and Vygotsky's understanding of language. They were both, for example, deeply interested in the social context of speech, explored language *in use*, and Bakhtin's (1975, 1981, 1984a, 1984b, 1986, 1994) interest in dialogue was matched by Vygotsky's (1960, 1978, 1986) interest in language as an inherently social process mediating among persons during their shared activity.

While insisting on this conceptual parallelism, one must clearly see the differences between the two theories. Bakhtin's point of departure and field of inquiry is primarily literature and literary text, whereas Vygotsky's is developmental psychology, especially as it relates to education. Furthermore, Bakhtin's discussion of dialogue more characteristically addressed verbal texts in both written and oral forms, whereas Vygotsky was interested in interactive activity between real interlocutors, usually in dyads or small groups. Moreover, in contrast to Bakhtin's view, Vygotsky understood oral communication as dialogical and written communication as primarily monological. "Written speech and inner speech," he wrote, "represent the monologue; oral speech, in most cases, the dialogue" (Vygotsky, 1986, p. 240). These similarities and differences should be remembered as one draws parallels between Bakhtin's and Vygotsky's ideas.

Bakhtin's theory of dialogue is the common thread that runs through his views on language, culture, and the self. Bakhtin's main philosophical theme is the dialogic relations between persons, between cultures, and between a person and culture. Morson and Emerson (1990) observed, for example, that, contrary to a widespread misconception, dialogue for Bakhtin is not simply a verbal act of interaction (p. 49). Dialogue, according to Bakhtin, is universal communication, which is the basic principle not only of culture but also of individual human existence (Gurevich, 1992, p. 90). Emerson (1997) thus commented on its meaning in Bakhtin's work:

> By dialogue, Bakhtin means more than mere talk. What interested him was
> not so much the social fact of several people exchanging words with one an-

other in a room as it was the idea that each word contains within itself diverse, discriminating, often contradictory "talking" components .... Understood in this way, dialogue becomes a model of the creative process. It assumes that the healthy growth of any consciousness depends on its continual interaction with other voices, or worldviews. (p. 36)

Far from being merely a linguistic phenomenon, dialogue is in fact a truth-generating process: "Truth is not born nor is it to be found inside the head of an individual person, it is born *between people* collectively searching for truth, in the process of their dialogic interaction" (Bakhtin, 1984a, p. 110). In other words, Bakhtin's concept of dialogue embraces at once many levels of human experience and links together the themes of consciousness, history, worldview, language, and communication.

In Bakhtin's philosophy of language, the concept of dialogue plays the most fundamental part. For him, dialogue creates the possibility of language; language emerges from dialogue and is its consequence. Language, in turn, is the essential medium of dialogue and self-formation. Emerson (2000) noted, for example, that "[Bakhtin] acknowledge[s] language as our most efficient socializing agent and repository of personality" (p. 29). Bakhtin's dialogue in the broadest sense comprises *relations* both in the sphere of culture and human consciousness (Samokhvalova, 1992, p. 191). These relations are based, in turn, on the concepts of identity and difference, of the self and the other. Bakhtin especially stressed the significant role of the "other" in linguistic consciousness.

He also emphasized three aspects of discourse, which he called "the concrete life of the word" (Bakhtin, 1984, p. 181):

Any word exists for the speaker in three aspects: as a neutral word of a language, belonging to nobody; as an *other's* word, which belongs to another person and is filled with echoes of the other's utterance, and, finally, *my* word, for, since I am dealing with it in a particular situation, with a particular speech plan, it is already imbued with my expression. (Bakhtin, 1986, p. 88)

All this makes Bakhtin's version of dialogue especially relevant for multilingual and multicultural contexts where the difference between the self and the other is not only a matter of individual idiosyncrasies but also is complicated by the linguistic and cultural divide.

Bakhtin proposed a new approach to the study of language, different from that of traditional linguistics. V. V. Ivanov (1999) observed that Bakhtin objected to all main tenets of de Saussure's (1974) theory. From Bakhtin's point of view, de Saussure's dichotomy between a unitary language (*langue*) and individual speech (*parole*) fails to capture the basic dialogical nature of language and is, therefore, misleading. Furthermore,

Ivanov pointed out, Bakhtin rejected de Saussure's understanding of a linguistic sign. Bakhtin opposed the dialogical nature of an utterance to the monological quality of linguistic signs. Bakhtin, wrote Ivanov, "was the first to discover the difference between an abstract linguistic system of signs and a concrete utterance in which each sign acquires a different function due to its role in the whole of discourse" (p. 3). Utterance is important for Bakhtin (1986) as "the real unit of speech communication" (p. 71). The dialogic and thus social nature of an utterance is obvious for him: "Our speech, that is, all our utterances [are] ... filled with the words of our others" (1986, p. 89). As speakers and writers, we do not create our own words out of nothing. We use and reuse what others have brought to us, what has been already known and said—now shaping those words differently, reflecting on them, evaluating them, and sending them further (or back) in our communication with others. Bakhtin (1981) described the dialogic structure of an utterance in the following terms:

> In the makeup of almost every utterance spoken by a social person—from a brief response in a casual dialogue to major verbal–ideological works (literary, scholarly and others)—a significant number of words can be identified that are implicitly or explicitly admitted as someone else's, and that are transmitted by a variety of different means. Within the arena of almost every utterance an intense interaction and struggle between one's own and another's word is being waged, a process in which they oppose or dialogically interanimate each other. (p. 354)

Bakhtin believed that the study of language requires an examination of questions that go beyond the usual scope of linguistics and encompass the philosophical, cultural, and ideological aspects of "language in its concrete living totality" (Bakhtin, 1984, p. 181). Furthermore, he insisted on an intimate connection between language and the living reality of a person's existence. "Every utterance makes a claim to justice, sincerity, beauty, and truthfulness (a model utterance), and so forth," he wrote. "And these values of utterances are defined not by their relation to the language (as a purely linguistic system), but by various forms of relation to reality, to the speaking subject and to other (alien) utterances (particularly to those that evaluate them as sincere, beautiful, and so forth)" (Bakhtin, 1986, p. 123). This is the genuine import of the study that he proposed to call *metalinguistics*. (Later authors changed this term to *translinguistics*; Clark & Holquist, 1984; Holquist, 1986; Todorov, 1984; Wertsch, 1991.)

The key concepts of Bakhtin's theoretical output have played an especially important part in sociocultural/sociohistoric approaches to various aspects of human experience (Holquist, 1986, 1990; Tulvister, 1991; Wells, 1999; Wertsch, 1990a, 1990b, 1991, 1997). These approaches interpret

phenomena as socially constructed, dynamic, and situated in multiple in-
terdependent contexts. The potential of Bakhtin's thought for such interpretations has already been recognized. Inspired by Bakhtin, Wertsch
(1990a) proposed the term *dialogicality* as a key concept of a sociocultural
approach to human development that seeks to explicate how mental functioning "reflects and shapes the cultural, historical, and institutional settings in which it occurs" (pp. 62–63; see also Wertsch, 1991, pp. 53–54).
This aspect of Bakhtin's thought may be fruitfully juxtaposed with
Vygotsky's.

Vygotsky is considered the founder of the cultural–historical approach to
human development. He argued that cognitive development and higher
order psychological functions are socially and culturally determined
(Vygotsky, 1978, 1986). This idea underlines the importance of intersubjective interaction in learning. Vygotsky (1978) understood language as
a sign-and-symbol system that embodies culture and thus determines consciousness and personality. "Thought development," he believed, "is determined by language, i.e., by the linguistic tools of thought and by the
sociocultural experience of the child .... The child's intellectual growth is
contingent on his mastering the social means of thought, that is, language"
(Vygotsky, 1986, p. 94). This view does not represent a contrast with
Bakhtin's, even though their terminology and frames of reference may be
different. Vygotsky viewed language as an intrinsically social phenomenon—but this means that it functions only on an interpersonal level. It is to
this that Bakhtin's emphasis on the dialogical nature of all communication
corresponds. The difference consists in the fact that, for Bakhtin (1984a),
dialogue is an ontological category ("To be," he wrote, "means to communicate" [p. 287]), whereas Vygotsky saw communication primarily in light of
his theory of psychological development and learning.

DIALOGUE OF CULTURES

The preceding discussion shows that, in Bakhtin's view, language is perme-
ated with dialogic relations on all its levels. An especially important aspect
of these relations is the interaction among participants in a dialogue that
brings out their differences. A major methodological discovery of Bakhtin
that describes the differences between participants in a dialogue is his concept of *outsideness* (1986, p. 7). This concept encapsulates the idea that in order to engage in meaningful communication one must remain distinct
from, and in a manner of speaking "outside" of, one's "other"—that is, a dialogue is possible, according to Bakhtin, only when we remain different
from our "others." Bakhtin's dialogue therefore presupposes a difference
between the interlocutors, that is, a certain distance between them. This is
what Morson and Emerson (1990) referred to when they observed that
"outsideness creates the possibility of dialogue" (p. 55). Each of the partici-

pants in a dialogue, wrote Bakhtin (1986), must retain his or her unique "self" and remain different from his or her counterparts (p. 7).

This concept was chosen by Bakhtin to reflect the need to maintain one's own identity in order to be able to speak to and to understand others precisely because there are many voices and, therefore, a multiplicity of dialogues involved in an act of communication. Bakhtin's (1986) view on this was quite explicit:

> There exists a very strong, but one-sided and thus untrustworthy, idea that in order to better understand a foreign culture, one must enter into it, forgetting one's own, and view the world through the eyes of this foreign culture .... Of course, a certain entry as a living being into a foreign culture, the possibility of seeing the world through its eyes, is a necessary part of the process of understanding it; but if this were the only aspect of this understanding, it would merely be duplication and would not entail anything new or enriching .... In order to understand, it is immensely important for the person who understands to be *located outside* the object of his or her creative understanding—in time, in space, in culture. (p. 6)

In other words, Bakhtin viewed intercultural understanding as simultaneously entering another culture and remaining outside it. The concept of outsideness allowed Bakhtin to consider intercultural dialogue in such a way that it did not threaten the identities of participating cultures. Moreover, Bakhtin viewed outsideness not as a limitation but as an incentive toward the broadening of one's perspective. Emerson (1997) commented thus on this aspect of Bakhtin's insight:

> Bakhtin ... would recommend that I not seek out people *just like myself* for the sake of security or identity. It narrows my scope and thus is too much of a risk; should I change or the environment change, I might become extinct .... Any instinctive clustering of like threatens to reduce my "I" and its potential languages to a miserable dot. Those who surround themselves with "insiders"—in heritage, experience, appearance, tastes, attitudes toward the world—are on a rigidifying and impoverishing road. In contrast, the personality that welcomes provisional finalization by a huge and diversified array of "authors" will command optimal literacy. It feels at home in a variety of zones; it has many languages at its disposal and can learn new ones without trauma. From its perspective, the world appears an invitingly open, flexible, unthreatening, and unfinalized place. (pp. 223–224)

One finds a fundamental link between the Bakhtinian outsideness, on the one hand, and the Vygotskian *zone of proximal development* (ZPD), on the other, in their shared conceptual structure. This conceptual structure can be explained as follows. Vygotsky (1978) defined the ZPD as "the distance between the actual developmental level as determined by independent problem solving and the level of potential development as determined through problem solving under adult guidance or in collaboration with more capable peers" (p. 86). He further stressed that interaction and cooperation are essential features of the ZPD (1978, p. 90). Thus, the ZPD is the developmental space where learning is dialogical. Both outsideness and ZPD involve (at least) two participants connected with each other by a process of communication or interaction. Bakhtin's dialogue presupposes a difference between the interlocutors, that is, a certain distance between them. If there is no such difference, then the interlocutors are simply identical to each other, and dialogue collapses into monologue. It is this state of the interlocutors' remaining different and unique with regard to one another that Bakhtin (1986) called *outsideness*. Similarly, participants in the learning process as described by Vygotsky's ZPD stand in the same relation to one another; that is, for learning to occur there must be a difference between them. A ZPD can exist only when the interlocutors are unequal: The expert must know more (about the subject of interaction) than the learner or novice.

Here it is appropriate to emphasize one important difference between the two thinkers. In Bakhtin's case, dialogue is a concept describing communication of equals in the sense that both or all participants have equally important things to share with one another, whereas Vygotsky addressed explicitly the interaction between the student and the teacher who cannot be seen as equal contributors to their mutual communication. At the same time, one cannot help noticing that the difference marked by Bakhtin's outsideness also implies a certain inequality between interlocutors: There is no point in communicating if they are identical in what they can share with each other. This means, in turn, that their respective levels of knowledge in the area that the dialogue addresses must be different, unequal. Be that as it may, the main thrust of Bakhtin's dialogue is toward the equality of its participants, whereas the indispensable condition of ZPD is inequality between the expert and the novice.

On a broader level, however, the parallels between their respective conceptions of culture are quite significant. Vygotsky (1978) conceived of culture as a product of social processes that are shaped by human interaction. Similarly, Bakhtin viewed culture as the product of human interaction. He was more interested, however, in the learning of other cultures as a way of enriching one's own rather than as replacing it with another culture or assimilating oneself to another culture. According to him, "a dialogic encounter of two cultures does not result in merging and mixing. Each retains his own unity and *open* totality, but they are mutually enriched" (Bakhtin, 1986, p. 7). The dialogue, he wrote, "transcends the enclosed and one-sided nature of the cultures' respective meanings" (Bakhtin, 1986, p. 508). A single culture may not notice certain things about itself, as Bakhtin pointed out, and needs another culture to underscore its peculiarities. In his view, knowledge of the one is inseparable from knowledge of the other. A person who speaks two or more languages is a bearer of two or more cultures. Such a person taps on several cultures at once, and can compare them, thus getting a deeper insight into each of them. When I learn about American culture I do become, to a certain extent, an American. This helps me to see myself, in turn, as a Russian from an American perspective. I realize things about myself that I have not realized before. I become "more Russian" through this process, "more myself," and therefore, paradoxically, even more "outside" American culture. This strange process has an intricate dialectic and may be hard to grasp in exact terms, but it is a process of enrichment and evolution rather than impoverishment and degradation of one's own cultural identity. These thoughts are in full concord with Bakhtin's (1986) view of the interaction between cultures:

> In the realm of culture, outsideness is a most powerful factor in understanding …. A meaning only reveals its depth once it has encountered … another foreign meaning …. We raise new questions for a foreign culture, ones that it did not raise itself; we seek answers to our questions in it; the foreign culture responds to us by revealing to us its new aspects and new semantic depths. (p. 7)

Moreover, in Bakhtin's view, interaction between cultures is a vital condition of their existence. "Every cultural act," he wrote, "lives essentially on the boundaries: in this is its seriousness and its significance; abstracted from boundaries, it loses its soil, it becomes empty, arrogant, it degenerates and dies" (Bakhtin, 1984a, p. 301).

For Vygotsky, too, the concept of culture was one of central concerns: He called his theory of human psychological development cultural–historical because he considered higher psychological functions as products of processes that take place in culture and history. He viewed culture from the developmental standpoint as the goal of learning: A learner's task is to make cultural values his or her own. A cultured mind, in Vygotsky's view, is one equipped with the appropriate psychological tools, first and foremost language.

SELF AND OTHER

If we now look at how Bakhtin and Vygotsky understood the formation of the self, we see that, for both of them, dialogue is the key factor in this process. Both Bakhtin and Vygotsky viewed the self in dynamic terms. In Bakhtin's work, the self is a changing entity, engaged in a dialogue. In Vygotsky's writings, the self participates in a learning process and is transformed by it. For both, the self is thus immersed in a communicative context. As noted earlier,

Bakhtin's dialogue is a universal form of human communication, and Vygotsky's learning process is a particular case of dialogue. In both cases, communication between two or more selves is the medium that forms and transforms the self. As a consequence, Bakhtin and Vygotsky view the self as open to other selves. Moreover, these other selves are active participants in the emergence of one's own self. "The role of these others," emphasized Bakhtin (1986), "for whom my thought becomes actual thought for the first time (and thus also for my own self as well) is not that of passive listeners, but of active participants in speech communication" (p. 94). In Vygotsky's model, the expert plays an even more pronounced role in the novice's formation, and the interaction between the two is the defining factor of the ZPD. Closely bound up with this interaction is the interest in how language participates in building people's identities. "Language arises initially," Vygotsky (1978) claimed, "as a means of communication between the child and the people in his environment .... [S]ubsequently, upon conversion to internal speech, it comes to organize the child's thought, that is, becomes an internal mental function" (p. 89). The concepts of language, consciousness, and communication with others are intimately intertwined in both Bakhtin's and Vygotsky's thinking. In fact, Bakhtin fully shared the idea of their mutual relatedness, expressed by Vygotsky (1986) in the climactic conclusion of his major work, *Thought and Language*:

> If language is as old as consciousness itself, and if language is a practical consciousness-for-others and, consequently, consciousness-for-myself, then not only one particular thought but all consciousness is connected with the development of the word. The word is a thing in our consciousness ... that is absolutely impossible for one person, but that becomes a reality for two .... Consciousness is reflected in a word as the sun in a drop of water .... A word is a microcosm of human consciousness. (p. 256)

There are, however, certain differences between Bakhtin and Vygotsky in how they formulated their ideas and how they understood the relations between the self and the other.

Bakhtin's understanding of the self evolved throughout his life. In his earlier work, *Art and Answerability* (1990), the self is markedly unfinalized and nondirectional; its "real centre of gravity," he wrote, "lies in the future" (p. 111). Later, in *Toward a Philosophy of the Act* (1993), he created a model of the self that is both nonsystemic and interpersonal. The unfinalized and open nature of the self reaches its apogee in Bakhtin's (1984b) study of Rabelais, where the self becomes carnivalesque. Vygotsky, on the other hand, theorized the self in a systematic way and saw it as evolving in a linear progression from one stage of maturation to another (Emerson, 2000, p. 23). Furthermore, what I mentioned earlier, in my discussion of outsideness, about the identity and difference between participants in a dialogue, applies in this context as well. Bakhtin viewed the selves engaged in a dialogue as equal to each other. For Vygotsky, by contrast, the selves that are engaged in a learning process are marked by difference: One possesses more knowledge than the other. Thus, the difference between the selves in Vygotsky's view assumes the form of unequal levels of knowledge, whereas in Bakhtin's view it is conveyed through the concept of cultural and historical difference (outsideness). By outsideness Bakhtin strove to maintain an irreducible difference between equal selves participating in a dialogue.

Bakhtin found in the musical concept of polyphony a model for the simultaneous uniqueness and equality of selves. Polyphony consists of combining different simultaneous melodies of equal interest in one composition. "Each individual 'voice' is uniquely valued and indispensable," wrote a commentator, "and as such is needed to the chorus" (Batischev, 1992, p. 125). On the other hand, however, the equality of these voices cannot be carried too far: There must be an overriding unity within a polyphonic composition. This is what Gogotishvili (1992) had in mind when she observed that absolute polyphony is impossible: "Polyphony can be realized," she remarked, "only through the monologic voice that holds it together, no matter how much this monologic voice may be weakened by other voices in the utterance" (p. 152). Furthermore, the expressly non-hierarchical relation of the selves in Bakhtin's dialogue gave rise to some relativistic interpretations of it. Bakhtin himself, however, was anything but a relativist; he wholeheartedly embraced universal humanistic values (Gogotishvili, 1992). Moreover, his reluctance to admit hierarchy and inequality into dialogue was a form of protest against the evil of Stalinism. Bakhtin was surrounded by a society that was ruled by an ideological hierarchy. Communism was the leading ideology; the Communist Party was the leading force in society and enjoyed the ultimate authority. Bakhtin understood only too well the danger of admitting hierarchical inequality in the relation between communicating selves. "A word, discourse, language or culture," he wrote, "undergoes 'dialogization' when it becomes relativized, de-privileged …. Undialogized language is authoritative or absolute" (Bakhtin, 1981, p. 427). This is why he strove to block the entrance of hierarchy into dialogue. It may weaken the theoretical possibilities of his model, but at the same time it testifies to the civic courage of the theorist.

There are certain differences between the ways in which the self emerges in Bakthin's and Vygotsky's respective models. In the course of his life, Bakhtin developed three models of the self. The first model, formulated in his early period (1919–1924), was focused on the self's ethical and creative aspects. The second model is variously called by commentators *dialogic, novelistic*, or *polyphonic*. It was created in Bakhtin's second period (1924–1930), predominantly in his work on Dostoevsky. The third model appeared at the time when Bakhtin was working on Rabelais (1930-1950) and is referred to as the *carnival* model (Emerson, 2000; Morson & Emerson, 1990). Summarizing these models, one could say that Bakhtin was interested in how the self emerges in a moral and creative act; how it manifests itself in a dialogical relation with other, equal selves; and how it rebels against the constraints imposed on it by official sociocultural hierarchies.

At the core of Bakhtin's view is the tripartite scheme of the self: (a) "I-for-myself," where the *I* is never finished, never closed, and never has a final evaluation; (b) "I-for-other," that is, the *I* as known by the other; and (c) "the other-for-me," that is, the other as known by the *I*. This scheme is closely paralleled by Vygotsky's Hegelian model of the self, which includes the *I* "in oneself," the *I* "for others," and the *I* "for oneself" (Emerson, 2000; Vygotsky, 1986). The contrast with Bakhtin consists in the fact that Vygotsky viewed the self as evolving in a progressive fashion and was primarily interested in the learning self. Nonetheless, as a particular case of dialogue, the communication that occurs in Vygotsky's ZPD necessarily presupposes a common ground, some form of identity, between its participants. In this, his model of the emergence of the self implicitly coincides with Bakhtin's emphasis on the equality of the self and the other in dialogue. Conversely, Bakhtin's outsideness marks a difference between the self and the other in dialogue and thus implicitly coincides with Vygotsky's view.

The main contrast between the respective ways in which Bakhtin and Vygotsky interpreted the formation of the self can be described as follows. For Vygotsky, the individual self is formed through the internalization of its sociocultural environment. "The true direction of the development of thinking," he claimed, "is not from the individual to the social, but from the social to the individual" (Vygotsky, 1986, p. 36). Commenting on this aspect of Vygotsky's theory, Solomadin (2000) emphasized that "in Vygotsky's understanding, 'inner speech,' or individual(ized) verbal thought—in other words, 'speech for oneself,' does not include 'the inner other'" (p. 33). Bakhtin's view is directly opposite to this idea:

> The very being of man (both external and internal) is the *deepest communion. To be* means *to communicate.* Absolute death (non-being) is the state of being unheard, unrecognized, unremembered. To be means to be for another, and through the other, for oneself. A person has no internal sovereign territory, he is wholly and always on the boundary. (Bakhtin, 1984a, p. 287)

Using Dostoevsky's characters as examples, Bakhtin strived to show how "separation, dissociation, and enclosure within the self [is] the main reason for the loss of one's self" (1984a, p. 287).

It should be noted here that the self that one finds in a second language classroom by definition emerges and exists precisely on the boundary between two languages and two cultures. If this boundary vanishes, the self becomes monolingual and monocultural and thus no longer a second language learner. The second language teacher is likewise a self produced by the boundary between languages and cultures. The value of Bakhtin's theory of the dialogic self consists in the fact that it accurately describes the realities of a second language classroom.

In sum, Bakhtin's and Vygotsky's models of the formation of the self share a partially explicit and partially implicit common content. They differ largely in the ways in which the two scholars placed emphases in their respective models within the common framework. From the point of view of language pedagogy, this common framework allows us to combine the two groups of concepts and supplement Vygotsky's pedagogical insights with the multicultural possibilities of Bakhtin's approach. At the same time, Bakhtin's ideas about dialogue as a literary phenomenon and a philosophical concept can be given a pedagogical dimension using Vygotsky's language.

UNDERSTANDING AS DIALOGUE

All the concepts associated with Bakhtin's theory of dialogue serve the purpose of elucidating the mechanism of understanding. "As Bakhtin perceives the world," remarked Emerson (1996), "outsideness, boundaries, noncoincidence, and a love for difference are the first prerequisites for creatively understanding another person or another culture, and for being creatively understood by them" (p. 110). Such a creative mutual understanding, for Bakhtin, was, in turn, an instrument of self-transformation. "The person who understands must not reject the possibility of changing or even abandoning his already prepared viewpoints and positions," he observed. "In the act of understanding, a struggle occurs that results in mutual change and enrichment" (Bakhtin, 1986, p. 142). The term *creative understanding* emphasizes the active role of a participant in a dialogue.

> Primacy belongs to the response ... it prepares the ground for an active and engaged understanding .... Understanding comes to fruition only in the response. Understanding and response are dialectically merged and mutually condition each other; one is impossible without the other. (Bakhtin, 1981, p. 282)

The concept of understanding gathers in itself language, culture, and the self, all of which are linked by the idea of dialogue. The tendency toward such a synthesis is equally characteristic of both Bakhtin and Vygotsky, but in Bakhtin's work it is brought under the umbrella of understanding. All these concepts turn out to be inextricably interconnected, and their unity culminates in understanding. Bakhtin (1986) himself eloquently expressed this idea in the following observation:

> I understand the other's word (utterance, speech work) to mean any word of any other person that is spoken or written in his own ... or in any other language, that is, any word that is *not mine*. In this sense, all words (utterances, speech, and literary works) except my own are the other's words. I live in a world of others' words and my entire life is an orientation in this world, a reaction to others' worlds (an infinitely diverse reaction), beginning with my assimilation of them (in the process of initial mastery of speech) and ending with assimilation of the wealth of human culture (expressed in the word or in other semiotic materials). The other's word sets for a person the special task of understanding this word. (p. 143)

It is quite striking how these words mirror what happens in a second language classroom. Here we deal with oral speech and written texts, students strive to master language and ideas of a different culture, and all this is undertaken for the sake of interpersonal and intercultural understanding.

CONCLUSION

The discussion in this chapter has addressed only a few Bakhtin's ideas that can be relevant to the problems of SLL. Many concepts that deserve careful study and detailed discussion have remained outside the scope of this chapter. The concepts of language, culture, and the self, however, are the cornerstones of the theoretical edifice created by Bakhtin, and a thorough grasp of them is needed in order to appreciate the significance of these other ideas.

The following thoughts suggest themselves. Bakhtin's dialogic model deeply resonates with the concerns of second and foreign language research and pedagogy. The desire for universal equality of participants in a dialogue speaks to the problems of the coexistence of languages and cultures in today's global context. The idea of intercultural dialogue has become a reality of second language classrooms. The theme of the formation of the self on the boundary between languages and cultures increasingly permeates second language learning and teaching. Second language classrooms have today become the place where intercultural understanding is built on the dynamic equilibrium of intersecting worldviews and values and where outsideness is a condition of creative understanding on the part of each participant in the dialogue.

Vygotsky's model loses none of its value either. To achieve a genuinely creative mutual understanding, individuals who wish to participate in the Bakhtinian dialogue must go through the process of learning and maturation that will make them equal to the task. Both Vygotsky and Bakhtin acknowledged the need for such evolution, which Bakhtin (1986) called "the initial mastery of speech" (p. 143). Bakhtin's model may be viewed in today's context as the goal toward which Vygotsky's model provides a path. Without this path, the Bakhtinian dialogue may forever remain a utopia. This is the sense in which the theories of the two scholars are mutually complementary and can be fruitfully combined for discussions of SLL.

REFERENCES

Bakhtin, M. M. (1975). *Voprosy literatury i estetiki* [The issues of literature and aesthetics]. Moscow: Khudozhestvennaia Literatura.
Bakhtin, M. M. (1981). *The dialogic imagination* (M. Holquist, Ed., C. Emerson & M. Holquist, Trans.). Austin: University of Texas Press.
Bakhtin, M. M. (1984a). *Problems of Dostoevsky's poetics* (C. Emerson, Ed. and Trans.). Minneapolis: University of Minnesota Press.
Bakhtin, M. M. (1984b). *Rabelais and his world* (H. Iswolsky, Trans.). Bloomington: Indiana University Press.
Bakhtin, M. M. (1986). *Speech genres and other late essays* (C. Emerson & M. Holquist, Eds.; V. McGee, Trans.). Austin: University of Texas Press.
Bakhtin, M. M. (1990). *Art and answerability: Early philosophical essays by M. M. Bakhtin* (M. Holquist & V. Liapunov, Eds., V. Liapunov, Trans.). Austin: University of Texas Press.
Bakhtin, M. M. (1993). *Toward a philosophy of the act* (V. Liapunov, Trans). Austin: University of Texas Press.
Bakhtin, M. M. (1994). *Raboty 1920-kh godov* [The works of the 1920s]. Kiev, Ukraine: Next.
Batischev, G. S. (1992). Dialog ili polifoniya? (Antitetika v filosofskom nasledii Bakhtina) [Dialogim or polyphonism? (Antithetics in philosophical legacy of Bakhtin)]. In L. Gogotishvili & P. Gurevich (Eds.), *Bakhtin kak filosof* (pp. 125–141). Moscow: Nauka.
Clark, K., & Holquist, M. (1984). *Mikhail Bakhtin*. Cambridge, MA: Harvard University Press.
Corder, S. P. (1967). The significance of learners' errors. *International Review of Applied Linguistics, 5*, 161–169.
de Saussure, F. (1974). *Course in general linguistics* (W. Baskin, Trans.). London: Fontana/Collins.
Emerson, C. (1986). The outer word and inner speech: Bakhtin, Vygotsky, and the internalization of language. In H. Daniels (Ed.), *An introduction to Vygotsky* (pp. 123–142). New York: Routledge.
Emerson, C. (1996). Keeping the self intact during the culture wars: A centennial essay for Mikhail Bakhtin. *New Literary History, 27*, 107–126.
Emerson, C. (1997). *The first hundred years of Mikhail Bakhtin*. Princeton, NJ: Princeton University Press.

Emerson, C. (2000). Bakhtin, Lotman, Vygotsky, and Lydia Ginzburg on types of selves: A tribute. In L. Engelstein & S. Sandler (Eds.), *Self and story in Russian history* (pp. 20–45). Ithaca, NY: Cornell University Press.

Firth, A., & Wagner, J. (1997). On discourse, communication, and (some) fundamental concepts in SLA research. *Modern Language Journal, 81*, 285–300.

Firth, A., & Wagner, J. (1998). SLA property: No trespassing! *Modern Language Journal, 82*, 91–94.

Gogotishvili, L. A. (1992). Filosofiya yazika Bakhtina i problema tsennostnogo relativizma [Bakhtin's philosophy of language and the problem of axiological relativism]. In L. Gogotishvili & P. Gurevich (Eds.), *Bakhtin kak filosof* (pp. 142–174). Moscow: Nauka.

Gurevich, P. S. (1992). Problema "Drugogo" v filosofskoi antropologii Bakhtina [The problem of "Other" in Bakhtin's philosophical anthropology]. In L. Gogotishvili & P. Gurevich (Eds.), *Bakhtin kak filosof* (pp. 83–96). Moscow: Nauka.

Hall, J. K. (1995). (Re)creating our worlds with words: A sociohistorical perspective of face-to-face interaction. *Applied Linguistics, 16*(2), 206–232.

Hall, J. K. (1997). A consideration of SLA as a theory of practice: A response to Firth and Wagner. *Modern Language Journal, 81*, 301–306.

Holquist, M. (1986). Answering as authoring: Mikhail Bakhtin's trans-linguistics. In G. S. Morson (Ed.), *Bakhtin: Essays and dialogues on his work* (pp. 59–71). Chicago: University of Chicago Press.

Holquist, M. (1990). *Dialogism: Bakhtin and his world.* New York: Routledge.

Ivanov, V. V. (1999, December). *Bakhtin's theory of language from the standpoint of modern linguistics.* Paper presented at the workshop "Bakhtin in Context(s)," Indiana University, Bloomington.

Kramsch, C. (Ed.). (2002). *Language acquisition and language socialization: Ecological perspectives.* New York: Continuum.

Lantolf, J. P. (Ed.). (1994). Special issue: Sociocultural theory and second language learning. *Modern Language Journal, 78*(4).

Lantolf, J. P. (Ed.). (2000). *Sociocultural theory and second language learning.* Oxford, England: Oxford University Press.

Lantolf, J. P., & Appel, G. (Eds.). (1994). *Vygotskian approaches to second language research.* Norwood, NJ: Ablex.

McKay, S., & Wong, S.-L. (1996). Multiple discourses, multiple identities: Investment and agency in second-language learning among Chinese adolescent immigrant students. *Harvard Educational Review, 66*(3), 577–608.

Morson, G. S., & Emerson, C. (1990). *Mikhail Bakhtin: Creation of a prosaics.* Stanford, CA: Stanford University Press.

Peirce, B. N. (1995). Social identity, investment, and language learning. *TESOL Quarterly, 29*(7), 9–31.

Pennycook, A. (1990). Towards a critical applied linguistics for the 1990's. *Issues in Applied Linguistics, 1*, 8–28.

Pennycook, A. (1994). *The cultural politics of English as an international language.* New York: Longman.

Phillipson, R. (1992). *Linguistic imperialism.* Oxford, England: Oxford University Press.

Rampton, B. (1995). Politics and change in research in applied linguistics. *Applied Linguistics, 16*, 233–256.

Rampton, B. (1997). A sociolinguistic perspective on L2 communication strategies. In J. Kasper & E. Kellerman (Eds.), *Communication strategies: Psycholinguistic and sociolinguistic perspectives* (pp. 279–303). London: Longman.

Samokhvalova, V. I. (1992). Soznanie kak dialogicheskoe otnoshenie [Consciousness as a dialogic relation]. In L. Gogotishvili & P. Gurevich (Eds.), *Bakhtin kak filosof* (pp. 83–96). Moscow: Nauka.

Selinker, L. (1972). Interlanguage. *International Review of Applied Linguistics, 10,* 209–231.

Solomadin, I. M. (2000). "Ya" i "drugoi" v kontseptsii Bakhtina i neklassicheskoi psikhologii Vygotskogo ["I" and "the other" in the theory of Bakhtin and nonclassical psychology of Vygotsky]. In *Dialog, karnaval, khronotop: M. M. Bakhtin v kontekste russkoi kul'tury XX veka* (pp. 28–35). Moscow: Yazyki Russkoi Kul'tury.

Todorov, T. (1984). *Mikhail Bakhtin: The dialogic principle* (W. Godzich, Trans.). Manchester, England: Manchester University Press.

Tollefson, J. (Ed.). (1995). *Power and inequality in language education.* Cambridge, England: Cambridge University Press.

Tulvister, P. (1991). *The cultural-historical development of thinking.* New York: Nova Science.

van Lier, L. (1996). *Interaction in the language curriculum: Awareness, autonomy, and authenticity.* London: Longman.

Vygotsky, L. S. (1960). *Razvitie vysshikh psikhiseskihk funktsii* [Development of higher psychological functions]. Moscow: Academy of Pedagogical Sciences, RSFSR.

Vygotsky, L. S. (1978). *Mind in society: The development of higher psychological processes* (M. Cole, V. John-Steiner, S. Scribner, and E. Souberman, Eds.). Cambridge, MA: Harvard University Press.

Vygotsky, L. S. (1986). *Thought and language* (A. Kozulin, Ed. and Trans.). Cambridge, MA: MIT Press.

Wells, G. (1999). *Dialogic inquiry: Towards a sociocultural practice and theory of education.* Cambridge, England: Cambridge University Press.

Wertsch, J. V. (1990a). Dialogue and dialogism in a socio-cultural approach to mind. In I. Markova & K. Foppa (Eds.), *The dynamics of dialogue* (pp. 62–82). New York: Springer-Verlag.

Wertsch, J. V. (1990b). The voice of rationality in a sociocultural approach to mind. In L. C. Moll (Ed.), *Vygotsky and education: Instructional implications and applications of sociohistorical psychology* (pp.111–126). Cambridge, England: Cambridge University Press.

Wertsch, J. V. (1991). *Voices of the mind: A sociocultural approach to mediated action.* Cambridge, MA: Harvard University Press.

Wertsch, J. V. (1997). *Mind as action.* New York: Oxford University Press.

Chapter 10

Dialogical Imagination of (Inter)cultural Spaces: Rethinking the Semiotic Ecology of Second Language and Literacy Learning

Alex Kostogriz
Monash University

In the last few decades, the work of Mikhail Bakhtin has gained wide dissemination in many parts of the world and has received an enormous amount of critical attention. In particular, his philosophy of language has spread to numerous fields of sociological inquiry, including current research into language and literacy education. The impact of his ideas on the research and pedagogy of second and foreign language, however, has been more gradual. One reason for this is that the field of second language acquisition is still predominantly informed by structural linguistics and cognitive psychology, focusing on the study of self-consistent systems of language and the workings of individual minds. Even though these studies contribute to the construction of second language acquisition as a discipline in its own right, a dominant positivistic approach underlying them obscures what it means to teach and learn a second language in the contemporary world: a world characterized not only by great sociocultural and linguistic heterogeneity but also by cultural domination, assimilation, and xenophobia. In this respect, Bakhtin's commitment to the profoundly social nature of language and consciousness, to the dialogical dynamism of cultural–semiotic life, to the recognition of the plurality of voices, and to the coexistence of differences offers fertile ground for researchers and practitioners who seek to make sense of second language and literacy learning in multicultural societies and classrooms. In this chapter, then, I endeavor to explore the relevance of Bakhtinian ideas for a socially critical approach to English-as-a-second-language (ESL) education, especially in current conditions when conservative and liberal notions of cultural diversity and difference claim to provide final vocabularies for adjudicating tensions in multicultural societies.

Conservative politicians discussing the funding of ESL education in major immigrant-receiving countries have historically followed an assimilationist and then integrationist agenda rooted in the cultural politics of maintaining the vision and practice of a single unified culture. The primary project of these agendas has been the acculturation of migrants to the cultural–linguistic capital of the dominant culture. ESL has been seen by the governments of these countries as one of the most influential means of propelling assimilation and normalization of cultural and linguistic difference within the broader politics of order-through-domination and unity-through-incorporation (Pennycook, 2001; Phillipson, 1992; Tollefson, 1995; Toohey, 2000). In spite of the insistence that schools are neutral and democratic institutions, a conservative power in governments has traditionally maintained the need for an ideologically charged mission of ESL in weaving the idea of a monolingual common culture into the fabric of public education. As a result, the roles of ESL programs have often been aligned with the construction of homogenizing cultural representations and have played a distinctive social role in shaping the subjectivities of culturally different students. This traditional view of the role of ESL education can thus be conceived as fundamentally nested within the broader production of a monosemic and unitary cultural space, in broad society and in schools, focused on the promotion of a common cultural literacy (Macedo, 2000).

The rationale behind the concept of cultural literacy proposed by Hirsch (1987, 1999) and the pedagogical model it informs lie precisely in the acquisition of unexamined, canonized, and universally shared information, seen as necessary for all competent speakers, readers, and writers to function effectively in society. In this view of literacy, the knowledge of canonical texts and information is a "ticket to full citizenship" or "one's membership card" to mainstream culture—"*the* basic culture of the nation" (Hirsch, 1987, p. 22). The transmission of canonical literacy in schools is then believed to play a key role in ensuring national development and communication among a diverse population divided by ethnic, political, and social differences. But the other side of the cultural literacy coin also implies the unconditional assimilation of ethnic and linguistic minorities to dominant cultural codes. In this view, there is no need for multicultural education because, as Hirsch (1987, p. 21) argued, it interferes with the primary focus of national education and schools' responsibility to ensure the children's mastery of the common cultural literacy—that is, the literacy canon of "the most democratic culture." Such a program of cultural literacy for a diverse populace therefore subjugates other cultural knowledge(s) in a rather undemocratic way and maintains existing inequalities. This presents one of the main hurdles for putting into practice an ESL pedagogy that recognizes and values literacies and knowledge(s) of the "Other"—a pedagogy that is needed in a society constantly evolving in a multiplicity of social forms and cultural practices.

At the same time, it is no less important to identify the ethnocentric blind spots and voluntaristic rhetoric in what were regarded as the most radical (liberal) critique of mainstream models of migrant and minority students' education. Although in general liberalism opposes the mystical essentialism of domination by saying that no culture, language, religion, or tradition is superior to any other, some liberals attempt to manage the crisis of cultural universalism through the politics of difference. In doing so, they construct establishment (celebratory) pluralism in which the Other is seen through a positivistic grid of static and discrete ethnic identities. This position is backgrounded in so-called "scientific culturalism" (McConaghy, 2000) that essentializes racial or ethnic binary oppositions. It describes minority groups as having ways of thinking, learning, and perceiving the world that are radically different from the mainstream. The diversity of cultural forms is seen as a natural condition of cultural existence rather than as the effect of an enunciation of difference that constitutes asymmetries of power in interethnic relations (Luke & Luke, 1999). As a result, such a vision of multiculturalism is complicit with the nationalist project of late capitalism that objectifies and reduces the Other to the "particular ethnic Thing" (Zizek, 1997, p. 43).

This celebration of the autonomy and uniqueness of local cultures and of minority and immigrant identities by liberals reinscribes patronizing attitudes to difference, treating "each local culture the way the colonizer treats colonized people—as 'natives' whose mores are to be carefully studied and 'respected'" (Zizek, 1997, p. 44). As Hall (1992) and Pennycook (2001) have observed, this multicultural strategy of the convenient Other-ing and exoticization of ethnicity merely confirms and stabilizes the hegemonic cultural order by naming the Other as marginal or peripheral to the mainstream. Because liberals celebrate cultural pluralism by essentializing the Other and by promulgating the myth of "equal opportunities," they also fail to see "the power-grounded relationships among identity construction, cultural representations, and struggles over resources" (Kincheloe & Steinberg, 1997). Neither the totalizing power of a dominant culture nor the educational governmentality of a nation–state can be underestimated or wished away through a mere celebration of the local embrace.

In general, then, neither a conservative nor a contradictory liberal model of multiculturalism is able to provide a feasible solution for language and literacy pedagogy in classroom communities of difference. It is clear that such communities of learners, characterized by a plurality of voices and meaning-making possibilities, can not be simply fused into a single or dominant consciousness without repressive silencing or marginalization of the Other. Undermining the polyphonic potential of multicultural classrooms in striving for a more just democratic society is exactly the main contradiction that needs to be addressed in the current climate of explicit cultural–linguistic coercion and political myopia inherent respectively in the traditional conservative and liberal frameworks of language and literacy education. Hence, the shift from the ESL pedagogy of cultural assimilation to the pedagogy of multiculturalism—as the coexistence of differences—is hardly possible without determining those relations of domination and subordination, incorporation and resistance that are at play in conditions of cultural complexity. Neither form of modern ethnic absolutism, both seeking cultural purity and root identity, is able to focus on multiple disjunctures and conjunctions that emerge not in fixed cultural places but in the dynamics of border-crossing events and semiotic exchanges, in radically local experiences and in human mobility.

To address these issues in ESL education, we need a theory (a knowledge) of the production of cultural–semiotic and intellectual spaces in multicultural conditions, one that injects a third dimension into thinking about the possibility of crossing, erasure, and "translation" of the boundaries in the cultural construction of identities and textual meanings. How can Bakhtin help us forge a socially critical approach that goes both beyond the politics of cultural–linguistic dogmatism and the politics of partial and asymmetrical recognition of monadic identities of ESL learners? How might the Bakhtinian conceptualization of dialogism and cultural–linguistic hybridity help us analyze the unsettling nature of second language learning and inform us how to learn and, in general, to live with difference?

It is important to point out that Bakhtin's conceptual heritage is rather particular in that it allows for a plurality of connotations and application (Brandist, 2002). The concept of "dialogue," for instance, not only has been used in numerous philosophical, linguistic, and cultural studies but has also received a variety of readings by the most diverse ideological currents, ranging from neo-liberal to more radical and critical interpretations. In what follows I explore the production of cultural spaces as semiotic environments for language use and literacy practices by drawing on the work of Bakhtin and Lotman. In the first instance, the concept of dialogue will be used as a basic unit of intra- and intercultural communication, encapsulating the need for the Other as a means of self-definition as well as the need for a cultural outside against which the semiotic practices of the inside can be defined as meaningful. Following that, dialogue is used as a critical tool, pertaining not only to how cultural–semiotic boundaries are produced to translate the foreign but also to how those boundaries become transgressed by cultural texts of the Other, unsettling the monologism of dominant texts and practices. The concept of dialogue is, in this way, inseparable first from the struggle against the cultural and linguistic centripetalism and for the recognition of difference and multiplicity, and, second, the living dialogical plurality of recognized cultural and linguistic differences is tantamount to the production of Thirdspace—a space in between self and the Other—in which new meanings and identities are dynamically constructed. In this critical mode, dialogue can be conceived as a condition for transcultural and translinguistic innovation that is inseparable from "the project of restoring freedom, multiplicity, democracy, expression" (Gurevitch, 2001, p. 88). Finally, I apply the Bakhtinian vision of dialogical life to explore the possibilities of what I call *Thirdspace pedagogy for ESL literacy education*, as an attempt to challenge dichotomizing tendencies in thinking about ESL learners, with the aim of locating their literacy learning in the borderland or on the fault line between cultures.

THE DIALOGICAL PRODUCTION OF INTERCULTURAL SPACE

It might be helpful to commence rethinking of current cultural and language politics in multicultural states by drawing on the Bakhtinian understanding of dialogue. For Bakhtin, dialogue is not just a mode of interaction but rather a way of communal existence in which people establish a multifaceted relationship of mutual interdependence. Yet this social unity is not a homogeneous cultural–semiotic space that is reducible to single authoritarian consciousness; it is conceived of in *ecological* terms as the "coexistence of socio-ideological contradictions between the present and the past, between different socio-ideological groups in the present, between tendencies, schools, circles, and so forth, all given a bodily form" (Bakhtin, 1981, p. 291). In this ecological model of social life, the polyphonic opposition of differences becomes a source of openness and "incompleteness" of cultural identities, leading to the productive enrichment of semiotic resources and enhancing possibilities in meaning-making.

Thinking along these lines, Bakhtin (1984, p. 293) argued that dialogue is a mode of "authentic human existence" that is central both to the sociohistorical emergence of consciousness and to the production of cultural–semiotic space. From a macrohistorical perspective, to live means to engage in dialogical relations and semiotic exchanges within the human and nonhuman world. It is within this complex material–semiotic unity of the dialogic that human consciousness emerges as a distinct force. Bakhtin explained this in spatial–ecological terms as the production of the intelligent living environment in which the human consciousness of "supra-I" affirms its social agency to know, judge, and change the world. At the same time, however, this "supra- I" is "someone who is no longer the person, no longer the I, but the other" (Bakhtin, 1986, p. 137). Thus, attributing the source of living energy to dialogical events, Bakhtin argued that developments in consciousness and self-awareness, the production of thought—like the production of being—can take place only through contact with an Other. Just as life forms in nature provide the modes of Otherness for humans to understand their own distinctive life form, so too do different cultures, cultural groups, or individuals require the Other to understand their particular identities.

On the microhistorical level of speech events, to be in a dialogue with the Other would mean to the individual consciousness getting out of itself and, in the space of "outsidedness," meeting another consciousness (Bakhtin, 1986). The space between self and the Other becomes a space of in-between-ness produced by the very act of inner distancing and pushing "one's consciousness to the limit of Otherness in order to meet the external, 'alien' Other" (Gurevitch, 2001, p. 90). This interaction is binary, asymmetrical and, at the same time, unitary.

If we conceive of self-distancing in a dialectical way as a tension between opposites, there are two possible outcomes. At one extreme, the self might project his or her own cultural space onto the Other, attempting to erase difference either by misrecognition or by repression. Bakhtin (1984, p. 292) identified this as an extreme form of monologism that "denies the existence outside itself of another consciousness with equal rights and equal responsibilities"—that is, another *I* with equal rights. In its pure form, the monological approach perceives the Other as an object of rational contemplation that does not have any particular value and hence does not require recognition as being unique. At the other extreme, the self may become so bestowed with the Other that his or her identity is in danger of negation. This form of self-negation, according to Bakhtin (1986), provides a possibility for understanding the foreign Other by seeing its culture through its eyes; "but if this were the only aspect of this understanding, it would merely be a duplication and would not entail anything new or enriching" (p. 7). Therefore, Bakhtin rejected the dialectics of extremes that implies a win-or-lose scenario, arguing for a shift from binarism to multiplicity as a dialogical coexistence of differences. This shift is a political strategy for overcoming the binary logic of self- and other-centeredness and is a necessary step for restoring the dialogical unity of polyphonic voices on the border between self and Other. In this sense, outsidedness becomes tantamount to being on the border where no one has an exclusive right to articulate the final meaning.

For Bakhtin, being outside of one's self is not something that occurs from time to time; rather, it is an everyday experience of participation in the dialogical events. In this treatment of the dialogic, the borderline experience is an inseparable feature of cobeing in which the only way to understand oneself is to look into, and with the eyes of, the Other. However, to live on the border does not mean losing one's individuality but rather reconstructing oneself and articulating new meanings. Therefore, with regard to intercultural encounters, Bakhtin (1986) argued:

> In the realm of culture, outsidedness is a most powerful factor in understanding. It is only in the eyes of another culture that foreign culture reveals itself fully and profoundly ... A meaning only reveals its depths once it has encountered and come into contact with another, foreign meaning; they engage in a kind of dialogue which surmounts the closedness and one-sidedness of these particular meanings, these cultures. (p. 7)

Participation in such an intercultural dialogue, then, implies the shift from fixed cultural meanings and toward the open space of in-between-ness in which the very fact of being located outside of monadic cultures and identities may result in the "surplus of vision" and creative understanding of both the self and the Other. Consequently, the border between self and the Other becomes a Thirdspace: a third category for understanding cultural dynamics as a process of creative hybridization.

Illustrative of this argument is a study by Harklau (1999), in which she analyzed how ESL students in their writing challenge practices that enforce foreignness and polarize cultural identities. She observed that in many topics of ESL writing instruction, some teachers tend to dichotomize cultural perspectives as mutually exclusive. By offering comparative–contrastive topics for reflective writing about things in "your/their" country and "our" country, these teachers expect ESL students to emphasize their essentialized difference. Although this desire for "perpetual foreignness" reflects the broader politics of identity, ESL learners experience a sort of cultural schizophrenia by having lived in, experienced, and identified themselves with two (or more) cultures. They reject stereotypes held about "their" country and their essentialized identities and take a position of in-between-ness.

In Harklau's (1999, p.119) study, a student from Vietnam, responding to the prompt "Are blue jeans popular in your country?", wrote, "Blue jeans are very popular in *my* own country and around the world. *They* wear it like *we* [wear] it in the United States" [italics added]. The ambivalent position of double identification with one's "own" (Vietnamese) culture and with "our" (American) culture leads to maintaining many different identities through which migrant students are able to express their resistance to the cultural politics that engulfs them. According to Said (1993), this is a marker of border-crossing innovation, transgressive intertextuality, and mobile textual self-fashioning. In writing on cultural topics, ESL students are constantly facing the dilemma of crossing linguistic and cultural boundaries, the dilemma of identity reconstruction, the dilemma of undecidability and choice actualized through a "politics of the local" (Hall, 1990). The hybridization of ESL learners' cultural identities in literacy practices is a response to the asymmetrical relations of power that they face. Also, hybridity itself represents a specific domain of semiotic power: "the transgressive power of symbolic hybrids to subvert categorical oppositions and hence to create the conditions for cultural reflexivity and change" (Werbner, 1997, p. 1). This brings up an important aspect: a concept of *dynamic* culture, which might be helpful both in problematizing the concept of static culture, as a common denominator for those who live within it, and in understanding cultural change and transformation on the larger scale, as the production of new meanings and cultural spaces.

A powerful counternarrative of a dynamic culture comes from the work of Yuri Lotman (1990), who offered an ecological vision of linguistic and textual processes in culture, defining its semiotic space as the *semiosphere*. The concept of the semiosphere can be understood as a living space of cultural semiosis or as an ecosystem of semiotic production and consumption characterized by a plenitude of linguistic and nonlinguistic resources for meaning-making. The semiosphere is a deeply postformalist notion in that Lotman tries to escape the gridlock of traditional structuralism by putting the Bakhtinian concept of dialogicality at the center. He argues that the tendency toward cultural uniformity is opposed by the tendency toward cultural "polyglotism." Because of the tension between these two forces, cultural conventions are historically disrupted in a dialogical communication with the Other, leading to the emergence of new meanings and, consequently, to new, unpredictable directions in cultural development.

The production of new meanings occurs on the boundaries between us and them, self and other, our culture and foreign culture. According to Lotman (1990), the external boundary of cultural semiotics separates our "own" space, which is safe and ordered, from "their" space, which is hostile and chaotic. Besides this function of ordering and organizing reality, the boundary is also the bilingual mechanism that translates external messages into the internal language of the semiosphere, and vice versa. Yet the boundary translation between "us" and "them" is *not* a perfect assimilation of difference but rather results in approximate equivalences, or new hybrid semantic connections and meanings. In this function, the boundary determines both the internal mechanism of textual production and the mechanism of translation through which the semiosphere of a culture can be in contact with other, alien cultural spaces.

The same basic boundary division occurs also *within* the semiotic sphere of a particular culture and reflects its asymmetrical nature, or the "bipolar asymmetry" (Lotman, 1990). The semiosphere has a center surrounded by increasingly amorphous areas moving in the direction of the periphery. If the center contains dominant sign systems that include sign users, texts, and codes that are elaborately organized, the periphery, on the other hand, is characterized by heterogeneity and fragmentation and is responsible for dynamics within the semiosphere of culture. However, the conception of the center and the periphery, in Lotman's (1990) words, is just a rough primary distinction:

> In fact, the entire space of the semiosphere is transected by boundaries of different levels, boundaries of different languages and even of texts, and the internal space of each of these sub-semiospheres has its own semiotic "I" which is realised as the relationship of any language, groups of texts, or separate texts, to a metastructural space which describes them, always bearing in mind that languages and texts are hierarchically disposed on different levels ... [creating] a multi-level system. (p. 138)

Lotman's perspective on cultural semiotics presupposes the presence of a center or origin in the play of signification, but he tends toward a poststructural conception by exploring relations between multiple centers and margins. Therefore, the fundamental culturally perceived differences and oppositions, such as native–foreign, high–low, left–right, white–black, good–evil, town/center–countryside/periphery, male–female, normal–abnormal, and so on, perforate the semiosphere by creating multiple inner boundaries that specify its regions (subsemiospheres). The play of signification and translation across those borders leads to the semiotic "irruption" of texts and signs into an alien territory and ultimately to the transformation and emergence of new meanings.

Lotman's (1990) speculations on translation and intersemiosis present the boundary as the semiotic and political "hot spot." The tension between us and them, inside and outside, is most evident at the boundaries. This tension maintains the semiosphere in a state of "creative ferment" and conflict, both separating and blending languages, genres, texts, and cultures. The boundaries of the semiosphere are sites of semiotic creativity that is facilitated by the flow of texts and the sociocultural dynamics of people. On the one hand, the notion of semiotic motion within and across the semiosphere of a culture cleaves open its hegemonic political discourse within the bounded notion of cultural space, mapping the turbulent patterns of "bilingual translation." In the process of intersemiosis between center(s) and margin(s), as well as in translation between "own" and "foreign," the authority of central discourses is constantly undermined and dispersed, shifting official meanings by the very process of being translated. On the other hand, the process of semiotic border-crossing for the marginal and the foreign involves the dialogical affirmation of identity. Yet this identity is neither immutable nor primordial. A tension between socially constructed differences results in a dialogical indeterminacy of identity that opens up a process of cultural–semiotic hybridization.

In sum, Bakhtin and Lotman understand *culture* not as a noun but rather as a verb, foregrounding the dynamics of cultural practices and identities between and across constructed and imagined boundaries. The dialogical principle of intra- and intercultural interaction emphasizes those processes that occur on the boundaries between the self and the Other or between cultural–semiotic spaces, resulting in the production of Thirdness—new texts, meanings, and identities. This phenomenon of hybridization, which is crucial for Bakhtin, Lotman and others, is often excluded from or bypassed in the political discourse of multicultural states. It is traditionally seen as a transitional stage *en route* to complete cultural assimilation. However, for Bakhtin and Lotman hybridity is neither a form of inferiority nor a transitional state but a mode of cultural–semiotic development itself. It is a contestatory energy that exists at and in between cultural boundaries and is, in fact, a source of productive cultural creativity and new meaning-making possibilities.

SEMIOTIC LANDSCAPING, DIASPORA, AND HYBRID LITERACIES

Bakhtin's concept of dialogicality and Lotman's analysis of the production of semiotic space are fundamentally important in understanding how the Other is (mis)recognized in the heated debates about immigration and the education of minority students. Through such spatial–semiotic markers as "high" and "low," "inside" and "outside," "center" and "periphery," "us" and "them," and so on, people not only make sense of themselves and of cultural spaces in which they live but also deploy these discursive topologies to construct a communal space that would be a permanent source of protection from fears of insecurity, isolation, estrangement, and the intrusion of aliens. In turn, this reifies a politics of difference that favors "us" (identities, meanings, and practices of the "inside") while marginalizing and excluding "them" (practices, meanings, and identities of the "outside"). Obviously, in the production of cultural–semiotic spaces and political locations, identities and meanings become consolidated and generalized. As Artiles (2000) argued, *us* comes to define a particular collective identity: homogeneous, hard-working, speaking proper English. In contrast, the individuals who comprise *them* are lazy, dirty, heterogeneous, misuse English, and take advantage of the welfare system.

Operating within the bipolar asymmetry of "us" and "them," the dominant "inside" identifies the Other—newcomers, strangers, and immigrants—as a lower category, threatening the cultural–linguistic canon and hence as something that requires disciplining and assimilation. The semiotic production of spaces of difference is directly related to those discourses in which difference is constructed and its presence is organized. The first step in this process, according to Bauman (1997), is the invention of the disruptive Other who does not fit into the linguistic, cognitive, moral, and aesthetic spaces of the dominant culture:

> By their sheer presence, [strangers] make obscure what ought to be transparent, confuse what ought to be a straightforward recipe for action, and/or prevent the satisfaction from being fully satisfying, pollute the joy with anxiety while making the forbidden fruit alluring; ... they befog and eclipse the boundary lines which ought to be clearly seen; if, having done all this, they gestate uncertainty, which in its turn breeds the discomfort of feeling lost—then each society produces such strangers. (p. 46)

The next issue becomes what to do with these strangers to make cultural–semiotic spaces orderly and meaningful again.

The reaction of the cultural "inside" to the presence of the Other results, as a rule, in broad semiotic landscaping involving, among others, political and educational initiatives that are directed at making the different similar. This can be seen in the persistent and historically recurrent efforts of the "inside" to produce cultural literacy crises, leading consequently to the actions that reduce the linguistic vitality of minority groups and diasporas. Semiotic landscaping includes language and literacy planning as one of its most important constitutive parts. Initiatives such as the English-only movement and the Hirschian model of cultural literacy in the United States, the move toward mainstreaming of ESL support after the Swann Report in the United Kingdom, and the phasing out of long-established bilingual programs for Aboriginal students in the Northern Territory of Australia are just some examples representative of the interplay between the broader Anglo-fundamentalist politics of assimilation and educational reforms intended to implement this agenda. In this process, linguistic standards are legitimized and commodified so that "language determines who has access to political power and economic resources" (Tollefson, 1991, p. 16). That is, language and literacy planning not only establishes the semiotic hegemony of the "inside" but also consolidates the cultural–linguistic deficit of the Other, both creating and perpetuating inequality.

When large-scale semiotic landscaping demands that all people in a multicultural state share a common language and literacy as "emblems of distinctiveness and national cultural identity" (Lo Bianco, 2000, p. 93), there is an inevitable tension. So, as we witness the implementation of assimilative language and literacy politics, there emerges a countertendency to revitalize efforts to sustain linguistic diversity. The logic of this process has made multiculturalism, polycentricity, and semiotic multimodality central to a critical rethinking of monolithic cultural–linguistic spaces. According to Soja (1999), the process of the social production of material–semiotic spatiality is a historical phenomenon that replicates the (re)distribution of power. Therefore, regional–geographic and local social and ethnic fragmentation is a political process aimed at creating oppositional semiotic spaces in which the vitality of multiple sociocultural identities is sustained through local literacies, social languages, and other cultural practices.

As Lave and Wenger (1991) argued, local communities of practice, to which we can add ethnic, aboriginal, and migrant communities, occur in coercive environments. The discourses of local practices are in many ways responses to that coercion. For instance, language and literacy practices in local socioethnic communities run parallel to the totalizing programs of language and literacy development in schools and broader society and are tools for the collective contestation and redefinition of meanings. Maintaining loyalties to their homelands helps migrants in collectively overcoming feelings of alienation, exclusion, marginalization, or other kinds of "difference."

There is ample evidence of diaspora members seeking to establish a legitimate place in new cultural spaces, largely through sustaining the vitality of their language, literate, religious, and other practices. Barker et al. (2001, p. 8) defined the parameters of linguistic vitality according to the degree to which the first language is used in everyday communicative and textual practices, as well as in the "external" means of communication, such as media, public signs and symbols, billboards, street names, mail advertising, government information, and so on. Through these diasporic strategies immigrants attempt to raise themselves to a position of sociocultural competitiveness. The native linguistic and cultural literacy vitality of migrants then becomes a matter of political activity for rights, status, and power. Hence, the semiotic exchange between diaspora and center is based on the semiotic vitality of the former and the controlling politics of the latter. Although the analysis of both polarities concentrates on essential features of cultural semiosis within their respective boundaries, Bakhtin and Lotman invite us to look beyond such identifications.

Their view of intercultural communication represents a turning point in the studies of language and literacy practices from a perspective of semiotic ecology, emphasizing that after a collision of differences (i.e., in semiotic exchanges between asymmetrical polarities), neither opposite remains the same. With regard to migrant and minority communities, the semiotic ecology of their language and literacy practices is formed not only in competitive cultural–semiotic locations but also in sociocultural dynamics, inevitably involving dis-location and border-crossing. Whether we consider the household and family literacy practices of immigrants or their religious and workplace textual practices, diasporic boundaries are constantly transgressed. It is obvious, then, that a diasporic space is a new sphere of semiotic practice which, because of its dialogical nature in intercultural communication and translation, involves a strategy of radical cultural creativity and hybridization. The unique practices of hybridization can be observed most vividly in the communicative and textual events. These practices represent a more subtle and tactical deployment of racial, ethnic, and linguistic categories of identification.

According to Modood, Beishon, and Virdee (1994), transgressing a diasporic boundary of cultural practice (e.g., a religious practice of a diaspora) signals a growing split between older and younger generations as well as tension between the collectivist and individualized forms of ethnic representations. Similarly, Baumann (1997) defined this process as the discursive praxis of negotiation between the *dominant* and *demotic* discourses of the diaspora. In his ethnographic study of a multi-ethnic urban neighborhood in West London, Baumann analyzed how residents deploy both the dominant discourses of the diaspora that reify a homologous ethnic identity and the demotic discourses that dissolve this equation of "community," "culture," and ethnicity. As a result, the South Asians in his study created a hybrid popular culture by fusing their identities. They intentionally subverted the normative boundaries of the diaspora set by their parents. However, on public occasions the same people reverted from the demotic discourses back to the dominant when there was an alien threat to the reifying discourse of community leaders.

Thus, the cultural–semiotic practices of a diaspora are negotiated by individuals "within, about and across their 'ethnic' identifications" (Baumann, 1997, p. 222). Just as identifications shift contextually on the nexus host culture–diaspora–country of origin, hybrid identities develop a dual discursive competence that allows them to participate in a variety of cultural–semiotic practices. It is not surprising, therefore, that the syncretization of cultural literacies is a complex problem with regard to ESL learners' intercultural becoming.

Solsken, Willet, and Wilson-Keenan's (2000) study unveils the relevance of hybridity to culturally responsive literacy education that seeks to make school practices more congruent with the home and community practices of minority children. Through the microanalysis of the oral and written texts constructed by a Latina student, Solsken et al. showed how the intermingling of home, school, and peer language practices serves a variety of sociocultural agendas. First and foremost, textual hybridization is connected to the construction of this girl's multiple identities: as a good student and literate member of the classroom community, by taking up the semiotic resources of classroom literacy practices; as a loving member of her family, by drawing on her family/community semiotic resources; as a respected member of the peer group, by taking up the semiotic practices of children; and, to support the social cohesion of the group, by bridging the topics and genres of others, that is, by intertextual hybridity.

However, Solsken et al. (2000) observed that conventional views of literacy do not leave space to acknowledge or appreciate the richness and complexity of hybrid textual constructions. The girl's semiotic creativity, based on the syncretism of family stories and a variety of other practices, went largely unnoticed. Because her stories failed to approximate the conventional genres privileged in school, the girl was seen as a literacy-deficient student. In contrast, in bringing a culturally responsive perspective to the student's participation in literacy events, these researchers were able to give an alternative vision of her literacy development. With a focus on meaning-making dynamics, rather than on textual form, she can be conceived of as an achieving, capable, and creative student. Thus, a culturally responsive perspective on the textual hybridity of migrant and minority students has a direct connection to critical perspectives on language and literacy education that see in hybridity the potential to transform the knowledge, texts, and identities of the mainstream curriculum.

TOWARD A PEDAGOGY OF THIRDSPACE

Given the dialogical process of cultural–semiotic spaces, the dynamic nature of border-crossing, and the hybridization of literacy practices by minority and migrant students, there is a need to formulate a Thirdspace perspective on ESL literacy education. This perspective originates from a sociocultural view of literacy as literacies, that is, different ways with texts within different sociocultural practices (Gee, 2001). However, by emphasizing differences between situated practices mediated by texts, the sociocultural approach does not attempt to produce yet another divide in literacy studies. Because different literacies sit in different relations of power, there is a great deal of mutual interpellation, ranging from the relations of complementation and adaptation to those of assimilation and opposition. Examples of such interpellations have been documented in the ethnographic studies of interaction between school literacy and literacy practices in different communities (e.g., Barton, Hamilton, & Ivanic, 2000).

There is no denial that a particular literacy practice can be re-enacted without obvious transformative changes across the relatively large time scales of history. The reproduction of linguistic and textual practices is due to the censorship of a community, the enculturation of newcomers to particular practice and text types, and the process of ongoing "autcommunication" within communal boundaries (Lotman, 1990). Yet communities of practice not only are in contact with other communities but also become "populated" by strangers and newcomers, "bombarded" by alien texts, or "invaded" by new technologies and discourses. One way or another, literacy events involve not only reproductive but also productive–transformative activities, resulting from intersemiosis. This feature is observable in those literacy events in which two (or more) literacy practices are interdiscursively and intertextually networked, generating "borderland Discourse" (Gee, 1996) and hence organic (unconscious) and dialogic (intentional) forms of semiotic hybridity (Bakhtin, 1968). These new hybrid discourses can be recognized as productive or as threatening, depending on the philosophy of a community—its constructed image, practice patterns and social goals, and the degree of its openness to difference and change.

Both neo-conservative and neo-liberal policymakers and educators have embraced the image of contemporary classrooms as communities. For the former, such an image provides the ideological basis for designing homogenous literacy learning environments; it is then easier to imagine what those communities need to know year by year. For the latter, this image provides an opportunity to organize chairs in a circle and to learn more about cultural differences and their attending values. Yet it soon appears that the cultural resources of the Other fall outside the knowledge and values of the dominant groups, on the basis of which curricula are designed. Thus, while recognizing that classroom communities will remain to a large extent imagined, a Thirdspace pedagogy of ESL literacy endeavors to reimagine them in a dialogical way as multivoiced collectives whose literacy learning is related to the practices, discourses, and "funds of knowledge" of other sociocultural communities (Moll, 2000).

Taking into account the implications of the Bakhtinian concept of dialogicality and Lotman's view of cultural–semiotic spatiality for literacy education, the challenge for second language researchers and practitioners is to develop a *critical pedagogy of space*, which would take into account both the multiple and contested nature of literacy learning in multicultural classrooms and intercultural innovations in meaning- and identity-making. This is needed not only to deconstruct the politics of assimilative language and literacy education but also to construct a practical Thirdspace alternative, overcoming a closed logic of cultural binarism that dominates current discourses in education. As Lotman (1990) and others (e.g. Bhabha, 1994; Foucault, 1986; Soja, 1996) have recognized, a parallel can be drawn between the production of discourse and the use of space. The discourses that are drawn on, built, and sustained in the course and context of literacy work are directly related to the social configuration of pedagogic space—that is, the way material artifacts, textual resources, students, and their activities are organized. Overcoming ethnocentric discourses and the exclusion of cultural–semiotic resources of the Other in the production of pedagogic space becomes then an essential part of (re)designing learning environments from a Thirdspace perspective.

Thirdspace pedagogy is informed by the practice of critical literacy, seeking to ameliorate educational disadvantage, promote social justice in and through education, and pursue democratic principles in a practical–pedagogic project of possibility, with regard to social transformation and change (Green & Kostogriz, 2002). Hence, the starting point of Thirdspace literacy education is the recognition of any learning environment as the heteroglossic space of struggle over meaning, a complex and contested arena in which numerous voices compete. This Bakhtinian position encourages a critical quest for culturally responsive practices in second language literacy education, those that would stress the incompleteness of our sense of self in communication with the Other and produce a mutual recognition of cultural difference. Such an intercultural dialogue would enable creation of a new pedagogic space in which the boundary between the dominant and the marginal is transgressed and differences are recognized as mutually enriching, by rejecting any form of ethnocentrism and exclusion and encouraging multicultural rhetoric and transformative learning.

Promoting learning and meaning-making through the recognition of cultural–semiotic differences requires a (re)design of the pedagogic space. This can be done by addressing three broad dimensions in the organization of literacy learning environment: the (a) *material-semiotic*, (b) *intellectual*, and (c) *discursive* spheres of classroom practices.

The material–semiotic sphere of Thirdspace pedagogy refers to the construction of second language learning environments through cultural–semiotic artifacts. Because the cultural resources of the Other in most cases fall outside the knowledge and values of the dominant groups, traditional ESL curricula authorize mainstream material–semiotic artifacts as a means of teaching, devaluing, or ignoring the importance of minority students' resources in literacy learning. This can result in the construction of learning environments that are enabling for some students and disabling for others. Therefore, by putting emphasis on the crucial role of cultural "tools" in learning (Vygotsky, 1978), the Thirdspace perspective on second language literacy calls for dramatic changes in the ways in which literacy learning is organized in multicultural classrooms.

First and foremost, the task of educators and policymakers should be to make cultural–semiotic diversity a resource rather than a liability (Gutiérrez, 2000). Literacy instruction practices that restrict students from using multiple semiotic resources (including their home and community resources) have negative social *and* cognitive consequences for second language learners (Cole, 1998). By contrast, the incorporation of the primary resources of migrant and minority students within the learning activities of a classroom will help mediate students' relationship to their cultural worlds by connecting classroom literacy learning to multiple textual practices and bodies of knowledge. High-quality literacy learning, from a Thirdspace perspective, is possible only in *semiotically rich* learning environments in which a classroom community of difference uses multiple mediating tools and makes use of all the social, cultural, and linguistic resources of its participants (Gutiérrez, 2000).

Furthermore, if we are to create rich learning environments that give minority students more (or equal) opportunities for participation, then those environments must also be *supportive*. A (re)design of pedagogic space, besides a pluralism of semiotic materials and texts, requires changes in the patterns of literacy learning as well, enabling genuine collaboration of students in which multiple voices are heard rather than the single voice is privileged. A critical task of second language literacy education is then to construct a social space that gives voice to those who have been strategically and historically silenced.

(Re)designing the material–semiotic sphere of pedagogical space is inseparable from a critical inquiry into knowledge/meaning representations—that is, the second dimension of Thirdspace pedagogy: an intellectual sphere of second language literacy learning. A critical analysis of the intellectual sphere is tied to the construction of knowledge and to the forms of social control over cultural–semiotic means of knowing. With regard to schooled literacy, technologies of knowledge and meaning production are synonymous with how the intellectual space of classrooms is understood and managed through expert talk (scientific and teacher discourses) as well as through the ordinary discourse of students. The Thirdspace perspective on literacy learning considers the intellectual dimension as pedagogic practice of cognitive scaffolding in a journey of becoming literate. However, the kind of cognitive scaffolds that are constructed, and the intellectual goals that are aimed at being achieved with their help are a matter of how literacy learning is understood. Therefore, by opposing cognitive reductionism in conceptualizing learning, which promotes acquisition of unexamined knowledge, Thirdspace pedagogy treats knowledge as socially constructed and knowing as dialogical.

The locus of literacy learning practice within a heterocultural space of meaning-making forces the abandonment of taken-for-granted knowledge and provides a rationale for collaborative learning based on multiple forms of knowledge. Unlike traditional models of collaborative learning, this dramatic shift in the organization of learning suggests a need also to explore the forces that produce what culture validates as knowledge. As such, a Thirdspace pedagogy of literacy advocates a political strategy of "reassembling" educational knowledge to bring about the active involvement of minority students in literacy learning. This activity is simultaneously critical and productive. Students are encouraged to examine the construction of knowledge and relations of power in textual representations (cf. Auerbach, 1995). At the same time, a critical Thirdspace position dismisses the polarization between a single center of power that produces dominant meaning and local disempowerment or a passive audience. In other words, a critical inquiry into textual representations is not about the unpacking of simplified dichotomies between a universalized oppressor and the oppressed, leading to the formulation of a counterhegemonic recipe for action. Rather, the pedagogic Thirdspace presupposes multiple axes of knowledge and difference production and, hence, a multisitedness of power and resistance.

In this respect, the transformation of meaning starts from a particular location of identity, or a speaking position, but then moves to an anti-essentialist strategy of "Thirding" that makes translation across cultural differences possible. Because "Thirding" for ESL students is often a life choice that ensures the survival of the marginalized and the disadvantaged and provides openings for border-crossing, the Thirdspace pedagogy of literacy offers a possibility for productive literacy learning through the construction of *rich collective zones of proximal development* (ZPD), in which students' cultural knowledge and textual practices are the starting point for transformative learning (Vygotsky, 1978).

Teaching and learning literacy in the collective ZPD, then, means working with the *multiple* funds of knowledge that can afford productive learning and meaning-making and, hence, high-quality intellectual and social outcomes needed for life in multicultural conditions. In terms of the recognition of epistemological diversity in the ZPD, it is important to create favorable conditions for the negotiation and renegotiation of meaning by students. Such an engagement in critical meaning-making is essential to enable the learner to see how knowledge is assembled and to articulate new meanings. However, the production of new meanings on the basis of diverse semiotic resources and funds of knowledge is not a "relativist picnic" (Bruner, 1986, p. 158); rather, this is a pedagogic technology of literacy education for remaking the wor(l)d (Green, 1997). It should foster practices of re-presenting and re-mediation, contributing to the development of responsible members within a classroom community of difference and a multicultural society at large. These considerations lead me to the third and final dimension of the pedagogical Thirdspace: the recognition of difference on the level of discursive interaction.

The discursive dimension of pedagogic Thirdspace is conceived as consisting of *living* dialogical events in literacy learning practices. It subsumes the previous two dimensions and is given here a sociopolitical priority. Both semiotic and intellectual pluralism are needed for students to explore new cultural locations from which they can articulate a sense of the world. At the same time, the coexistence of diverse material–semiotic artifacts and epistemologies requires a specific model of Thirdspace teaching. In this model, a teacher's social role is to skillfully navigate and coordinate alternative and competing discourses in the classroom in order to transform the conflict between differences into productive learning.

This task is difficult and challenging, because it requires a recognition of new hybrid meanings that arise from the "sociology of consciousness" and from the dialogical tension between contradictory discourses (Bakhtin, 1984). One of the features of teaching ESL literacy in Thirdspace lies precisely in the public deliberation of this tension by drawing on and analyzing the conflicting discourses. This implies a bottom-up perspective on the critical empowerment of students (and teachers) in which everyone takes responsibility for understanding and for critically reflecting on his or her own actions, desires, and perspectives that might be similar to and different from others (Kincheloe, Slattery, & Steinberg, 2000). Significant here is that *critical* represents not a single consciousness but *multiple* perspectives born in the intercultural symposium of voices that are searching for new meanings collectively and dialogically.

One last point must be made clear: The pedagogical move from traditional ESL literacy pedagogy toward a critical Thirdspace stance is not easy. It involves the subversion of authoritarianism into multiple uses and users of authority; rigid cultural hegemony into critical multiculturalism; traditional understandings of literacy and empowerment into critical literacy for empowerment; and negative competition into positive, mutually enriching collaboration. It is also not easy because transformation of the traditional practices of language and literacy learning is a political act. The choice and decision of how and where transformations should be made are constrained by the tension between the multifarious power centers embodied in teachers' and students' actions. The desire for change is in tension with the pressure for conformity to unequal relations of race, class, and gender. Hence, challenging representations and practices that "name, marginalize, and define difference as the devalued Other" (Giroux, 1988, p. 174) requires the relearning and externalization of what has been previously internalized (Vygotsky, 1978). In this regard, the concept of Thirdspace pedagogy can play a modest role in a broader attempt to subvert oppressive practices in ESL education. It endeavors to apply a Bakhtinian vision of literacy learning as the development of intercultural consciousness, in classrooms that use different perspectives and semiotic resources. As a pedagogy of cultural and critical empowerment, it sees learning as a transformative practice in which meaning is rearticulated dialogically. The opportunity to jointly experience diversity through a genuine dialogicality of unmerged voices leads to Thirdspace, something that goes well beyond an antagonistic binarism of the dominant and the subjugated.

REFERENCES

Artiles, A. (2000, July). *The inclusive education movement and minority representation in special education: Trends, paradoxes, and dilemmas.* Paper presented at the International Special Education Conference, Manchester, England.

Auerbach, E. (1995). The politics of the ESL classroom: Issues of power in pedagogi-cal choices. In J. Tollefson (Ed.), *Power and inequality in language education* (pp. 9–23). New York: Cambridge University Press.

Bakhtin, M. (1968). *Rabelais and his world*. Cambridge, MA: MIT Press.

Bakhtin, M. (1981). *The dialogic imagination* (M. Holquist, Ed.). Austin: University of Texas Press.

Bakhtin, M. (1984). *Problems of Dostoevsky's poetics* (C. Emerson, Ed.). Minneapolis: University of Minnesota Press.

Bakhtin, M. (1986). *Speech genres and other late essays* (C. Emerson & M. Holquist, Eds.). Austin: University of Texas Press.

Barker, V., Giles, H., Noels, K., Duck, J., Hecht, M., & Clement, R. (2001). The Eng-lish-only movement: A communication analysis of changing perceptions of lan-guage vitality. *Journal of Communication, 51*, 3–37.

Barton, D., Hamilton, M., & Ivanic, R. (Eds.). (2000). *Situated literacies*. London: Routledge.

Bauman, Z. (1997). The making and unmaking of strangers. In P. Werbner & T. Modood (Eds.), *Debating cultural hybridity* (pp. 46–57). London: Zed Books.

Baumann, G. (1997). Dominant and demotic discourses of culture: Their relevance to multi-ethnic alliances. In P. Werbner & T. Modood (Eds.), *Debating cultural hybridity* (pp. 209–225). London: Zed Books.

Bhabha, H. (1994). *The location of culture*. London: Routledge.

Brandist, C. (2002). *The Bakhtin circle: Philosophy, culture and politics*. London: Pluto.

Bruner, J. (1986). *Actual minds, possible worlds*. Cambridge, MA: Harvard University Press.

Cole, M. (1998). Can cultural psychology help us think about diversity? *Mind, Cul-ture, and Activity, 5*, 291–304.

Foucault, M. (1986). Of other spaces. *Diacritics, 16*, 22–27.

Gee, J. (1996). *Social linguistics and literacies: Ideology in discourses* (2nd ed.). London: Taylor & Francis.

Gee, J. (2001). A sociocultural perspective on early literacy development. In B. Neuman & D. Dickinson (Eds.), *Handbook of family literacy research* (pp. 30–42). New York: Guilford.

Giroux, H. (1988). *Teachers as intellectuals: A critical pedagogy for practical learning*. Westport, CT: Bergin & Garvey.

Green, B. (1997). Reading with an attitude; or deconstructing "critical literacies." In M. Muspratt, A. Luke, & P. Freebody (Eds.), *Constructing critical literacies: Teaching and learning textual practices* (pp. 227–242). Sydney, Australia: Allen & Unwin.

Green, B., & Kostogriz, A. (2002). Learning difficulties and the New Literacy Stud-ies: A socially critical perspective. In J. Soler, J. Wearmouth, & G. Reid (Eds.), *Contextualising difficulties in literacy development* (pp. 102–114). London: RoutledgeFalmer.

Gurevitch, Z. (2001). Dialectical dialogue: The struggle for speech, repressive si-lence, and the shift to multiplicity. *British Journal of Sociology, 52*, 87–104.

Gutiérrez, K. (2000). Teaching and learning in the 21st century. *English Education, 32*, 290–298.

Hall, S. (1990). Cultural identity and diaspora. In J. Rutherford (Ed.), *Identity: Com-munity, culture, difference* (pp. 222–237). London: Lawrence & Wishart.

Hall, S. (1992). New ethnicities. In J. Donald & A. Rattansi (Eds.), *"Race," culture and difference* (pp. 252–260). London: Sage.

Harklau, L. (1999). Representing culture in the ESL writing classroom. In E. Hinkel (Ed.), *Culture in second language teaching and learning* (pp. 109–130). New York: Cambridge University Press.

Hirsch, E. D. (1987). *Cultural literacy.* Boston: Houghton Mifflin.

Hirsch, E. D. (1999). Americanization and the schools. *The Clearing House, 72,* 136–139.

Kincheloe, J., Slattery, P., & Steinberg, S. (2000). *Contextualzing teaching: Introduction to education and educational foundations.* Boulder, CO: Westview Press.

Kincheloe, J., & Steinberg, S. (1997). *Changing multiculturalism.* Philadelphia: Open University Press.

Lave, J., & Wenger, E. (1991). *Situated learning: Legitimate peripheral participation.* Cambridge, England: Cambridge University Press.

Lo Bianco, J. (2000). Multilingualism and multiliteracies. In B. Cope & M. Kalantzis (Eds.), *Multiliteracies* (pp. 92–105). Melbourne, Australia: Macmillan.

Lotman, Y. (1990). *The universe of the mind: A semiotic theory of culture* (A. Shukman, Ed.). Bloomington: Indiana University Press.

Luke, C., & Luke, A. (1999). Theorizing interracial families and hybrid identity: An Australian perspective. *Educational Theory, 49,* 223–249.

Macedo, D. (2000). The colonialism of the English only movement. *Educational Researcher, 29*(2), 15–24.

McConaghy, K. (2000). *Rethinking indigenous education: Culturalism, colonialism and the politics of knowing.* Flaxton, Queensland, Australia: Post Pressed.

Modood, T., Beishon, S., & Virdee, S. (1994). *Changing ethnic identities.* London: Policy Studies Institute.

Moll, L. (2000). Inspired by Vygotsky: Ethnographic experiments in education. In C. Lee & P. Smagorinsky (Eds.), *Vygotskian perspective on literacy research: Constructing meaning through collaborative inquiry* (pp. 256–268). Cambridge, England: Cambridge University Press.

Pennycook, A. (2001). *Critical applied linguistics: A critical introduction.* Mahwah, NJ: Lawrence Erlbaum Associates.

Phillipson, R. (1992). *Linguistic imperialism.* Oxford, England: Oxford University Press.

Said, E. (1993). *Culture and imperialism.* New York: Knopf.

Soja, E. (1996). *Thirdspace: Journeys to Los Angeles and other real-and-imagined places.* Cambridge, MA: Blackwell.

Soja, E. (1999). Thirdspace: Expanding the scope of the geographical imagination. In J. Massey, J. Allen, & P. Sarre (Eds.), *Human geography today* (pp. 260–278). Cambridge, MA: Polity Press.

Solsken, J., Willet, J., & Wilson-Keenan, J. (2000). Cultivating hybrid texts in multicultural classrooms: Promise and challenge. *Research in the Teaching of English, 35,* 175–197.

Tollefson, J. (1991). *Planning language, planning inequality.* London: Longman.

Tollefson, J. (Ed.) (1995). *Power and inequality in language education.* Cambridge, England: Cambridge University Press.

Toohey, K. (2000). *Learning English at school: Identity, social relations and classroom practice.* Clevedon, England: Multilingual Matters.

Vygotsky, L. (1978). *Mind in society: The development of higher psychological processes* (M. Cole, V. John-Steiner, S. Scribner, & E. Souberman, Eds.). Cambridge, MA: Harvard University Press.

Werbner, P. (1997). Introduction: The dialectics of cultural hybridity. In P. Werbner & T. Modood (Eds.), *Debating cultural hybridity* (pp. 1–26). London: Zed Books.

Zizek, S. (1997). Multiculturalism, or, the cultural logic of multinational capitalism. *New Left Review, 225*, 28–51.

Chapter 11

Japanese Business Telephone Conversations as Bakhtinian Speech Genre: Applications for Second Language Acquisition

Lindsay Amthor Yotsukura
University of Maryland, College Park

Bakhtin (1986) claimed that a speaker's command of a given language is demonstrated through his or her ability to use the heterogeneous and dynamic speech genres of that language. Native speakers exhibit varying degrees of competence in the use of these genres, depending on their experience. Through socialization and contact with others, native speakers acquire these genres over time. This has important repercussions for second and foreign language pedagogy, in that we cannot expect learners to acquire a facility with these genres without careful modeling, guided rehearsal, and feedback regarding their performance. In this chapter I explore some of the ways in which tokens of one particular genre of spoken Japanese—Japanese business telephone conversations—may be used in second language classrooms to foster the development of learners' pragmatic competence in that language.

According to Bakhtin (1986), "Speech genres are much more changeable, flexible, and plastic than language forms are, but they have a normative significance for the speaking individuum, and they are not created by him but are given to him" (pp. 80–81). From the perspective of the language learner, then, the acquisition of speech genres is somewhat analogous to the study of roles for an actor in the theater; that is, an actor might shadow the person whose life is the basis for a particular part, in order to learn more about the nuances of the part he or she will play on the stage. At first, the actor may not feel comfortable in his or her role, but with practice and feedback from directors in rehearsal (and perhaps from the model as well), the actor's performances become more smooth and convincing. With time, the actor develops a sense for the role, and once the part is well learned, usually introduces his or her own style into the role. In much the same way, the learner in the second language classroom is given his or her lines to rehearse and initially looks to model conversations in a textbook and to his or her instructors in order to observe how this "part" has been enacted before.

Speech genres vary in shape and form, from the more tightly constrained, ritual genres, such as greetings and farewells, which leave little room for individuality apart from expressive intonation and the choice of the genre itself, to artistic genres, which allow for more individual expression. Bakhtin (1986) pointed out that, regardless of which speech genre is at issue:

> The better our command of genres, the more freely we employ them ... the more flexibly and precisely we reflect the unrepeatable situation of communication—in a word, the more perfectly we implement our free speech plan. (p. 80)

In other words, the better one's mastery of the speech genres of a given language, the better one's ability to participate in the activities of a given society. One may better express oneself, and one will be better *understood* by the members of the culture who speak that language. This ensures smooth communication among participants, both native and non-native alike.

Bakhtin (1986) was quick to point out that his view of speech genres and the notion of the utterance differs sharply from that of Saussure and, actually, the majority of the world's linguists:

> The single utterance, with all its individuality and creativity, can in no way be regarded as a *completely free combination* of forms of language, as is supposed, for example, by Saussure (and by many other linguists after him), who juxtaposed the utterance (*la parole*), as a purely individual act, to the system of language as a phenomenon that is purely social and mandatory for the individuum. The vast majority of linguists hold the same position, in theory if not in practice. *They see in the utterance only an individual combination of purely linguistic (lexical and grammatical) forms and they neither uncover nor study any of the other normative forms the utterance acquires in practice* [italics added]. (p. 81)

Bakhtin (1986) also noted in this regard that we select words based on our knowledge of their use in *other utterances*; hence, "we choose words according to their generic specifications":

> A speech genre is not a form of language, but a typical form of utterance; as such the genre also includes a certain typical kind of expression that inheres in it. In the genre the word acquires a particular expression. Genres correspond to typical situations of speech communication, typical themes, and, consequently, also to particular contacts between the *meanings* of words and actual concrete reality under certain typical circumstances. Hence also the possibility of typical expressions that seem to adhere to words. (p. 87)

In short, we choose our words on the basis of how they have been used by other speakers on similar but particular occasions, for similar purposes, in similar contexts. Bakhtin (1986) argued that:

> The unique speech experience of each individual is shaped and developed in continuous and constant interaction with others' individual utterances. This experience can be characterized to some degree as the process of *assimilation*—more or less creative—of others' words (and not the words of a language). (p. 89)

This is how our utterances acquire their situated meaning—the "echo of the generic whole that resounds in the word" (Bakhtin, 1986, p. 88). This meaning can of course change over time as speakers change their usage; in turn, speech genres, which are flexible and open ended, can and will change as well. As Bakhtin (1986) put it, "Speech genres in general submit fairly easily to re-accentuation" (p. 87).

Although native speakers benefit from the fact that they grow up in a society where these models of how language is put to similar purposes are all around them, second language learners do not have this opportunity unless they can manage an extended period abroad. The question for us as instructors is thus how we may bring those models into the classroom and, moreover, how we might go about enabling our students to develop appropriate pragmatic intuitions and expectations in order to behave in a culturally nuanced manner in the target language. These are the issues I will address in this chapter.

FOCUS OF ANALYSIS: JAPANESE BUSINESS TELEPHONE CONVERSATIONS

Rationale

One of the most daunting tasks for a learner of any language is to interact with a native speaker on the telephone. Whereas in face-to-face conversation participants can partially rely on nonverbal cues—such as gaze, gestures, head nods, and the like—to convey nuances of meaning and to check comprehension, on the telephone communication is limited to the oral channel. The potential for misunderstanding is therefore significant. Moreover, in the case of business telephone calls (as compared to mundane, everyday conversations), missteps may have both transactional and interactional consequences. It is thus critical for learners interested in conducting business in the target language that they undergo substantial training in the genre of business telephone conversations.

The Data: Telephone Conversations as "Texts" for Analysis

In the following sections I present and discuss some of the features of Japanese business transactional telephone conversations, or JBCs, based on a corpus of more than 540 such calls collected for a recent ethnomethodological study (Yotsukura, 1997, 2003a). Bakhtin (1986, p. 60) noted in his discussion of speech genres that what makes exemplars of a given genre hold together as a group are their thematic, structural or compositional, and stylistic similarities. No two tokens of a genre are alike, of course, but a constellation of similar features makes them recognizable and identifiable to experienced speakers of a particular language. In the case of JBCs, thematically what these calls all have in common is the fact that they involve the initiation, continuation, or resolution of a business transaction, such as the purchase and shipment of books, airline tickets, food, and the like. Structurally, they follow a similar pattern, as summarized in Fig. 11.1. The calls begin with an opening section, in which identification of the participants and the reason for the call are established; followed by a discussion of business; and a closing section, in which matters previously agreed upon are restated and a promise of future contact may be extended. Stylistically, they tend to incorporate formal, polite linguistic forms, as opposed to the direct, casual style forms more commonly found in everyday conversations between familiars.

Because these "texts" include a number of ritualized conversational routines (Coulmas, 1979, 1981) such as opening and closing sequences and transitional statements, they are ideal for classroom use (Hall, 1999). Studies examining the opening segments of conversations have identified certain interactional tasks that most conversationalists will seek to accomplish at the outset of a call, such as identification and/or recognition and greetings, regardless of the language of the exchange. However, local variations in terms of how these sequences unfold in individual languages can usually be attributed to situational factors or rituals specific to a particular sociocultural setting (Haegeman, 1996; Halmari, 1993; Hopper & Koleilat-Doany, 1989; Houtkoop-Steenstra, 1991; Lindström, 1994; Luke & Pavlidou, 2002; Schegloff, 1968, 1979, 1986; Whalen & Zimmerman, 1987). These findings are relevant here because recent research in interlanguage pragmatics on the development of pragmatic competence

I. Opening

   1. (Opening greeting and) Company and/or self-identification by both parties

       (Exchange of personal greetings)

   2. Salutations

   3. (Request to speak with different person = "switchboard request")

       (Request for or confirmation of self-identification)
       (Indication that requested person is not available)

           (Offer to have different person call back)
           (Offer by caller to call again later)

       (Transfer to different person)
       (Recursion to identification, greetings, and/or salutation steps)

II. Transition to discussion of business transaction(s) (= *maeoki* 'prefatory phrase ')

   4. Attention focuser

   5. General statement of business matter to be discussed

III. Discussion of business transaction(s)

IV. Pre-closing

   6. Summary/restatement of matters agreed upon within the conversation

       (Recursion to Section II and/or III for another item of business)
       (Promise of future contact)

V. Closing

   7. (Request for self-identification of one or both parties)

       (Self-identification by one or both parties)

   8. Leave-taking

FIG. 11.1. **Overall structure of Japanese business transactional telephone conversations.**

has suggested that it is not sufficient for learners to merely be exposed to second language forms in order to acquire them. Rather, additional explicit instruction through, for example, consciousness-raising activities can help to direct students' attention to sociocultural distinctions between the target second language and their native language and thereby heighten students' pragmatic awareness (Kasper, 1997, 2001). These sorts of activities can then be followed by guided communicative practice through role plays with careful feedback from the instructor, together with regular opportunities for additional discussion.

The opening segments of JBCs are a case in point and are the focus of my discussion here. Classroom-based analyses of these opening sequences can be particularly useful for American learners of Japanese, because the Japanese openings typically include a range of forms for self and/or company identifications, as well as ritual business salutations, that are not as frequently used in English. Moreover, the opening sequence is followed by a prefatory, transitional phrase I will refer to here as a *maeoki*, following Kashiwazaki (1993). *Mae* in Japanese can be glossed "before" or "ahead," and *oki* is the nominal form of the verb *oku*, "to place" or "to put," so the compound word refers to an utterance that one "places ahead" in the discourse. In a cross-linguistic study comparing the production of requests in face-to-face interactions by learners and native speakers of Japanese, Kashiwazaki found that the native speakers were far more likely to use a *maeoki* prior to uttering a request when opening a conversation. For example, native speakers would initiate their requests by first apologizing (e.g., *sumimasen ga* ["I'm sorry, but …"]) or by providing a preliminary explanation by way of background for the request (e.g., *rejume o insatsu shitai n desu kedo …* ["It's that I'd like to print [my] resumé, but …"]).

My research on JBCs has shown that in business transactional contexts on the telephone, when callers either explicitly or implicitly seek assistance from customer service representatives, similar forms of prefatory *maeoki* are just as critical to the interaction, because in JBCs the *maeoki* introduces the general reason for the call. Thus by including JBCs in classroom activities, we not only acquaint students with a particular genre of telephone call; more specifically, we can provide them with models and opportunities for hands-on practice in the essential skill of topic management (Yotsukura, 2003b).

One final pedagogical advantage to introducing JBCs in the language classroom relates to what Bakhtin (1986) called the *addressivity* of the utterance, or "the quality of turning to someone" (p. 99). He pointed out that:

> If an individual word or sentence is directed at someone, addressed to someone, then we have a completed utterance that consists of one word or one sentence, and addressivity is inherent not in the unit of language, but in the utterance. A sentence that is surrounded by context acquires addressivity only through the entire utterance, as a constituent part of it. (Bakhtin, 1986, p. 99)

Putting this slightly differently, when a word or a sentence is not situated in context, and is not directed to a particular addressee, it does not "reverberate" with the dialogical overtones it acquires in actual practice. More specifically, Bakhtin (1986) noted:

> Language as a system has an immense supply of purely linguistic means for expressing formal address: lexical, morphological … and syntactical ….

But they acquire addressivity only in the whole of a *concrete* [italics added] utterance. (p. 99)

We can apply Bakhtin's observations about the differences between the abstract signifying units of a language versus the situated meaning of an utterance in particular contexts to the classroom analysis of Japanese discourse. As I show in the next two sections, by examining the stylistic conventions that Japanese conversationalists adopt when addressing an interlocutor, in response to utterances by previous speakers, we necessarily bring to the fore a number of situational and cultural factors for our students. This is because the Japanese language morphologically and lexically encodes information regarding the relationship between speaker and addressee on the one hand, and speaker and referent (who may or may not be the addressee) on the other. *But because this information is deictically dependent on the situational context, without discussing who those speakers, addressees, and referents are to each other*—in terms of relative status, in-group/out-group relationships, and so on—*it is difficult if not impossible to convey the full meaning of individual words, not to mention complete utterances.* In addition to illustrating how abstract "signifying units" are contextualized in authentic discourse, such discussions add depth and breadth to the classroom experience and can better prepare learners for future interactions with Japanese speakers, both at home and abroad.

SOME NOTES ABOUT STYLE IN JAPANESE

There are a number of stylistic contrasts in Japanese, but most fundamentally there are two axes for indexing what English speakers might refer to as "politeness." The first stylistic contrast, *distal–direct* (also referred to as *formal–informal*), indexes the relationship between speaker and addressee in terms of linguistic or social distance. Often, one's role in a given interaction influences what one's stylistic stance should be; for example, in a conversation between a subordinate and his boss, traditionally the subordinate would be expected, because of his junior status, to use distal style, whereas the boss could opt for either direct or distal style. This contrast is not necessarily reciprocal. Indeed, if a boss chooses to address his subordinate in direct style, it would not usually be seen as appropriate for the subordinate to respond in kind. Similar contrasts hold for relationships between professors and students in universities,[1] and between a *senpai* (one's senior at school or at work) and *koohai* (one's junior) as well. The rel-

---

[1] It is particularly notable that this practice continues beyond graduation from college, such that students will usually still address their teachers as *sensei* ("Professor") long after graduation. This contrasts with the American custom adopted by many students of addressing their professors by first name, even before completion of their studies.

ative formality of a situation can also influence conversationalists' choice of style, with more formal, public occasions (e.g., an academic conference) calling for the use of distal style and more informal, private functions calling for the use of direct style.

The second axis, *polite–plain*, indexes the relationship between the speaker and the referent. The referent could be the speaker, the addressee, or a third party who may or may not be participating in the interaction. Simplifying the situation somewhat, we may note that it is primarily one's relationship to that referent, together with the relative formality of the discourse context, that influence the choice of whether to use a polite or plain form. Between familiars of the same age or peer group, the plain form might be preferable (although some older women may adopt honorific, direct-style utterances toward each other). However, when a junior addresses his senior, in principle he would be expected to mark references to that senior either lexically and/or morphologically with honorific-polite style. If the junior refers to himself, on the other hand, he might adopt humble-polite style. The senior would then have the option to adopt plain or polite forms.

As Bakhtin (1986, p. 99) suggested, by considering linguistic forms as they appear within larger utterances in particular conversational contexts, we can reveal the aspects of addressivity that they acquire in those contexts. For example, each of the verbals in the following three conversational exchanges is a semantic equivalent of the plain form of the verbal *iku* (go); the verbals differ only stylistically. I have provided loose English equivalents in order to evoke some of the nuances conveyed by each utterance as a whole. A key for the abbreviations used in the transcriptions is presented in the Appendix.

    1A: *Irasshaimasu ka?*
            go-HON-DIST-IPF Q
            "Will you go?"
    2B: *Ee, mairimasu.*
            yes go-HUM-DIST-IPF
            "Yes, I'll go."

A conversation such as Example 1 might take place at a workplace between colleagues who are not well acquainted or between employees of two different companies. The use of distal style (marked with the morpheme *mas*) by both speakers invokes a degree of linguistic distance between them, and the contrasting honorific and humble polite forms (represented by the verbal stems *irasshai-* vs. *mairi-*, respectively) suggest that each speaker is referring to the other in a careful, respectful manner.

(2) 1A: *Iku?*
          go-PLN-DIR-IPF
          "Are you gonna go?"
     2B: *N, iku yo.*
           yeah go-PLN-DIR-IPF SP
           "Yeah, I'm goin', ya know."

The interaction in Example 2 differs from that of Example 1 in that it would likely occur between peers or well-acquainted colleagues who are of similar rank. In a context outside of the workplace, this exchange might occur between friends or classmates. Note that both speakers adopt the plain verbal form *iku*, as opposed to one of the polite forms, *irassharu* or *mairu*, used in Example 1.

Another variation we can consider is an interaction such as that presented in Example 3, which could also take place between colleagues. In this case, however, Speaker A might be female, based on the use of the honorific, direct style form *Irassharu?* Another possible scenario would be a wife addressing her husband in an everyday (nonprofessional) conversation.

(3) 1A: *Irassharu?*
          go-HON-DIR-IPF
          "You'll go?"
     2B: *N, iku yo.*
           yeah go-PLN-DIR-IPF SP
           "Yeah, I'm goin', ya know."

One other polite form that appears frequently in JBCs is the *neutral polite* form, used in reference to inanimates or in-group members, including oneself. Neutral polite forms show respect to one's addressee but do not exalt or humble the referent. As I show in the next section, the neutral polite form of the copula, *de gozaimasu*, appears regularly in company and self-identifications. Its honorific equivalent, *de irasshaimasu*, is used when speaking to or about out-group members.

What is most important to consider when analyzing these as well as other stylistic contrasts in Japanese not described here (e.g., *masculine–feminine*, *blunt–gentle*) is the fact that there are no neutral utterances in the language. One must always choose among linguistic forms that index a particular interactional stance toward one's addressee and/or the referent (if different from the addressee). Stylistic conventions of use have changed over time, of course, with differences arising across generations, but despite what some may call a recent weakening of *keigo* (polite language) usage, appropriate selection of these forms can demonstrate one's understanding and recognition of the interconnectedness of relationships in Japan (Wetzel, 1993, 1994, 2004; Wetzel & Inoue, 1996).

Bakhtin made a similar observation about languages in general, at least as far as the issue of neutral utterances is concerned:

> There are no "neutral" words and forms—words and forms that can belong to "no one"; language has been completely taken over, shot through with intentions and accents. For any individual consciousness living in it, language is not an abstract system of normative forms but rather a concrete heteroglot conception of the world. All words have the "taste" of a profession, a genre, a tendency, a party, a particular work, a particular person, a generation, an age group, the day and hour. *Each word tastes of the context and the contexts in which it has lived its socially charged life; all words and forms are populated by intentions. Contextual overtones (generic, tendentious, individualistic) are inevitable in the word* [italics added]. (Holquist, 1981, p. 293)

The examples I consider in the next section, which are taken from authentic Japanese business discourse, are indeed imbued with intentions and contextual overtones. I show that even though JBC participants may be faced with similar interactional tasks (i.e., presenting themselves on the telephone and negotiating the topics of business to be discussed), they use different utterances depending on who their addressee is at the moment (stranger vs. known acquaintance) and whether the participants share some sort of business relationship—and, if so, what sort of relationship obtains between them (e.g., in-house colleagues vs. customer–client). I also discuss how differing intentions on the part of callers have linguistic consequences in terms of the forms adopted by speakers for their *maeoki* utterances.

THE OPENING SEQUENCE OF JBCS

Self- and Company Identifications

As noted previously, the opening sequence of JBCs contains a number of ritualized elements that lend themselves easily to classroom discussion, modeling, and practice. The first of these is the self- or company identification. Park (2002) and Yotsukura (2003a) have observed that there appears to be a stronger interactional preference among Japanese as compared to American English speakers to provide self-identifications on the telephone. Moreover, Schegloff (1979) has noted that company identifications by call recipients are a regular feature of business telephone conversations. The "interactional practice" of self- and company identifications is therefore a critical element for Japanese learners studying business conversations to observe or notice (Hall, 1999). It is also a routine that builds on one with which even beginning students should already be familiar, namely, the exchange of self-introductions.

One way to effectively heighten students' awareness of the ways in which JBCs reflect situational factors is to present a series of opening segments for comparison and subsequent discussion. Consider, for example, the following three excerpts from the JBC corpus:

(4) Opening segment of Tokyo Books #1B-33
((phone rings))
   1A: *Hai, Tookyoo Shoten de gozaimasu.*
           yes Tokyo bookstore COP-DIST-IPF (+)
           "Yes, (this) is Tokyo Books."
   2C: *A, Hirano desu keredomo ....*
           oh Hirano COP-DIST-IPF but
           "Oh, it's Hirano, but ...."
   3A: *A, otsukaresama desu.*
           oh tired person (+) COP-DIST-IPF
           "Oh, [you must be working hard."] [*lit.,* "you are a tired person."]
(5) Opening segment of Kansai Imports #1-7
((phone rings))
   1A: *Kansai Yunyuu de gozaimasu.*
           Kansai Imports COP-DIST-IPF (+)
           "(This) is Kansai Imports."
   2C: *E: Kobe-ginkoo no Sannomiya no Igarashi desu GA:*
           HES Kobe bank CN Sannomiya CN Igarashi COP-DIST-IPF but
           "Um, (this) is Igarashi of the Sannomiya (branch) of Kobe Bank, but ..."
   3A: *A, hai, osewa ni narimasu:.*
           oh yes assistance GL become-DIST-IPF
           "Oh yes, [(we are/I am) obliged (to you) for your assistance."]
   4B: *Osewa ni natte- 'masu:*
           assistance GL become-GER be-DIST-IPF
           ["Thank you for your continued assistance."]
(6) Opening segment in Kansai Imports #1B-24
   1A: *XX desu.*
           XX COP-DIST-IPF
           "(This) is XX."
   2C: *A, Kansai Unyu to mooshimasu:,*
           oh Kansai Shipping QT be called-HUM-DIST-IPF
           "Oh, this is " [*lit.,* "(I)'m called] Kansai Shipping,"

3A: *Osewa-sama// desu:*
        assistance-person COP-DIST-IPF
        "[Thank you for your assistance.]"
4C: *Hai, osewa ni narimasu:.*
        yes assistance GL become-DIST-IPF
        "Yes, [(I) am obliged for your assistance.]"

After first playing the recordings of these opening sections and asking students to transcribe what they have heard, the instructor can launch the discussion by asking students to look for similarities and differences on a line-by-line basis across the three conversations. In doing so *without* providing any more specific information about the identities of the participants, this becomes an inductive-reasoning exercise. It encourages students to listen for and pay attention to small but important distinctions that reflect the ways in which speakers fine tune their utterances for their addressees—in short, how they incorporate the notion of addressivity in their utterances.

Looking at line 1A for the first two conversations, we see that the individuals who answer the telephone adopt the same basic pattern, that is, /name of company/ followed by the neutral–polite form of the copula, *de gozaimasu*. However, they do not volunteer their names. If we then compare these utterances to the answerer's initial utterance in the third conversation (Example 6), we note one distinction in form: the answerer in Example 6 adopts the plain form of the copula (*desu*) rather than the neutral polite *de gozaimasu*. In addition, she does not clearly enunciate the word preceding the copula; hence it is transcribed as *XX*. (It is likely that what this speaker uttered was the name of her company, Kansai Yunyuu, because hundreds of similar exchanges in the corpus begin in this manner. I return to this question in a moment.)

Moving on to line 2C of these exchanges (the callers' first utterances), differences begin to emerge across calls. In Example 4, the caller gives a family name *(Hirano)*[2] followed by the plain copula *desu* and a clause particle *(keredomo)*. In contrast, the caller in Example 5 provides a more detailed self-identification, first providing a company name *(Kobe-ginkoo)*, followed by the branch location *(Sannomiya)*, and then a surname *(Igarashi)*. We might speculate, therefore, that less of an information gap exists between the speakers in Example 4 as compared to Example 5, because the first caller does not deem it necessary to provide parallel company and branch information in his self-introduction. We might then contemplate *why* such an information gap might exist—for example, the two speakers in Example 4 might be better acquainted, and/or in more frequent contact, than the speakers in Example 5. Thus it is possible that differences in the degree of shared experience between these pairs of

---

[2]Pseudonyms are used here for individuals and institutions in order to protect their identities.

speakers have linguistic repercussions for the ways in which they address each other at this initial instant on the telephone.

If we now compare the callers' first utterances in Examples 4 and 5 with that of the caller in Example 6, another difference appears: Instead of adopting the pattern /company name + copula/ for the predicate, this third caller provides a company affiliation (*Kansai Unyu*) followed by a quotative particle (*to*) and the verbal *mooshimasu*, which is the humble–polite equivalent of the verbal *iu*, "to be called." When discussing this example with students, it may help to point out to them (if they are not already aware) that the pattern ... *to mooshimasu* is one that is used in many formal face-to-face self-introductions. Because the form ... *to mooshimasu* means "I am called ...," it functions deictically to suggest that the speaker is presenting him- or herself to the addressee for the first time. In the case of this telephone call, then, we might surmise that the caller is similarly unacquainted with his addressee and is signaling (i.e., indexing) that fact by selecting this form for the predicate.

We can now return to the comment made earlier that the answerer's initial utterance in Example 6 appears to have been partially inaudible. If we assume that the utterance was only partially audible to the transcriber and to the caller as well, it then makes sense that the caller would use the form ... *to mooshimasu* to present himself—that is, if the caller is not sure who has just answered the telephone, an appropriate response would be to announce one's company affiliation in a way that does not presume that the caller and answerer are acquainted. Moreover, by adopting a humble–polite form rather than a plain form such as the copula *desu*, the caller also minimizes any potential face threat in his utterance (Brown & Levinson, 1987), should there turn out to be a distinction in rank between the two participants. In Bakhtinian terms, this caller's utterance illustrates the concept of addressivity, because it is *responsive* to the particulars of the answerer's previous utterance and *anticipates* potential issues between them.

Salutations and Greetings

Now consider line 3A of these opening segments, which represents salutations or ritual greetings. In Example 4, the answerer says *otsukaresama desu*, which is a ritual utterance often used in face-to-face encounters to greet a colleague who has just returned from an errand or task performed outside the office (McClure, 2000, p. 276). This utterance therefore provides us with an important clue regarding the relationship between the answerer and the caller, for it suggests that the two are likely to be coworkers. The likelihood that they are acquainted is underscored by the fact that both the caller in line 2C and the answerer in line 3A begin their utterances with "*A*, ...", which may indicate recognition by the speaker of the addressee. Thus

these individuals, in their respective ways, are fine tuning their utterances
to suit the context of the moment (the workplace) as well as the particular
people they are addressing. Put another way, these utterances, when considered in their entirety, acquire aspects of addressivity that would not have
been evident had we examined each individual word in isolation.

If we then compare line 3A of Example 4 (*A, otsukaresama desu*) with those
of Examples 5 (*A, hai, osewa ni narimasu*) and 6 (*Osewa-sama desu*), we can
identify another distinction among these calls and their respective participants. Although these utterances all represent ritual greetings, *osewa ni
narimasu*, as well as its linguistic variants—*osewa ni natte-(ori)masu* and
osewa-sama—acknowledges an obligation on the part of the speaker to the
addressee. More specifically, on the telephone, *osewa ni narimasu* is conven-
tionally uttered after the exchange of introductions by speakers who do not
belong to the same company but who are acknowledging an ongoing business relationship. Thus, the utterances *otsukaresama desu, osewa ni narimasu*,
and *osewa-sama desu*, when considered in their respective discourse contexts, reveal that the participants in Example 4 are likely to be members of
the same in-group, whereas the speakers in Examples 5 and 6 are not. In
other words, the participants in these calls signal their respective identities
and relationships to each other by exchanging these ritual phrases and by
tailoring their utterances in a manner appropriate to their addressees and
the larger situational context.

MAEOKI TRANSITIONAL STATEMENTS

Another issue that can be taken up in discussions with students is the question of how callers negotiate a transition to the matter of business through
their *maeoki* utterances. *Maeoki* in the JBC corpus varied in terms of their
degree of specificity. Some were extremely general, whereas others were
more specific. The following are some examples of the ways in which relatively general inquiries may be used to signal a shift to more specifics in an
upcoming utterance. As I suggested in the earlier discussion of opening
segments, such excerpts can be presented in the classroom for inductive
comparisons by the students, with guidance from the instructor. Alterna-
tively, a more explicit, instructional approach may be used to explain the
pragmatic and structural components of these utterances.

(7) a.   *Chotto, oukagai-shitai n desu keredoMO*
         a little ask-HUM-DES-IPF EP-DIST-IPF but
         "It's that (I)'d like to ask a little (something), but …"
    b.   *A, sumimasen, chotto okiki-shitai koto ga aru*
         oh be sorry a little ask-HUM-DES-DIR-IPF thing SUB
         have-DIR-IPF

    n desu keredomo
    EP-DIST-IPF but
    "Oh (I)'m sorry, it's just that there's something (I)'d like to
    ask, but ..."

c.   *Ano desu nee! Chotto oshirabe itadakitai*
    ATF a little investigation receive-HUM-DES-DIR-IPF
    n desu ga
    EP-DIST-IPF but
    "Well you see! It's that (I)'d just like to have you investigate
    something, but ..."

All three of these utterances (which are representative of this type of
maeoki in the JBC corpus) have several features in common. First, they share
elements that Kashiwazaki (1993) identified in her study of requests in
face-to-face encounters, namely, apologies, explanations, and other mitigating devices. From a Bakhtinian standpoint these elements represent
some of the addressive aspects of speech that come to the fore and make
sense only in the larger discourse context—that is, within complete utterances. Considered in isolation, these elements are difficult to analyze. For
example, the word *chotto* literally means "a little," as in a small amount. But
when *chotto* appears within an utterance that requests something of one's
addressee, it acquires a slightly different nuance, which might be glossed as
"just" in English—that is, it functions as a mitigating device.

    In terms of structure, each of the *maeoki* in Examples 7a through 7c in-
cludes the desiderative morpheme *–tai*, followed by what is known as the extended predicate (EP) or *no desu* construction. The EP is another element of
the *maeoki* that makes sense only in the larger discourse context rather than
in isolation. In essence, the EP functions to ground the speaker's ongoing
utterance in the situation in which it is uttered by providing an explanation.

    As with the business salutation *osewa ni narimasu*, it is difficult to render
this commonly occurring Japanese form into a smooth English equivalent.
The best approximation is perhaps the cleft construction "it's that ...," as
shown in the English glosses provided. In JBCs, the EP as it appears in the
maeoki helps explain the reason for the call and functions much like the
phrase sometimes heard in English: "What I'm calling about is ...." The EP
thus acts as a very important metalinguistic framing device for the ensuing
discourse and as a response to the preceding discourse. Here again, then,
we have a signifying unit of language that acquires meaning and overtones
through its use in context.

    If we consider the situational context for utterances such as those ap-
pearing in Example 7, we find that these relatively vague *maeoki* tokens appear in two very different types of interactions: (a) in cold calls or general
inquiries, known as *toiawase* in Japanese (e.g., in calls to request a cata-

logue from a particular firm or to ask about the availability of an item), and
(b) in calls involving the presentation of problems related to shipping and
other transactions. In the latter type of call it is interesting to note that
callers do not rush to present specific details as to the problem at the outset and instead appear to prefer to follow these initial *maeoki* with a
stagelike presentation of details that will be salient and easily recognizable
to the call recipient (Yotsukura, 1997, 2002, 2003a, 2003b). Thus, between company representatives who are in regular contact, the mention of
a shipping date, location of origin and destination, type of shipping
method, and invoice or tracking number can signal to the interlocutor
what the subsequent matter of business might involve, for example, a shipment that has not reached its destination.

In fact, many calls that turned out to be problem reports were initially presented by callers in the form of a shipping confirmation. *Experienced callers*
would provide the information they knew the call recipient would require in order to
look into the problem, and then wait to find out what the results of the call recipient's investigation would be, rather than stating baldly at the outset that, for
example, a package had never arrived at its intended destination. Such calls
are excellent illustrations of the ways in which experience with a particular
genre of interaction enables participants to develop a repertoire of expectations and intuitions as to how to negotiate these interactions. They also illustrate how skilled participants design their utterances in a way that suits their
addressees, from an informational, interactional, and cultural standpoint.

Developing similar sets of expectations among our students for a variety
of speech genres is not an unreasonable goal, provided that we can introduce a sufficient number of authentic texts into the classroom—for example, in the form of digitized audio- and/or videofiles—for students to
observe how these interactions unfold on a regular basis. We can then include a number of practice opportunities to develop students' performances in the target language. Allowing students the chance to make
inductive observations such as those presented earlier, rather than merely
presenting the information in a traditional teacher-fronted classroom, can
also make the learning experience more meaningful (Kasper, 1997).

As noted earlier, not all *maeoki* are as general as those presented in Example 7. In some cases, a *maeoki* will make reference to items or issues mentioned in a previous conversation, or even in the present call itself:

(8)   *Ano: sakihodo nooki no koto*
        HES a little while ago shipment delivery date CN matter
        de otoiawase ga atta n desu kedo
        COP-GER inquiry SUB have-PF EP-DIST-IPF but

"Um, it's that we had an inquiry a little while ago concerning the matter of the appointed delivery date of the shipment, but ..."

This example served as the *maeoki* preface for a follow-up call from a shipping company that was responsible for the shipment referenced in the inquiry in Example 7. At first glance, the utterance may still appear to some readers to be rather vague and lacking in detail, but to the experienced ear of an operations staffer who handles such problem reports regularly, it is possible to respond appropriately.

Another interesting type of *maeoki* are those I have termed "formulations of place and self-reference," following Schegloff (1972). In these utterances, a caller provides information that she feels will help the call recipient to understand how her present location or personal connection to the firm she is calling relates to the purpose of her call. Consider the following example.

(9)   *Ima Kansai Yunyuu-san no mae ni iru n desu kedo*
        now Kansai Imports-Mr. CN front LOC be-DIR-IPF
        EP-DIST-IPF but
        "It's that (I)'m now in front of your company Kansai Imports,
        but ..."

This was an excerpt from a call from a supplier who had previously called for directions to Kansai Imports in order to make a delivery. The present call served to announce that he had finally arrived at their doorstep.

Other *maeoki* provide more specific details about transactions or shipping confirmations, but in a manner that still echoes the basic format outlined by Kashiwazaki (1993), namely, some sort of apology and/or explanation that prefaces a request:

(10)   *Eeto, gomen nasai, kono aida no kayoobi ni hassoo shita bun no*
        HES be sorry the other day CN Tuesday GL dispatch
        do-DIR-PF portion CN
        nimotsu no kakunin o chotto: onegai-shita n desu keDO:
        package CN confirmation OBJ a little beg-HUM-DIR-PF
        EP-DIST-IPF but
        "Um, excuse me, it's just that (I) requested a confirmation of
        the portion of the shipment that was made the other day on
        Tuesday, but ..."

Finally, there are occasions when a caller will explicitly enlist the assistance of the call recipient through *maeoki* utterances such as the following:

(11)   *Ano: hon no chuumon it-ten onegai-itashimasu:.*
          HES book CN order one item beg-HUM-DIST-IPF
          "(I)'d like to place a book order (for) one item."

These last types of *maeoki* are extremely formulaic, recurring in almost identical format with the exception of an occasional variation in the form of the verbal
(e.g., *onegai-shitai* vs. *onegai-itashimasu*). This makes sense, because these types of
transactions are quite ritualized, recurring as they do on a daily basis in the lives
of employees who regularly place orders for various goods and services.

CONCLUSIONS

In this chapter I have considered a number of excerpts from the opening segments of JBCs that illustrate some of the transactional and interactional tasks
participants negotiate on an everyday basis in their professional lives on the
telephone. I examined company and self-identifications and noted that the
linguistic forms that speakers select to predicate their utterances index their
relationships with their interlocutors and thereby demonstrate what Bakhtin
(1986) referred to as the *addressivity* of the utterance. Likewise, I observed
that the ritual salutations adopted in the opening segments of JBCs may vary
according to the type of call; in-house conversations often include the saluta-
tion *otsukaresama desu*, whereas calls between employees of different companies are likely to include an exchange of the phrase *osewa ni narimasu* or one
of its variants. Last, I sampled a range of *maeoki* utterances of varying degrees
of specificity in order to show that these too are produced by speakers with
their recipients and the immediate discourse context in mind.

For our students who do not have significant pragmatic competence in
the target language, I have suggested that one way to foster a greater awareness of the preferred interactional strategies in Japanese is to present them
with a number of authentic segments of conversations and to use notions
such as the addressivity of the utterance as a heuristic to explore how participants design appropriate utterances for their audiences. Ideally, these segments should initially be drawn from interactions that are more tightly
constrained in terms of their function and the latitude afforded the speaker
when responding to others. However, with time and significant exposure to
parallel contexts and participant frameworks, we can expand our learners'
understanding of these speech genres and help them to develop expectations and intuitions that will assist them in responding more flexibly and
creatively to the circumstances around them.

REFERENCES

Bakhtin, M. M. (1986). *Speech genres and other late essays* (V. W. McGee, Trans.). Austin:
     University of Texas Press.

Brown, P., & Levinson, S. C. (1987). *Politeness: Some universals of language use.* Cambridge, England: Cambridge University Press.

Coulmas, F. (1979). On the sociolinguistic relevance of routine formulae. *Journal of Pragmatics, 3,* 239–266.

Coulmas, F. (Ed.). (1981). *Conversational routine: Explorations in standardized communication situations and prepatterned speech* (Vol. 2) (J. Mey, Trans.). The Hague, The Netherlands: Mouton.

Haegeman, P. (1996). *Business English in Flanders: A study of Lingua Franca telephone interaction.* Unpublished doctoral dissertation, University of Gent, Belgium.

Hall, J. K. (1999). A prosaics of interaction: The development of interactional competence in another language. In E. Hinkel (Ed.), *Culture in second language teaching and learning* (pp. 137–151). New York: Cambridge University Press.

Halmari, H. (1993). Intercultural business telephone conversations: A case of Finns vs. Anglo-Americans. *Applied Linguistics, 14,* 408–430.

Holquist, M. (Ed.). (1981). *The dialogic imagination: Four essays by M. M. Bakhtin* (C. Emerson & M. Holquist, Trans.). Austin: University of Texas Press.

Hopper, R., & Koleilat-Doany, N. (1989). Telephone openings and conversational universals: A study in three languages. In S. Ting-Toomey & F. Korzenny (Eds.), *Language, communication and culture* (pp. 157–179). Newbury Park, CA: Sage.

Houtkoop-Steenstra, H. (1991). Opening sequences in Dutch telephone conversations. In D. Boden & D. H. Zimmerman (Eds.), *Talk and social structure: Studies in ethnomethodology and conversation analysis* (pp. 232–250). Berkeley: University of California Press.

Kashiwazaki, H. (1993). Hanashikake koodoo no danwa bunseki: Irai, yookyuu hyoogen no jissai o chuushin ni [Discourse analysis of requests with phatic communication]. *Nihongo kyooiku, 79,* 53–63.

Kasper, G. (1997). *Can pragmatic competence be taught?* (*NetWork #6*). Retrieved December 28, 1998, from http://www.nflrc.hawaii.edu/networks/nw06/

Kasper, G. (2001). Learning pragmatics in the L2 classroom. *Pragmatics and Language Learning, 10,* 1–25.

Lindström, A. (1994). Identification and recognition in Swedish telephone conversation openings. *Language in Society, 23,* 231–252.

Luke, K. K., & Pavlidou, T.-S. (Eds.). (2002). *Telephone calls: Unity and diversity in conversational structure across languages and cultures.* Amsterdam: John Benjamins.

McClure, W. T. (2000). *Using Japanese: A guide to contemporary usage.* Cambridge, England: Cambridge University Press.

Park, Y.-Y. (2002). Recognition and identification in Japanese and Korean telephone conversation openings. In K. K. Luke & T.-S. Pavlidou (Eds.), *Telephone calls: Unity and diversity in conversational structure across languages and cultures* (pp. 25–47). Amsterdam: John Benjamins.

Schegloff, E. A. (1968). Sequencing in conversational openings. *American Anthropologist, 70,* 1075–1095.

Schegloff, E. A. (1972). Notes on a conversational practice: Formulating place. In D. Sudnow (Ed.), *Studies in social interaction* (pp. 75–119). New York: Free Press.

Schegloff, E. A. (1979). Identification and recognition in telephone openings. In G. Psathas (Ed.), *Everyday language: Studies in ethnomethodology* (pp. 23–78). New York: Irvington.

Schegloff, E. A. (1986). The routine as achievement. *Human Studies, 9,* 111–151.

Wetzel, P. J. (1993). The language of vertical relationships and linguistic analysis. *Multilingua, 12,* 387–406.

Wetzel, P. J. (1994). Contemporary Japanese attitudes toward honorifics (*keigo*). *Language variation and change, 6,* 113–147.

Wetzel, P. J. (2004). *Keigo in modern Japan: Polite language from Meiji to the present.* Honolulu: University of Hawai'i Press.

Wetzel, P. J., & Inoue, M. (1996, April). *Just folks: Native speaker theories of honorifics.* Paper presented at the Annual Meeting of the Association for Asian Studies, Honolulu, HI.

Whalen, M. R., & Zimmerman, D. H. (1987). Sequential an institutional contexts in calls for help. *Social Psychology Quarterly, 50,* 172–185.

Yotsukura, L. A. (1997). *Reporting problems and offering assistance in Japanese business transactional telephone conversations: Toward an understanding of a spoken genre.* Unpublished doctoral dissertation, Ohio State University.

Yotsukura, L. A. (2002). Reporting problems and offering assistance in Japanese business telephone conversations. In K. K. Luke & T. Pavlidou (Eds.), *Telephone calls: Unity and diversity of conversational structure across languages and cultures* (pp. 135–170). Amsterdam: John Benjamins.

Yotsukura, L. A. (2003a). *Negotiating moves: Problem presentation and resolution in Japanese business discourse.* Oxford, England: Elsevier.

Yotsukura, L. A. (2003b). Topic initiation in Japanese business telephone conversations. *Japanese/Korean Linguistics, 12,* 75–87. Stanford, CA: CSLI.

APPENDIX

Key to Abbreviations in Transcriptions

ATF	attention-focusing utterance
COP	copula
CN	connective
DES	desiderative form
DIR	direct style
DIST	distal style
EP	extended predicate (*no desu*)
GER	gerund form
GL	goal particle
HES	hesitation noise
IPF	imperfective form
(+)	neutral–polite form
HON	honorific–polite form
HUM	humble–polite form

lit.	literally
LOC	locative particle
OBJ	object particle
PF	perfective form
PLN	plain form
Q	interrogative particle
QT	quotative particle
SP	sentence particle
SUB	subject particle
//	indicates point at which a subsequent utterance begins to overlap with the current one
:	indicates elongated vowel length
'	indicates a contracted phrase, such as 'masu for imasu
CAPS	indicates louder pitch or additional stress
XX	indicates portions unintelligible to the transcriber
[ ]	indicates material not normally uttered in parallel English contexts
( )	indicates material provided for a smooth English translation of the Japanese but not present in the original utterance

Author Index

Subject Index